FREE VERSUS REGULATED BANKING

Three Centuries of Crisis and Stability

in Great Britain and North America

(for the general reader)

D1738068

CHRISTOPHER DAVID SILBER

Cover: Bank of England façade. Threadneedle Street, London

English banking crises during Scottish free banking (1716-1845):

1721, 1745, 1763, 1772, 1793, 1797, 1810, 1815, 1825, 1837

Scottish banking crises during Scottish free banking:

None

American banking crises during Canadian free banking (1817-1935):

1819, 1837, 1839, 1857, 1873, 1884, 1890, 1893, 1896, 1907, 1930, 1931, 1933

Canadian banking crises during Canadian free banking:

None

TABLE OF CONTENTS

Preface   7

PART ONE: ENGLAND

1. Introduction and Orthodoxy   11
2. British Parliament and the Bank of England   15
3. The Bank of England: Post-Napoleonic Reforms and Peel's Act   23
4. The Bank of England: Bagehot's Dictum and Stability Achieved   29
5. Addendum: Do Modern Central Bankers Really Abide by
    Bagehot's Dictum?   35

PART TWO: SCOTLAND

6. Scotland's Free Banking Era, Part 1   45
7. Scotland's Free Banking Era, Part 2   51
8. Scotland's Free Banking Era, Part 3   57
9. Scotland's Free Banking Era, Part 4   63

PART THREE: THE UNITED STATES

10. Introduction to the United States and Canada   71
11. The United States: Crippled by Unit Banking Regulations, Part 1   75
12. The United States: Crippled by Unit Banking Regulations, Part 2   83
13. The United States: Crippled by Unit Banking Regulations, Part 3   91
14. The First Bank of the United States   97
15. The First Bank of the United States and the Revolutionary War Debt   103
16. The First Bank of the United States and the Panic of 1792   109
17. The First Bank of the United States and the Panic of 1797   117
18. The Second Bank of the United States and the Panic of 1819, Part 1   125
19. The Second Bank of the United States and the Panic of 1819, Part 2   131
20. Andrew Jackson, Nicholas Biddle, and the Bank War   137

21. The American Panic of 1837   145

22. The American "Free Banking Era" of 1837-1862   153

23. The U.S. National Banking System of 1863-1914, Part 1   160

24. The U.S. National Banking System of 1863-1914, Part 2   167

25. The U.S. National Banking System and the Panic of 1893   173

26. The Panic of 1893 Retires a Banker Conspiracy Theory   181

PART FOUR: CANADA

27. A Glancing History of Canadian Banking   187

28. Canada's Free Banking Era: Deregulation and Stability   195

29. Did Canadian Free Banking Have Any Regulations? Part 1   203

30. Did Canadian Free Banking Have Any Regulations? Part 2   209

31. Present-Day Criticism and the Post-Keynesian School, Part 1   215

32. Present-Day Criticism and the Post-Keynesian School, Part 2   220

33. Present-Day Praise and Disagreement   231

34. Why Was the Bank of Canada Established?   239

35. Canada's Post-1935 Success and the USA's Failures   244

36. Did Canada's Glass-Steagall Safeguard its Banks in 2008?   253

37. What Does Silicon Valley Bank's Collapse Tell Us About Depositor Losses Under Canadian Free Banking?   263

POSTSCRIPT: THE GREAT DEPRESSION

38. What Really Started the Great Depression? Part 1   273

39. What Really Started the Great Depression? Part 2   279

40. What Really Started the Great Depression? Part 3   287

Notes   296

Sources and Credits   302

Index   308

Preface

This book is a compilation of several dozen articles written over the course of more than two years for the current events page "Cautious Optimism." (Facebook)

The subject of the series is a general history of Anglo-North American banking regulation and its effects on financial stability. My ambition is to translate historical and theoretical texts that may appear cryptic and opaque to some into terms more easily understood by the general reader.

Although at the time of writing these periodic entries they were not intended to be chapters in a book, the articles themselves, whose histories were originally posted in largely chronological order, proved easy to compile into a logical book form.

However the reader may find the short nature of their paragraphs, a more conventional format for easier reading of online articles, a bit unbookish in appearance. I hope with only a little persistence the reader will find the slightly unorthodox layout quickly becomes second nature and easy to follow.

I have attempted to minimize editing to preserve as much of the original content as possible, but one consequence of this "hands off" approach for the reader will be repetition. As the articles were originally posted weeks and sometimes months apart I felt it then necessary to remind the original audience of certain requisite notions in order to formulate the next chapter. Readers of this book will notice frequent restatement of concepts such as the number of financial crises in England and the United States, the negative repercussions of unit banking laws, or provisions of Gilded Age America's National Banking Era regulations.

But even the most adept Cautious Optimism readers—those who were able to recall such details weeks or even months later—also needed these reminders simply due to the nature of Facebook's distribution algorithms: specifically that many of them never saw the original posts to begin with.

As a Cautious Optimism page publisher with administrator rights I was able to see distribution data for each post; data that revealed zero chance that any one reader, even an active page follower, would ever receive all the over thirty-five columns in their feed. The odds that any user had missed important introductory concepts was high which necessitated revisiting them again and again.

Even more importantly Cautious Optimism post distribution was routinely throttled by Facebook whenever the page was deemed guilty of violating "community standards" that were never specified at the time of an alleged offense. During these probations I knew the platform was distributing my posts to precisely zero of the page's nearly thirty-thousand followers and only those who were deliberate about visiting Cautious Optimism directly would ever see them.

Distribution and views data confirmed this. Articles that before had routinely reached several thousand people were only being viewed by a few dozen during these suppression periods. Hence a second or third reiteration of important requisite concepts was often being read for only the first time by many page followers.

Despite this chapter-to-chapter redundancy I hope the reader will still find the material as a whole informative and the repetition even reinforcing, particularly in the U.S. and Canadian sections.

Finally, I'd like to acknowledge the work of many scholars whose writings and lectures I've drawn from here. Although a fuller list is available in the sources section, I wish to thank in particular professors George Selgin, Lawrence H. White, and Charles Calomiris for not only their prolific academic work which I've relied upon heavily, but also for inspiring my interest in the subject of free versus regulated banking.

Chris Silber
San Francisco, CA
April 28, 2023

PART ONE: ENGLAND

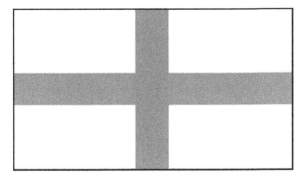

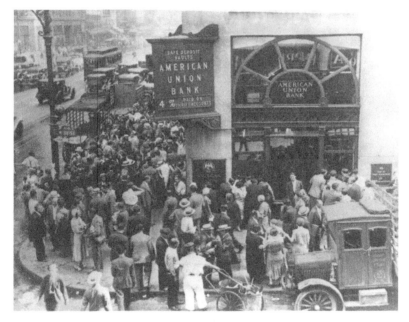

Great Depression bank run

Chapter 1

Introduction and Orthodoxy

The Cautious Optimism Correspondent for Economic Affairs launches a new series of historical articles challenging the popular assertion that private banks competing in a truly free-market environment—devoid of government financial regulation, privileges, bailouts, backstops, protectionism and restrictions—inevitably produce financial instability and systemic banking panics.

It's widely accepted by policymakers, academics, and even the general public that banks must be regulated by government overseers to avoid catastrophes like the 2008 financial crisis. After all, banks make loans which are inherently risky and, given the undisciplined greed and self-interest of bankers, must be controlled by impartial experts at America's various bank regulatory agencies: the Federal Reserve, OCC, and FDIC.

New York Times columnist and economist Paul Krugman gives us an articulate summary of the mainstream position, writing that:

> "History tells us that banking is and always has been subject to occasional destructive 'panics,' which can wreak havoc with the economy as a while... ...It's clear, then, that we need to restore the sorts of safeguards [i.e. regulations] that gave us a couple of generations without major banking panics."

-"Why We Regulate," *New York Times* (2012)

But a serious study of history shows that some countries have never experienced a banking panic at all, that the most deregulated banking systems have actually been the most stable, and that virtually every banking crisis in history can be traced directly back to some perverse government regulation.

History also provides us with another insight: those very same destabilizing bank regulations are nearly always enacted to either raise revenue for the government itself, to tilt the playing field in favor of some politically connected banks at the expense of others, or to benefit certain interest groups at the expense of the general public.

As evidence, far from "always being subject to destructive panics" Scotland and Canada, the two least regulated banking systems in the history of the industrialized world, suffered zero crises during their respective century-plus "free banking" eras of 1716-1845 and 1817-1935.

That's 129 and 118 crisis-free years despite almost no regulations in Scotland and very few in Canada.

Meanwhile England and the United States, far more regulated than their northern neighbors, suffered from roughly ten and thirteen crises.

Great Britain during Scottish free banking (1716-1845):

-English crises: 1721, 1745, 1763, 1772, 1793, 1797, 1810, 1815, 1825, 1837
-Scottish crises: None

North America during Canadian free banking (1817-1935):

-U.S. crises: 1819, 1837, 1839, 1857, 1873, 1884, 1890, 1893, 1896, 1907, 1930, 1931, 1933
-Canadian crises: None

Furthermore during the Great Depression, the United States, operating in what Paul Krugman calls a "deregulated" era (it wasn't as we shall later see) with a supervisory central bank, suffered over 9,000 bank failures. In Canada, with scant few regulations and no central bank, not a single bank failed.

That wasn't "Canada avoided a crisis." It was "No Canadian banks failed during the Great Depression and over 9,000 American banks did."

It's also important to note that in this age where governments regulate banks more than ever, and central banks dominate banking systems with vast powers like never before, the world is in an unprecedented age of crisis.

According to Charles Calomiris of Columbia University, if we define a banking crisis as total industry losses in excess of 1% of GDP then between 1978 and 2009 there have been 140 such episodes around the world (2010).[1]

During the allegedly unstable, deregulated age of the classical gold standard (1875-1913), only four such banking crises occurred. And one would have to eliminate the 20 largest crises of the 1978-2009 period before reaching the largest crisis of the 1875-1913 period as measured by share of GDP.[2]

That's a comparison of two periods of over 30 years each:

-The deregulated classical gold standard era (1875-1913): 4 banking crises.

-The regulated fiat/central bank era (1978-2009): 140 banking crises.

The worldwide prevalence of modern-day banking crises also dispels any dismissals of the contrasting experiences from Great Britain and North America as isolated phenomena limited to only English-speaking countries.

Already just a cursory look at the historical track records of free and regulated banking systems casts Krugman's evidence-free assertion into doubt as well as the conventional wisdom that's been disseminated by the media, politicians, and of course the regulators themselves.

In a new series of articles on the history of banking and financial instability, the Economics Correspondent will tell the important stories of Anglo-North American banking that the New York Times and its loyal readers appear to be completely unaware of: finance in England, Scotland, Canada, and the United States. There will be many chapters in these histories, and the Correspondent will give readers at minimum a "break" between the European record and North America's.

The chapters on England will be first in forthcoming columns.

January 30, 2021

Chapter 2

British Parliament and the Bank of England

As part of his new series on the success and failure of free versus regulated banking systems the Cautious Optimism Correspondent for Economic Affairs offers a brief history of the Bank of England.

The history you will read here is noncontroversial. All capable monetary economic historians are aware of the depicted events, many of which can be confirmed on the Bank of England's own website attached at this chapter's end.

England's perversely regulated banking system, which bore roughly seventeen banking crises over two centuries, stands in stark contrast to deregulated Scotland which experienced none during its own 129 year "free banking" era.

THE BANK OF ENGLAND'S FOUNDING: A ROCKY START

The Bank of England was established in 1694, the conception of a king and parliament desperately in need of funds to wage war against France.

The Glorious Revolution (1688) had deposed King James II and nearly a century of House of Stuart Catholics from the English throne. The crown was transferred to James' protestant daughter Mary and her husband the Dutch King William III, aka. William and Mary.

Unfortunately, the deposed James was also first cousin to French monarch and fellow catholic Louis XIV and his ousting undid England's alliance with France. War broke out, but the Royal Navy was inferior to

France's fleet at the time and was soundly beaten at the Battle of Beachy Head (1690).

With Anglo-French conflicts erupting in North America and alliances being forged with continental European nations, a new era of longer, more protracted, more global, and more expensive wars was beginning. Nations were learning that money was as important in war as battlefield tactics.

As one contemporary English financier and Treasury advisor wrote:

> "If we in England can put our affairs into such a posture, as to be able to hold out in our expense longer than France, we shall be in a condition to give the peace; but if otherwise, we must be contented to receive it."

> "For war is quite changed from what it was in the time of our fore-fathers when in a hasty expedition, and a pitched field, the matter was decided by courage. But now the whole art of war is in a manner reduced to money and now-a-days, that prince, who can bell find money to feed, clothe, and pay his army, not he that has the most valiant troops, is surest of success and conquest."

> -Charles Davenant, "An Essay Upon Ways and Means for Supplying the War" (1695)

Unfortunately the English public of 1694 was already overtaxed and tax evasion was rife. The government's credit among its own citizenry was poor. As a revenue workaround there were attempts to implement a poll tax, a lottery, and a failed land bank, all of which fell far short of raising the estimated £1,200,000 believed needed to effect the war.

Hence the Bank of England scheme was proposed by a brilliant and patriotic financier named William Paterson and championed by King William's Chancellor of the Exchequer Charles Montagu.

The Bank's founders launched today's equivalent of an IPO with the added incentive of patriotic exhortations, and those funds raised would be loaned to the government. Queen Mary herself subscribed to £10,000 as part of a marketing campaign that enticed not only the Bank's directors and wealthy merchants but also everyday citizens to invest.[3]

The share offering was a success. The Bank quickly raised the £1,200,000 it sought, mostly in silver coinage (i.e. specie) and loaned its new paid-in capital to the government primarily as written banknotes and sealed bills which served as claims on specie. In return the Bank received government bonds which were used as security against its private commercial lending while holding a smaller gold and silver reserve.

The Bank's first several years were tumultuous and it suffered several crises and suspensions, although some of these can be blamed on interventions by both the English and overseas governments.

An ill-conceived silver recoinage in 1696 led to a brief shortage of coins and a run on Bank specie, forcing it into an embarrassing suspension of its banknotes' convertibility into precious metal.

Jealous goldsmiths hoarded Bank of England notes and coordinated simultaneous redemptions to ruin the Bank, forcing another suspension as the directors scrambled to call in loans and secure more silver.

Multiple attempted invasions by the deposed Catholic king's son James Edward Francis Stuart (James III or "The Old Pretender") fomented panic and rumors of his army landing in Scotland caused a run on the Bank.

And the Bank's own worst enemy was King William himself who demanded more and more loans, each time larger than before, stretching the Bank's finances so thin that it was left with an increasingly inadequate and vulnerable silver reserve.

After vowing in 1694 that the Bank's £1,200,000 loan would settle the conflict, William's annual war expenses had swelled to £8,000,000 by 1696.[4] And in one particularly brazen act he demanded another large advance of banknotes, then immediately returned them to the Bank for redemption, nearly bankrupting it of its silver coinage.[5]

THE DIRECTORS DEMAND REDRESS: THE "SIX PARTNER RULE"

When the Bank's charter came up for renewal in 1707 the directors argued they had accommodated the government up to the point of near ruin on multiple occasions and demanded some sort of concession in return for their loyalty to the Crown.

So in a series of quid-pro-quo arrangements between business and government which were so common in those days of mercantilism, Parliament granted the Bank a monopoly on joint-stock banking. Written into the Bank of England Act of 1708 was the so-called "Six Partner Rule" decreeing:

> "It shall not be lawful for any body politic, or corporate whatsoever…
> … exceeding the number of six persons, in that part of Great Britain called England, to borrow or take up any sum or sums of money on their bills or notes payable at demand, or at any less time than six months from the borrowing thereof." [6]

This monopoly, the original and only definition of monopoly that reigned for over three hundred years before Standard Oil—the sole right to operate in a market at the exclusion of any would-be competitor and enforced by the power of the State—would set the stage for a series of financial crises and bank failures that would plague England for well over a century.

The Bank was also handed a total monopoly on note issuance within London making it the only source of paper money in the business and financial center.[7]

The Act's desired and very successful objective was to prevent any competing bank from gaining enough scale and influence to challenge the Bank of England, thus preventing funds from moving elsewhere and depriving Parliament of its handpicked source of reliable and ample wartime credit. While other private banks could not raise capital from any more partners (i.e. shareholders) than six, the Bank of England's shareholder base was unlimited.

Thus outside of London the English countryside became scattered with dozens and eventually hundreds of tiny banks that, even where well-managed, were legally restricted from growing to any meaningful size or servicing any large geographic area.

The preponderance of small country banks gave rise to at least four destabilizing factors:

(1) Small banks with limited geographic scale were unable to diversify their loan portfolios. Dependent on only the local industry or crop, a

downturn in a single economic sector could ruin a bank since it had no loans from any other industry or region.

(2) Small banks were also unable to diversify their depositors. Dependent on only the local community, a single wealthy depositor could bring down a bank with one large withdrawal, something even more likely to occur during times of trouble.

(3) The restriction precluded the most capable businessmen from entering banking. Successful entrepreneurs in the textiles, agricultural, machinery, or overseas trades were excluded from finance as their lucrative enterprises were already joint-stock companies, thus leaving banking to less competent upstarts. As William Dodgson Bowman's Bank history (1937) tells us:

> "In the provinces, people of many different occupations took up the trade—grocers, bakers, drapers, graziers, chemists and tailors," but only a few banks "were founded by prudent business men, who understood the business and were alive to the importance of maintaining an adequate cash reserve against their paper issues." [8]

and...

> "A number of the banks were run by people with inadequate capital, with little knowledge of banking principles and methods. These mushroom concerns were responsible for large issues of notes, which were found to be merely wastepaper as soon as there was a sudden demand for cash." [9]

(4) The legal restrictions placed on the size of country banks made each bank's notes issuance small and localized. Thus Bank of England notes so dominated English circulation that they came to be treated as a reserve themselves, much as Federal Reserve notes were legal reserves during the Fed gold standard era of 1914-1933 and remain fiat paper legal reserves today. This added an additional macroeconomic destabilizer as the entire country's credit policy tended to expand and contract with that of the Bank of England, leading to larger and more widespread boom-bust cycles.

In the span of 125 years from the enactment of the Six Partner Rule to its final repeal in 1833 England suffered from no less than ten banking panics including major ones in 1721, 1772, 1797, 1815, and 1825.

Meanwhile north of the border in Scotland, where neither the Six Partner Rule nor any central bank existed, a nearly 100% unregulated system of private, competitive, nationally branched and highly diversified banks experienced no financial crises during the same 125-year period (sole exception: the Napoleonic Wars suspension which will be explained in a chapter on Scotland).

Nonetheless, Parliament did nothing to reform the Six Partner Rule as its overriding concern was guaranteeing itself a reliable source of credit to finance England's century-plus series of on-again, off-again conflicts with France. Economic and financial stability consistently came second to war.

Stay tuned for next week's second chapter on lessons learned from the experience of Parliament and the Bank of England.

Bank of England's history at bankofengland.co.uk:
https://www.bankofengland.co.uk/about/

February 2, 2021

British Parliament and the Bank of England

Parliament repeatedly debates Bank of England reform
during the 19th century

Chapter 3

The Bank of England: Post-Napoleonic Reforms and Peel's Act

The Cautious Optimism Correspondent for Economic Affairs continues with a brief history of repeated crises and failures in 19th century England's regulated banking system—in stark contrast to the resilience and stability of Scotland's unregulated one.

1825-1873: ENGLAND UNEVENLY ADDRESSES ITS BANKING PROBLEMS

After Napoleon's 1815 defeat at Waterloo Britain and France finally cemented a lasting peace after 127 years of on-again, off-again war. As the century-long era of Pax Britannica began, Parliament's focus on the Bank of England's mission shifted from that of longtime war financier to steward of economic development.

After another crushing banking panic and depression in 1825 (which Scotland again avoided), Parliament fiercely debated reforms to impose upon the Bank in exchange for its charter renewal.

Lord Liverpool, conservative Prime Minister and proponent of reform, argued the right of joint-stock banking should be extended to all private banks.

According to Professor Andreades' classic 1909 history, Liverpool...

> "criticised severely... ...the Act of 1709, which limited the number of partners in a bank of issue to six, so that any small provincial trades-man, a fruiterer, a grocer or a butcher, might open a bank whilst the right of issue was refused to genuine companies, well deserving of confidence." [10]

In the House of Commons conservative MP and future Prime Minister Sir Robert Peel urged his fellow ministers to learn from the free Scottish system which had suffered not a single crisis since its first private bank—the Bank of Scotland—received its charter in 1695.

Here Andreades records that Peel...

> "...contrasted the monopoly which existed in England with the free Scotch system. He pointed out that in England 100 banks had failed in 1793, 157 between 1810 and 1817, and 76 during the recent crisis...
> ...whilst in Scotland, on the contrary, there was only a single bank failure on record, and even in that case the creditors had ultimately been paid in full." [11]

Furthermore Peel lamented that...

> "...the Bank of England's monopoly lay like a dead hand on the organization of credit in this country, and demonstrated the superiority of the Scottish system." [12]

Parliament relaxed the Six Partner Rule in 1826, ending 118 years of crippling legal restrictions and finally permitting joint-stock banking across all of England except within a critical 65-mile radius around London. [13] By 1833 joint-stock banking was finally permitted everywhere in England and the central bank's longstanding monopoly on London banknotes was ended.

But the Bank of England warned it would not do business with any bank that attempted to issue notes within London. As the small country banks would require several years to grow and eventually compete with the Bank of England head-on, the central bank's threat alone kept the circulation of its own notes paramount for a while longer, particularly in the capital and financial center.

And in a foreshadowing of eventual abandonment of the liberalization trend, the 1833 charter renewal bestowed Bank of England notes legal tender status for redemption of private/country banknotes. Having long been treated as a de facto reserve asset by private banks, the central bank's notes were now a de jure monetary reserve and became a form of high-powered money. [14]

Nevertheless progress slowly began. Freed from 125 years of Six Partner Rule constraints, well-managed small banks undertook expansion, several of them eventually into successful conglomerates.

Taylors and Lloyds, a small Birmingham bank founded in 1765, eventually grew into Lloyds Bank, a modern household name.

In 1736 a small non-issuance London bank founded in 1690 took on a Quaker businessman named James Barclay as partner and renamed itself "Freame, Gould and Barclay." Once permitted to add more than six capital partners the bank grew over time to become British multinational Barclays Plc.

Unfortunately the 1833 reforms didn't come in time to prevent another major panic just four years later, brought on by the statutory treatment of Bank of England notes as a reserve and such incompetent central bank negligence that Scottish economist Henry Dunning Macleod lamented "Of all the acts of mismanagement in the whole history of the Bank, this is probably the most astonishing." [15]

To address the causes of the Crisis of 1837 Parliament should have encouraged and waited for the small country banks to expand into a system of large, nationally branched note issuing institutions whose scale would diminish the Bank of England's outsized influence. Instead the British government took a major step backwards and enacted the ill-advised Peel Act of 1844.

PEEL'S ACT

It was thought that the continued panics were caused by overissuance of notes by both the Bank of England and private country banks. But the applied remedy was to prohibit private competitive banknote issuance altogether and grant a complete monopoly to the Bank of England. Furthermore, the central bank's note issuances would be limited to the balance of its government debt holdings and no more than 100% of the Bank's gold reserves.

Prime Minister Robert Peel had himself forgotten the experience of the Scottish system he had championed in 1826. For free and universal note issuance had been allowed in Scotland for 128 years and in all that time never once destabilized the money trade.

Unlike in England, Scotland was ruled by unfettered market forces, free from government-backed monopolies and Six Partner Rules, and it was market competition that prevented Scottish banks from overissuing. The constant threat of redemption calls, often from competing banks, and an efficient private clearinghouse system kept them all in line.

Moreover Peel and Parliament were persuaded by the Bank of England governor and deputy governor that the tight regulatory straitjacket foisted upon both central and private banknote issuance would solve the problem. The directors favored a statutory reassertion of their bank's dominance and according to economist Lawrence H. White…

> "…had been searching for a simple non-discretionary rule that would govern their circulation in such a way as to insulate the bank from public criticism of its monopoly." [16]

Hence the general trend of steady liberalization that had prevailed from 1826 to 1844 was reversed with a dose of heavy-handed government control over national finance.

With the Act's passage Parliament adopted a de facto national credit policy dictated entirely by the Bank of England. Whereas before national credit had been incidentally influenced by the central bank now it would be completely regulated by it.

With private banks no longer able to issue banknotes and forced to accept Bank of England paper as reserves, the entire banking system began to expand and contract credit in perfect concert with the central bank. As Bank of England note circulation increased so did private bank lending and interest rates fell. When Bank of England note circulation contracted private credit dried up, interest rates rose, and panic and depression ensued.

This arrangement, a pyramiding where private banks amplify the credit movements of the monopoly central bank, is much like that of today's relationship between U.S. commercial banks and the Federal Reserve System.

Most perversely of all, whenever depositors became nervous and increased their cash holdings, private banks were forced to crawl begging on knee to the Bank of England for more of its exclusive notes. But the

Peel Act forbade the central bank from accommodating since it was prohibited from issuing beyond 100% of its gold reserves.

Unable to obtain paper money to meet customer demands and restricted from issuing their own, many perfectly solvent English banks failed needlessly due to short-term illiquidity.

Thus even with the Six Partner Rule repealed, Peel's Act restrictions and a renewed consolidation of the Bank of England's note monopoly continued to generate crises in 1847, 1857, 1866, 1878, and 1890, bringing the number of crises since the Bank's founding to at least seventeen (post-Peels' Act plus crises in 1696, 1715, 1721, 1745, 1763, 1772, 1793, 1797, 1810, 1815, 1825, and 1837).

So bad a problem had the Peel Act created that on four occasions Parliament was forced to suspend its own law—the 100% gold reserve note restriction—starting with the Crisis of 1847 and lastly at the onset of World War I.[17]

With each suspension the Bank of England was briefly permitted to purchase assets or loan cash beyond the value of its gold holdings, and the Bank's directors slowly adopted the institutional role of lender of last resort—albeit by happenstance—a subject we will cover in the last installment on England.

February 7, 2021

❝ To avert panic, central banks should lend early and freely, to solvent firms, against good collateral, and at high rates ❞
WALTER BAGEHOT

Walter Bagehot (1826-1877)

Chapter 4

The Bank of England: Bagehot's Dictum and Stability Achieved

The Cautious Optimism Correspondent for Economic Affairs concludes with the third and final installment examining the history and failings of England's crisis-prone banking system.

BAGEHOT CLEANS UP

With each successive suspension of the 1844 Peel Act's banknote restriction the Bank of England gradually adopted a policy of providing liquidity to strained private banks by lending its notes on a short-term basis. Each new ensuing crisis, while still serious and disruptive to the economy, ended progressively faster and with less economic damage than the great panics of 1825 and 1837.

By 1873 banker and The Economist editor Walter Bagehot (pronounced "badge-it") could see clearly both the causes of and remedies to England's now fifteen banking panics stretching back to 1694, and he outlined two proposals for monetary reform in his seminal book *Lombard Street: A Description of the Money Market.*

In Bagehot's opinion the Bank of England's banknote monopoly was at the root of the problem. England, he said, should do away with the central bank completely and move towards a free, unrestricted, competitive and decentralized banking system like that which Scotland had enjoyed without a single crisis from 1716 to 1845.

But the Bank of England was now so ingrained in English culture for nearly two centuries, Bagehot opined, that it had become as impossible an institution to dislodge as Queen Victoria herself.

Thus his second best solution was for the Bank to use its considerable powers to clean up its own mess.

When the central bank creates a crisis, he argued, it should stand ready to help solvent but temporarily illiquid private banks weather the storm by lending generously on good collateral at high rates of interest, a prescription famously referred to today as "Bagehot's Dictum" or "Bagehot's Rule." After the crisis abates and calmed depositors replenish the banks' reserves, he said, they can then settle their emergency loans with the central bank.

Bagehot's book was well received by the public, the industry, and lawmakers and the Bank of England officially assumed a "lender of last resort" policy, the first adopted nationwide anywhere.

Although U.S. Treasury Secretary Alexander Hamilton and English economist Henry Thornton are believed to have anticipated and proposed similar remedies in 1792 and 1802, Bagehot gets official credit having both articulated it so well in 1873 and providing impetus for the policy's official adoption in Great Britain.

England suffered an incipient crisis in 1878 and one last brief but shallow crisis in 1890 (the Barings Crisis) which was only a blip on the radar compared to the Great Crises of 1825, 1837, and even 1857. Both emergencies were quickly stemmed by Bank of England liquidity loans.

Further strengthening the industry were the continued expansions and mergers of small country banks into stronger, widely branched and highly diversified national banks—a trend that had begun with the Banking Copartnership Act of 1826.

Hundreds of country banks operating only five branches on average in 1844 consolidated into fewer than 100 banks with 58 branches on average by 1899 (Turner-2014).[18]

In 1900 25% of all U.K. deposits were controlled by the emergent "Big Five" banks including Barclays, Lloyds, Midland, National Provincial, and Westminster Bank. The Big Five's market share grew to 40% by World War I.

Combined with an effective lender of last resort policy, England successfully avoided panics for 118 years following the Barings Crisis and its banking system even weathered the Great Depression without a crisis.

The contrast is striking. At least seventeen banking crises from 1694 to 1890, then zero from 1891 to 2007 with the scourge only returning in 2008.

SUMMARY

So what lessons do we learn from the English banking experience of 1694-1890?

Far from unregulated laissez-faire, English banking was beset by a government-granted monopoly, perverse regulations, and legal restrictions on bank expansion for well over a century—regulations that were the root cause of the nation's multiple financial crises.

At first private banks were kept small and fragile by Parliament's Six Partner Rule, tying their hands, making them unable either to widely branch or diversify their loan portfolios and deposit bases, and excluding the most competent businessmen from entering banking.

But even as Six Partner Rule restrictions were relaxed the central bank was granted an absolute banknote monopoly and assumed an indomitable role in the issuance of national credit. This artificially imposed pre-eminence led to a single institution's credit policy expanding and contracting money and lending across the entire country, amplifying the boom-bust cycle.

All these dysfunctional, counterproductive regulations were imposed on the private sector in their first 126 years for the benefit of the British government itself, providing it with a reliable banker and compulsory credit line that would never be diminished by competing upstarts.

The Bank of England and its directors would also continue to benefit from the monopoly and suppression of competition for another century-plus, profiting from its close relationship with government benefactors in a prime example of mercantilism or what so many of us today refer to as "crony capitalism."

The central bank was nationalized in 1946 and instead of enriching private shareholders its operating profits were transferred to the British government, just as the U.S. Federal Reserve diverts its earnings after member bank dividends to the U.S. Treasury today.

Later on the English experience teaches us that even the destabilizing effects of the monopoly central bank's machinations can still be reasonably contained provided that:

(1) Its discretion to inflate is partially constrained by an honest gold standard (such as the classical gold standard).

(2) Its directors are competent, apolitical, and act honestly.

(3) It acts quickly as lender of last resort to mitigate crises of its own creation.

(4) The private banking system is allowed to freely operate branch networks and conduct its own lending policies with minimal interference from government.

(5) The private banking system is allowed to reap the profits or losses of its policies, free from government privileges, guarantees, bailouts, and regulations that introduce moral hazard or otherwise distort market incentives.

Such an arrangement was Walter Bagehot's next best blueprint for stability—second only to dissolving the central bank itself—and the formula promoted soundness in English banking for 118 years, even when Great Britain abandoned the gold-exchange standard in 1931.

Unfortunately in today's era of fiat money, zero and subzero interest rates, "Greenspan puts," "Too Big to Fail" doctrines, federal deposit insurance and moral hazard, mortgage-hoarding and repackaging GSE's, and Parliaments and Congresses commanding banks to lower lending standards for the benefit of special interest groups and uncreditworthy homebuyers, Bagehot's rule can no longer stave off panic as the United Kingdom painfully learned during the 2008 global financial crisis.

In upcoming chapters we'll examine the parallel history of Scotland, England's northern neighbor that allowed the closest to a laissez-faire, unregulated banking system the post-Renaissance world has ever seen.

With no central bank and no restrictions on shareholders, branching, note issuance, liability, or geographic scale, Scotland experienced not a single banking crisis during its free banking era of 1716-1845 while its larger neighbor to the south was crippled again and again by repeated waves of financial turmoil.

February 13, 2021

Walter Bagehot: Never far from Federal Reserve
Chairman Ben Bernanke's thoughts

Chapter 5

Addendum: Do Modern Central Bankers Really Abide by Bagehot's Dictum?

From the Cautious Optimism Correspondent for Economic Affairs.

In the Economics Correspondent's previous series on banking instability in England we learned the Bank of England's first two centuries and a slew of destructive banking regulations imposed by British Parliament led England to weather no fewer than seventeen financial crises.

Ultimately a proposal for stability was penned by banker and The Economist editor Walter Bagehot (pronounced "badge-it") in his famous 1873 book *Lombard Street.*

Bagehot blamed the Bank of England itself, its centralization of gold reserves, and the banknote monopoly bestowed upon it by Parliament for repeated systemic financial crises. Furthermore he recommended throwing out the central bank and emulating the decentralized, deregulated, and nearly laissez-faire private Scottish system of 1716-1845 that had produced not a single crisis during its 129 years.

However Bagehot knew that it was politically impossible to dismantle the Bank of England since it had become so ingrained in the British psyche. Therefore his next best solution, assuming the central bank was to be retained, was that it cleans up its own mess, acting in a lender of last resort (LOLR) capacity: lending freely and early to solvent but illiquid banks at high interest rates during times of stress.

Since then central bankers the world over have lauded Bagehot as a visionary, pioneer and champion of central banking, and they've cited Bagehot's Dictum repeatedly as justification for their aggressive bailouts of troubled institutions.

In his book *The Courage to Act*, former Federal Reserve Chairman Ben Bernanke recounts the 2008 financial crisis and cites Bagehot more than any other nonliving economist (including Milton Friedman), justifying the Fed's aggressive emergency lending programs by invoking Bagehot's name over and over.

Bernanke even goes so far as to suggest that if Bagehot were alive today he would wholeheartedly approve of such massive bailout programs. After detailing not only emergency lending and asset purchases for banks but also TALF program lending on millions of auto loans, student loans, small business loans, and credit card loans he writes "Walter Bagehot would have been pleased." [19]

There's no shortage of other central bankers asserting they were only following Bagehot's antidotes and that Bagehot himself would have approved.

It may be no surprise to CO Nation that the Economics Correspondent disagrees.

BAGEHOT'S RULE ITSELF

We don't have to look far to see what's wrong with Bernanke's characterization of archangelic Bagehot smiling down upon the 2008 Fed with patrimonial approval. We only need look closer for a moment at Bagehot's Rule itself.

The Federal Reserve's website repeats Bagehot's Rule as:

> "[T]o avert panic, central banks should lend early and freely (ie without limit), to solvent firms, against good collateral, and at 'high rates.'"

This is an accurate summation, and Bernanke also states:

> "To calm panic, Bagehot advised central bankers to lend freely at a high interest rate, against good collateral, a principle now known as Bagehot's dictum." [20]

So why did Bagehot recommend central bankers "lend freely" (without limit), to "solvent firms," "against good collateral," "at high rates?"

"Lending freely" should be obvious. If many banks fail simultaneously due to illiquidity then panic and widespread depositor withdrawals might spread to other stressed banks. Thus Bagehot argued the central bank should not skimp on short term lending assistance to bolster liquidity.

As for "solvent firms" and "against good collateral," that's not too hard to understand either.

Bagehot didn't want the central bank pouring good money after bad into banks with negative equity. If banks were well managed but failing due to a simple liquidity run in times of panic, then the central bank would help savable institutions with its loans secured on good collateral. But for the minority of banks that were just badly managed and effectively bankrupt, they should be allowed to fail and not take central bank money down with them in the process.

And "high rates" (sometimes referred to as "punitive rates") were to ensure that illiquid banks regretted having managed their reserves so poorly. If they remembered paying a high price for liquidity loans they were less likely to repeat their mistakes in the future (i.e. moral hazard).

Also a punitive rate of interest ensured only truly needy banks would request central bank lending. If the interest rate was too low, healthy liquid banks would take advantage of the crisis to secure cheap funding and impose unnecessary leverage upon the central bank's balance sheet.

As Bagehot himself wrote, a punitive rate of interest...

> "...will prevent the greatest number of applications by persons who do not require it... ...that the [central] Banking reserve be protected as far as possible." [21]

Lastly Bagehot wrote only of assisting commercial banks, making no mention of lending to insurers and other nonbank institutions.

RULEBREAKERS

So just how faithfully did Bernanke, the Fed, and the world's central bankers adhere to Bagehot's Rule in 2008?

(1) "Lend freely (without limit)."

There's no question they adopted this policy and took it to new heights. Not only did the Fed lend hundreds of billions of dollars to troubled banks, it gladly allowed investment banks, insurance companies, and other nonbanking firms to change to commercial bank status overnight and secure bailout lending. General Electric springs to mind, having hurriedly bought a tiny Connecticut community bank in the depths of the crisis and then receiving a $16 billion Fed loan that dwarfed its newly acquired bank's entire balance sheet.[22]

Major insurers also changed their status such as The Hartford, Lincoln Financial, Genworth, and most notoriously AIG. And as Bernanke acknowledges in his book, the lending extended to hundreds of billions of dollars for auto loans, student loans, small business loans, and credit card loans.

(2) "Lend... ...to solvent firms."

Not only were the largest, most troubled institutions in 2008 illiquid, many were also insolvent. Loaded up to the hilt with nonperforming mortgages and bad securitized loans, firms like Citigroup, Merrill Lynch, countless regional and superregional banks, and nonbank institutions like AIG all received huge discount loans from the Fed despite their solvency coming into question or simply being bankrupt.

As evidence the Fed advanced credit to several commercial and investment banks that ultimately failed anyway or had to be saved through acquisition such as Washington Mutual (failed) and Wachovia (failed) or Bear Stearns, Merrill Lynch, and National City (all acquired).

But if the Fed loaned to many firms that were insolvent and never acquired, why are some of them still with us today? Because the Fed not only granted emergency liquidity loans, it also purchased their lousy mortgage securities in open market operations, the first time in its century-long history that the central bank bought mortgage paper instead of traditional, safer U.S. Treasuries.

Buying assets directly from banks, particularly lousy assets, was never on Bagehot's list of remedies either.

(3) "Lend… on good collateral."

Obviously lending to banks that are offering failing subprime and Alt-A mortgages as collateral also violates Bagehot's Rule.

And…

(4) "Lend… …at high rates [of interest]."

As everyone already knows, the Fed loaned hundreds of billions of dollars through its discount window at nearly zero percent.

(Federal Reserve discount rates history at https://fred.stlouisfed.org/graph/?g=yD9r)

One can hardly call zero or even 0.5% interest a high or punitive rate, and in fact securing so much money so cheaply would have been impossible for banks during the preceding boom years.

And with Fed lending rates so low, countless healthy and liquid banks lined up for cheap credit, something Bagehot specifically wished to avoid. Even banks that didn't want rescue money were coerced by the Treasury, most famously Wells Fargo whose CEO was threatened with punitive government action if his bank didn't accept a $25 billion TARP injection that the bank ultimately repaid with interest.[23]

So if Bagehot were alive today he'd perceive the world's central bankers fulfilling only one of the four commandments of his doctrine while brazenly contravening the other three, all in his name.

MORE BAGEHOT DISAPPROVAL

Furthermore, if we look closer into Bagehot's book we find he was a staunch hard-money gold standard advocate who hated any suggestion of unbacked or overissued paper money. Bagehot went out of his way to criticize central banker John Law's 1719 Mississippi Company paper money scheme that inflated the world's first stock market bubble which burst a year later and threw France into a protracted depression.[24]

He also sneered at the unbacked paper "greenbacks" circulating in America during and following the Civil War, although Congress began redeeming greenbacks for gold two years after Bagehot's death (1879).[25]

And as we've already mentioned, Bagehot wanted to get rid of the Bank of England completely, but reluctantly accepted that doing so was politically impossible. His argument in *Lombard Street* is rather lengthy but the key corroborating passages read:

> "I shall have failed in my purpose if I have not proved that the system of entrusting all our reserve to a single board, like that of the Bank [of England] directors, is very anomalous; that it is very dangerous; that its bad consequences, though much felt, have not been fully seen; that they have been obscured by traditional arguments and hidden in the dust of ancient controversies."

> "But it will be said 'What would be better? What other system could there be?' We are so accustomed to a system of banking, dependent for its cardinal function on a single bank [the Bank of England], that we can hardly conceive of any other. But the natural system that which would have sprung up if Government had let banking alone is that of many banks of equal or not altogether unequal size. In all other trades competition brings the traders to a rough approximate equality..."

> "I shall be at once asked 'Do you propose a revolution? Do you propose to abandon the one-reserve System and create anew a many-reserve system [private competitive Scottish system of 1716-1845]?' My plain answer is that I do not propose it. I know it would be childish. Credit in business is like loyalty in Government. You must take what you can find of it, and work with it if possible..."

> "...Just so, an immense system of credit, founded on the Bank of England as its pivot and its basis, now exists. The English people, and foreigners too, trust it implicitly... ...Nothing would persuade the English people to abolish the Bank of England; and if some calamity swept it away, generations must elapse before at all the same trust would be placed in any other equivalent. A many-reserve system, if some miracle should put it down in Lombard Street, would seem monstrous there. Nobody would understand it, or confide in it..."

> "...On this account, I do not suggest that we should return to a natural or many-reserve system of banking. I should only incur useless ridicule if I did suggest it."

-*Lombard Street,* pp.32-34

So in conclusion, whatever one thinks of the emergency measures employed in 2008, the claims by Bernanke and modern central bankers that they were only doing Bagehot's bidding fall flat in light of even a cursory glance at the evidence.

They only followed one of the four tenets of Bagehot's Dictum while blatantly breaking the other three.

And while the gold standard or animus towards monopoly central banks are not addressed directly in Bagehot's Dictum, an unwavering support of the gold standard is present throughout his writings, and his calls for abolishment of the Bank of England in favor of a private, decentralized, competitive banking system appear within *Lombard Street* itself.

Bagehot would have expressed outrage and indignation at the Fed and particularly the Bank of England issuing fiat monies and computerized reserves without gold backing, blowing up the very asset bubbles he had blamed the monopoly central bank for inflating in his own time.

So after scrutinizing Bernanke's claims of devotion to Bagehot's Dictum a bit more closely, we can safely conclude that "No Mister Chairman, Walter Bagehot would not have been pleased. He would have been very, very displeased by the conduct of central banks not only in 2008, but for many decades prior."

February 20, 2021

PART TWO: SCOTLAND

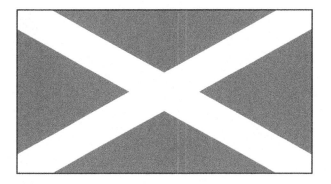

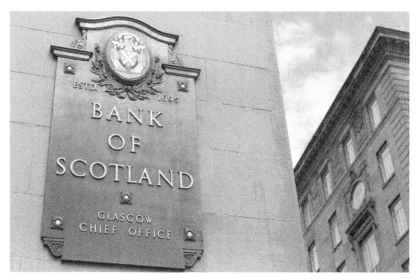

The Bank of Scotland, est. 1695

Chapter 6

Scotland's Free Banking Era, Part 1

The Cautious Optimism Correspondent for Economic Affairs suggests the next time a champion of statism tells you free markets can't work in banking, ask them first for an example.

If they say the United States, remind them the USA had the most heavily and adversely regulated banking system in the industrialized world from the Civil War through the Great Depression—regulations that precipitated panics in 1873, 1884, 1890, 1893, 1896, 1907, 1930, 1931, and 1933 (more on the USA in future columns).

If they don't cite the historical experiences of Scotland, Canada, or Sweden, educate them first about Scotland which, from 1716 to 1845, operated the closest to a laissez-faire banking system the modern world (post-Renaissance) has ever seen and was uncoincidentally crisis-free for the entire 129 years.

SCOTLAND'S FIRST BANKS AND THE NOTE DUEL

As we've learned in previous columns the Bank of England received its charter from English Parliament in 1694 to begin immediate wartime lending to the government before acting as a quasi-central bank.

One year later in 1695 Scottish Parliament chartered its first bank, the Bank of Scotland. Far from being a central bank, the Bank of Scotland was simply a commercial bank that took deposits in silver coin and issued deposit claims and loans primarily in the form of its own written banknotes.

Scotland was a much different place from England in 1695. Backwards and rural, Scotland was much poorer than its southern neighbor. It also had a great degree of autonomy and even its own parliament until the 1707 Act of Union merged the two countries into the United Kingdom of Great Britain.

And although late 17th century Scotland was immersed in the same mercantilist policies that were so common throughout Europe, it was intellectually on the cusp of the Scottish Enlightenment, an era dominated philosophically and legally by principles of reason, natural rights, sanctity of the individual, liberty, and free markets that would later inspire founding fathers of the United States such as Thomas Jefferson, James Madison, Benjamin Franklin, and John Adams.

True to the mercantilist backdrop of 1695, Parliament granted the Bank of Scotland a 21-year monopoly, the original and only definition of monopoly that reigned for over three hundred years before John D. Rockefeller's Standard Oil: the sole right to operate in a market at the exclusion of any would-be competitor, enforced by the power of the State.

Uncoincidentally Scottish Parliament also passed a law declaring it illegal for any Scottish bank to lend to governments without approval from Edinburgh. The Scots clearly saw King William III's strategy of financing war against France using private banks and wanted no part of it. William, surveying Scotland's poverty, backwardness, and the legal difficulties he would face in securing loans from the Bank of Scotland, decided it wasn't worth the effort and settled for relying on the Bank of England.

With a government-sanctioned monopoly commercial bank, Scottish finance could hardly be deemed a free market in 1695. However, the bank's monopoly expired in 1716 by which time Scottish and English Parliaments had merged in the Act of Union. The now British Parliament suspected the Bank of Scotland of Jacobite (House of Stuart Catholic) sympathies and was not amenable to granting any more privileges.

Mindful of Parliament's reluctance to extend its monopoly status and mistakenly believing the prospects for competition to be low, the Bank of Scotland's directors chose not to press the matter further and operated in a marketplace now devoid of government barriers to competitive entry.

The era of free banking in Scotland had begun.

Despite the Bank of Scotland's established position and virtual 100% market share, a new competitor emerged. In 1724 the Royal Bank of Scotland opened for business and received a charter in 1727. Henceforth we will refer to the original and upstart banks as the Old Bank and the Royal Bank.

The Old Bank was none too pleased at the appearance of a competitor and schemed to promptly put it out of business. Immediately its directors advised customers they would not accept the Royal Bank's notes for deposit and believed the new rival could be ousted with their incumbent market power.

The Royal Bank countered by advertising it would accept not only its own notes for deposit but those of the Old Bank as well. It then stockpiled Old Bank notes, later submitting them all for silver coin redemption and forcing the Old Bank into an embarrassing suspension as its directors scrambled to call in loans and even resorted to borrowing.

While the Old Bank scurried to raise coinage under cover of suspension the Royal Bank publicly announced "The Old Bank is not paying in silver, we are the only bank honoring its commitments" and stole many customers away.

Months later the Old Bank was able to resume redemption and plotted to exact revenge. It began accepting the Royal Bank's notes, hoarding them as well, and submitted them en masse to antagonize its competitor in turn.

The Old Bank also added a clause on its notes giving it the option to delay redemption by up to six months but pay noteholders 5% annual interest as compensation for their inconvenience. This "option clause" was the first of what would be many financial innovations borne from the fierce competition between Scottish banks.

The Royal Bank had anticipated the Old Bank's plot and held a large silver reserve as a defense. Soon both banks were hoarding specie as a precaution against surprise attacks.[26]

However before long both banks realized they were forgoing significant profits by holding such large reserves when they could be issuing more interest-bearing loans, so they agreed it was in their best interests to cooperate. They met once a week to trade notes and settle balances excluding offsetting claims. Soon they were meeting twice a week, and eventually every day. The world's first private bank clearinghouse system was born.

With the clearinghouse system established, Parliament outlawed the banknote option clause in 1765 in one of the very few interventions of the time enacted by government.

Later a third bank was chartered in Edinburgh, the British Linen Company; named so since its original business was textile trading and its routine credit dealings led it naturally into the banking business.

Scotland's history of private banknotes remains so renowned that the country is one of only four regions in the world—alongside Hong Kong, Macau, and Northern Ireland—where private note issuance is still permitted. Bank of Scotland, Royal Bank of Scotland, and Clydesdale Bank notes still circulate, although domestic gold convertibility was ended in 1914 and private banknotes must now be 100% backed by inconvertible Bank of England banknotes.

BANK COMPETITION IN THE SCOTTISH FREE MARKET

Throughout the remainder of the 18th century and the first half of the 19th century Scotland had no central bank, private banking was completely open to entry, the right of note issuance was universal, and government bestowed no special privileges, protections, or bailouts upon any bank. Although the English and Scottish parliaments were joined in the Act of Union, Scotland still enjoyed a great degree of economic autonomy and the anti-mercantilist, free market ideas of the Scottish Enlightenment had taken hold.

In this nearly laissez-faire environment where banks succeeded or failed on their own merits, competition was fierce, profit margins were thin, and enormous incentives to innovate prevailed.

In May of 1728 the Royal Bank of Scotland invented the account overdraft, a service regarded as commonplace today.[27]

Soon after the next logical step was established: the line of credit, filling a need by the banks' merchant customers who couldn't predict precisely when the need for advances would arise and in what amount.

Scottish banks printed Europe's first color banknotes, the world's first double-sided printed banknotes, and pioneered widespread payment of interest on demand deposits.[28]

Along with the private clearinghouse and option clause these new services didn't go unnoticed. In 1752's "Of the Balance of Trade" Scottish

Enlightenment philosopher David Hume praised the influx of financial innovations that emerged from the free, competitive banking system.[29]

Initially banks operated in the largest city of Edinburgh with its diverse economy and leading population. At midcentury branches only operated within Edinburgh, but by the 1770's both the Bank of Scotland and Royal Bank of Scotland had opened branches in Glasgow and the British Linen Company had already built a small branch network.[30]

Scotland was not subject to the mercantilist Six Partner Rule of England that sought to keep banks small and impotent, so by the turn of the century branch offices were operating throughout the nation, the first such network of its kind.

Unlike in regulated England nationwide branching was not restricted and Scottish banks diversified their loans and deposits across a wide array of trades and geographies, promoting greater credit resilience and industrywide stability.

Today consumers take nationwide branch banking for granted, but the concept was born in the bitterly competitive landscape of early 19th century Scottish finance. By the time British Parliament put an end to the free banking era in 1845 Scotland had over 50 banks with names like the National Bank of Scotland, Glasgow Bank, Dundee Bank, Clydesdale Bank, and Union Bank of Scotland. Of these, 19 were note-issuing institutions with 363 total branches.[31]

Today 363 branches may not seem like very many when Chase Bank alone operates over 5,000 in the USA. But in 1845 Scottish banks operated one branch per 6,600 people, greater than the one per 9,405 in England and one per 16,000 in the United States.

In fact Scotland's 1845 branch-to-population ratio was only slightly less favorable than the one FDIC insured branch per 4,320 people operating in the USA today. Scots had greater per-capita access to credit and financial services than Englishmen and Americans during the time of Queen Victoria or Texas' admission to the Union.

In Part 2 we'll discuss Scottish banking stability and the industry's contribution to economic development.

March 1, 2021

Contemporary accounts of English (L) and Scottish (R)
experiences during the Great Financial Crisis of 1825

Chapter 7

Scotland's Free Banking Era, Part 2

The Cautious Optimism Correspondent for Economic Affairs gets to the heart of financial stability under Scotland's free-market banking system of 1716-1845, when regulated England suffered at least ten financial crises and unregulated Scotland experienced none.

OVERISSUANCE, RISK, AND ECONOMIC DEVELOPMENT

From 1716-1845, Scottish banking operated in the closest to a laissez-faire environment the industrialized world has ever seen.

There was no central bank. There were no government privileges, protections, or barriers to entry. Banks were free to issue their own notes and lend any share of their reserves they chose. There was no deposit insurance, there were no bailouts, and failed banks that could not pay depositors made up the difference from their owners' pockets (i.e. full liability).

Critics of capitalism contend that under such a system unregulated banks, left free to their own devices, will leverage themselves to the hilt, issue too many risky loans, notes, and deposits, and their recklessness will bring the entire banking system down in crisis.

Yet Scottish bank failures, especially due to overleverage, were rare and credit quality was excellent.

The reason once again was unfettered market competition, unmarred by government-granted privileges, monopolies, backstops, and restrictions that are later called "the free market" by politicians after they've created full-blown crises.

Unlike in England there was no monopoly central bank to overextend and rapidly contract credit for the entire system, and any private Scottish bank that issued too many banknotes had to worry about large quantities of its notes returning for redemption and depleting its specie reserves.

The private clearinghouse networks also settled mutual banknote obligations daily, so any bank felt the consequence of overissuance very quickly. Once again, absent bailouts from central banks and central governments, it was precisely market competition that kept the banks prudent.

Adam Smith, himself a Scottish resident of Edinburgh, marveled in *The Wealth of Nations* (1776) at how efficiently both the threat of redemption and the private clearinghouse system enforced bank discipline.[32]

Some clearinghouses even set standards of financial soundness for banks to become and remain members. Moreover, the mechanism of prompt mutual banknote redemption also effectively protected its members in the event of one bank's unexpected failure. Since most of any failed bank's note obligations were already paid, other member banks were largely insulated from the financial repercussions of its demise, stemming the contagion of panic.

Unlike in England Scottish banks were free to widely branch and diversify their depositor bases and lending portfolios.

Also given that there was no central bank standing by to make emergency loans, no government bailouts, and no deposit insurance, banks had great incentive to lend to only the most creditworthy clients and promising enterprises.

Furthermore most Scottish banks operated in a full liability environment. If enough of a bank's loans soured and depositors were not fully paid off the difference came from the owners' personal estates.

The Economics Correspondent is no expert on liability and imagines there are advantages to our present system of limited liability that promote economic growth. However there can be no doubt that having their own assets at stake proved very effective at focusing the banks' owners like a laser on sound lending.

Finally, while the Bank of England dominated English finance and diverted funds to the Crown for war, leaving small English country banks to scrape up what little capital they could muster, larger Scottish banks were concerned with the needs of commerce and contributed greatly to the nation's economic development.

In 1745 Scotland's per-capita GDP was only half that of England's. A century later it was equal to England's.

Considering England was undergoing the first Industrial Revolution and an unprecedented expansion at the time, the pace of Scotland's economic growth must be considered all the more impressive as Adam Smith also noted and credited largely to the free banking system.[33]

STABILITY IN SCOTTISH BANKING

But absent the discipline and omniscient wisdom of government regulators, didn't Scottish banks succumb to greed, lower credit standards, lend recklessly, and spawn constant banking panics like the 2008 financial crisis? After all, we're told by politicians, regulators, academics, and the media that a private, competitive system left to its own devices is a recipe for disaster and collapse.

As we've mentioned in previous columns, not a single systemic banking crisis struck Scotland during its 129 years of free banking.

By contrast England, dominated by a monopoly central bank and hobbled by Six Partner Rule regulations that kept private banks small, weak, and undiversified, suffered from at least ten banking panics during Scotland's free banking period: in 1721, 1745, 1763, 1772, 1793, 1797, 1810, 1815, 1825, and 1837.

During the tumultuous period of wars with Revolutionary and Napoleonic France, 300 English banks failed in the thirty years between 1791 and 1821.

Scotland was tranquil by comparison. Of the joint-stock banks that dominated the market, not a single one failed in the even wider forty-year span of 1786-1826. What few failures did occur were limited to a handful of small private non-issuing banks. In the 1809-1830 period White estimates a Scottish failure rate of 3.7 banks per decade versus 148 per decade in England.[34]

During the English Crisis of 1825, the largest banking panic in British history before 2008, 80 banks failed in England and 700-800 more appealed to the Bank of England for assistance which was effectively every bank in the country.[35] In Scotland only four banks were even impacted, all smaller nonissuing houses. One was acquired by a larger bank, two paid their liabilities in full in 1825 and 1826, and only one outright failed in 1829.[36]

J.R McCulloch, heir to the Ricardian school after David Ricardo's death, wrote in 1826 of Scotland's "comparative exemption of this part of the empire from the revulsions that have made so much havoc in England." [37]

And as we've noted in previous chapters on England, conservative Prime Minister Lord Liverpool and future Prime Minister Sir Robert Peel urged their parliamentary colleagues to consider the free banking system in Scotland as a model for England's post-1825 crisis reform. Peel even noted in House of Commons debate that 300 English banks had failed in the previous thirty-three years while he could only find a single Scottish bank failure on record in the same period.

Another large panic struck England in 1837 and even spread to the United States which, with its own perversely regulated system (more on that in a future column), suffered the American Panic of 1837. Yet Scotland, even sitting on England's border with a tightly integrated economy and common currency union, was again unaffected and its resilience once more did not go unnoticed.

Economist Robert Bell recorded in 1838 "While England, during the last year, has suffered in almost every branch of her national industry, Scotland has passed paratively uninjured through the late monetary crisis." [38]

And economic historian William Graham noted in 1911 that "In the heavy losses and banking failures [of 1837] which ensued, Scotland had little share." [39]

Scotland's crisis-free record is even more impressive considering its close economic ties to a much larger neighbor. A major banking crisis in England could more easily spread to the north than a Scottish crisis could destabilize the south, yet the Scottish system was so durable that it was practically immune to English dysfunction with a sole exception (the 1797 suspension) that we'll examine in a future installment.

So the British experience completely contradicts the conventional wisdom that unregulated banking leads to industry recklessness and crisis while government regulation promotes stability.

Scotland's zero crises during its 129 years of free banking stands in stark contrast to regulated England's ten crises during the same period. The reasons aren't hard to understand once history is revealed.

In Part 3 we'll talk about what few regulations did exist in Scotland, its few isolated bank failures, and the end of the free banking era.

Note: The Cautious Optimism Economics Correspondent credits Lawrence H. White's book *Free Banking in Britain: Theory, Experience, and Debate* for much of the material within the first two chapters of "Scotland's Free Banking Era."

March 6, 2021

Demonstrators protest the U.K. Treasury's 2008 bailout
of the Royal Bank of Scotland

Chapter 8

Scotland's Free Banking Era, Part 3

After being temporarily preoccupied with the Biden $1.9 trillion Covid stimulus package the Cautious Optimism Correspondent for Economic Affairs returns to the history of free market banking in Scotland with the series' third and penultimate column.

Up until now we've discussed the origins of the Scottish free banking system, its propensity for financial innovation, contribution to economic development, and most of all its remarkable stability especially compared to England.

Given Scottish free banking's remarkable performance readers might pose a few logical questions:

(1) Were there literally zero bank regulations all that time?
(2) Did Scottish free banking end?
(3) If so how, and what became of the industry?

We'll cover these questions in this week's column.

WHAT SCOTTISH BANKING WAS AND WASN'T

It's important to note that no serious student of the free banking era claims it was 100% free of all and any government control, although it was the closest to a laissez-faire banking system the post-Renaissance world has witnessed.

The Economics Correspondent has only found three interventions (excluding the 1797 Suspension—to be covered last) in the entire 129-year period.

First, as noted in a previous column, British Parliament in 1765 outlawed use of the "option clause" that banks wrote onto their notes to delay specie redemption for up to six months while paying interest to noteholders for their inconvenience.[40]

Second, as part of the same 1765 Act, the private issuance of banknote denominations under one pound was outlawed throughout all of Great Britain, a regulation intended to protect the poor, to theoretically forestall inflation, and to prevent the tiniest and potentially unscrupulous ventures from entering the bank of issue market. It may also have been a rare act of cronyism for the benefit of established banks across all of England, Wales, Ireland, and Scotland.

Third and lastly, of the 50+ banks operating in Scotland by the end of its free banking era, three were granted limited liability protection via state charter. The remainder operated under full liability until British Parliament began the process of legislating limited liability for the financial industry in 1855.

However, by 1855 Scotland's free banking era had already been overturned de jure for a decade so universal limited liability never existed during the unregulated era.

None of these three, relatively small regulations can be viewed as indispensable safeguards that shielded the industry from some otherwise inevitable crisis. Nevertheless their existence inclines Scottish banking expert Professor Lawrence H. White to describe the system as "very lightly regulated" while the Correspondent considers even White's characterization an understatement.

Also no reader of Scottish free banking would venture to argue that it was a panacea or completely free of failures. Banks did fail in Scotland from time to time, virtually always badly managed ones.

But substandard bank failures are a salutary event. Present day critics of bank bailouts rightly object that bad banks should be allowed to fail and well managed banks to replace them. Champions of statist control in banking counter that large failures can't be permitted else a major crisis will ensue.

Yet imprudent banks were allowed to fail in Scotland, and the result was no systemic crisis ever took place while the system was made better off for shedding poorly managed institutions.

In fact there was one large Scottish joint-stock bank that failed spectacularly in 1772: the Douglas Heron & Company, better known as the Ayr Bank (pronounced "air" bank).

The Ayr Bank was contemptuous of what it considered the stodgy, conservative practices of the established chartered banks and upon opening in 1769 sought to outsize them with more aggressive lending practices.[41] Within just two years the Ayr had grown into one of Scotland's largest banks, but to achieve its rapid ascent had overextended itself with bad loans and was already surviving on just-in-time revolving credit from the Neal, James, Fordyce and Down Bank in London.[42]

When the Crisis of 1772 struck England the Neal, James, Fordyce and Down Bank failed. With its London lifeline cut off the Ayr Bank quickly collapsed which is precisely what should have happened. Savings and capital were shifted away from a wasteful institution that was channeling funds to value-destroying enterprises and redirected to more productive investments. After all, the replacement of failing firms with efficient ones is a fundamental tenet of progress under capitalism, and it's precisely how the market disposed of the Ayr Bank.

Today the Ayr Bank would be deemed "too big to fail" and rescued by government regulators. Yet even with its spectacular collapse, the Ayr Bank produced no systemic crisis.

The private clearinghouse system had largely prepaid the Ayr Bank's obligations to other joint-stock banks thus limiting the contagion. Several smaller Edinburgh nonissuing private houses with accounts at the Ayr were brought down, but none of the larger banks were ever in danger nor was the larger system as a whole. No banks outside Edinburgh failed and the Ayr actually approached the Bank of Scotland and Royal Bank of Scotland for what it slyly depicted as a routine liquidity advance. Sensing something more was amiss the two banks wisely refused, but ultimately the failed Ayr's creditors were all paid 240 pennies on the pound with any shortfalls covered by the personal assets of the bank's owners.[43]

Furthermore the Ayr Bank's failure served as a warning to other large Scottish banks that mismanagement would not be rewarded by government rescue. Its collapse taught other bankers a valuable lesson in accountability and it's no coincidence that no large joint-stock bank failed again for the 73-year remainder of Scotland's free banking era.

THE END OF THE SCOTTISH EXPERIMENT

Eventually free banking ended in Scotland.

The English Peel Act of 1844 was extended to Scotland in 1845 and Scottish banks were placed under the veritable domination of the Bank of England.

No new banks of issue were allowed to open, private banknote circulation was limited to that of May 1, 1845 (£3 million, an insignificant amount today but raised steadily over time), and the Bank of England obtained a monopoly on all remaining banknote issues above the Bank of Scotland, Royal Bank of Scotland, and Clydesdale Bank's limits.

In 1914 all of Great Britain went off the domestic gold standard and the Bank of England suspended gold payments to foreign central banks in 1931.

Ironically once Scottish banking was placed under the Bank of England's note monopoly, Scottish banks not only lost their resilience to panics but in a dramatic reversal they themselves became instigators of British crises—notably when the Western Bank of Scotland and City Bank of Glasgow failed, setting off the Crises of 1857 and 1878 respectively.

Once the Bank of England adopted Bagehot's Dictum British banking under the gold standard generally stabilized, but by the late 20th century the United Kingdom had transitioned to a total fiat standard and its banks were more heavily regulated.

Deposit insurance, introduced by the British government in 1979, encouraged moral hazard with both bankers and customers who were no longer as concerned with their banks' financial soundness. And political interest groups had begun affecting lending policies although not nearly to the same degree as in the United States.

As the Bank of England coordinated a real negative interest rate policy with the world's central banks in the early 2000's, they collectively inflated dangerous housing bubbles in at least 32 countries—including the U.K.—which burst in 2006-07.

When the global financial crisis of 2008 struck, the Bank of Scotland and Royal Bank of Scotland were no longer the solid, financially sound exemplars of the 19th century free banking era. Both were large U.K.

market mortgage players. Both had also expanded into overseas mortgage markets; the Bank of Scotland primarily in Ireland, Australia, and continental Europe, the Royal Bank in the U.S. subprime securitization market.

Loaded up with bad loans and holding lousy British, Australian, European, and particularly American mortgages the two venerable firms posted huge losses and quickly became insolvent.

These storied institutions, two of the world's oldest banks with proud heritages of soundness and innovation, were forced to seek massive rescue packages from the British government. In an AIG-like bailout, the British Treasury bought 43% and 80% stakes in the Bank of Scotland and Royal Bank of Scotland.[44]

Five years later the Treasury sold its Bank of Scotland stake for a tiny £65 million profit. However twelve years after rescuing the Royal Bank of Scotland the British Treasury still sits on losses in the tens of billions of pounds.

Yet there is no shortage of critics on both sides of the Atlantic who continue to blame the Scottish banks' failures on "deregulation," "free market dogma," and "unfettered capitalism."

The Bank of Scotland and Royal Bank of Scotland names live on, the former as a unit of the Lloyds Banking Group.

The Royal Bank of Scotland name is now more hated in the U.K. than the entirety of AIG, Goldman Sachs, and Lehman Brothers in the USA. Thus in 2020 RBS Group holding company rebranded itself as NatWest Banking Group (the Scottish banking unit remains RBS) which, despite an English title, remains an Edinburgh-headquartered enterprise.

However NatWest is effectively government owned, the lingering aftermath of its Treasury equity investment, and the British government has no plans to divest its share ownership to private hands until at least 2025.

April 4, 2021

Prime Minister William Pitt the Younger commands the Bank of England to hoard gold and shower Britain with irredeemable paper

Chapter 9

Scotland's Free Banking Era, Part 4

The Cautious Optimism Correspondent for Economic Affairs concludes his series on Scottish free banking, addressing the controversial gold suspension of 1797.

Scotland's free banking era of 1716-1845 was the most unregulated financial system in modern history. Absent a central bank, deposit insurance, government granted monopolies, bailouts, backstops, and legal restrictions Scottish banks engaged in fierce competition for customers and pioneered a plethora of innovative financial services that are considered commonplace today.

And in contrast to the heavily regulated English system which endured ten banking panics in the same period Scotland was remarkably stable, suffering not a single systemic crisis for 129 years.

THE CONTROVERSY OF THE 1797 SUSPENSION

More sophisticated critics of the Scottish free banking system argue that it did in fact suffer one banking crisis in 1797, that it was a major and lengthy disruption, and that the alleged stability of free banking is undermined by this event.

Before we examine this accusation more closely it's worth noting that even if there was one bona fide crisis in 1797, a single panic during the 1716-1845 free banking era is still vastly superior to the ten that occurred in regulated England during the same period.

Moreover if the price of free banking really is to endure one panic every 129 years then it's a very small price to pay indeed. The United States has seen ten banking crises in its last 129 years and seventeen crises since its Constitution was ratified. Even with some success in mitigating emergencies since deposit insurance was introduced in 1934 the U.S. has still experienced two crises in the 87 years since (1990, 2008).

Most Americans would gladly trade their current banking system's track record for one that produces just one crisis every 129 years.

But the most pivotal aspect of the 1797 suspension is that it wasn't even induced by free banking at all but once again by an overt government intervention.

Here's how the story unfolded.

France declared war on Great Britain in 1793 and again in 1797 in what became the French Revolutionary and Napoleonic Wars, a lengthy series of expensive conflicts that would last until 1815.

Alarmed by a French landing in Wales and runs on several private English banks, British Parliament passed the Bank Restriction Act of 1797 suspending the gold standard and granting the Bank of England and Bank of Ireland the right to refuse gold payment.[45]

However the Restriction Act did not apply to Scotland.

Perhaps readers can already see the impossible situation this was destined to create. Scotland and England were joined in a pound-standard currency union and banknotes from each country circulated freely within the other. Private Scottish banknotes circulated in England, particularly in the north, and some Bank of England notes circulated in Scotland.

When the Bank of England hoarded gold as was so common at the outbreak of war, it called in every Scottish banknote it could find, draining gold reserves from the Scottish system.

Normally this would not be problematic since Scottish banks were likewise redeeming Bank of England notes for gold leading to offsetting claims and relatively small net gold transfers. But now with a government intervention annulling the Bank of England's contractual obligations, redemption became an asymmetric affair. Gold flowed out of Scottish banks rapidly but Parliament forbade it from flowing back in.

Under this arrangement the Scottish banks could be bankrupted in a matter of months, weeks perhaps.

Imagine if you will Chase bank collecting on deposited checks drawn upon Citibank, but Citibank being restricted by law from collecting on checks drawn upon Chase. Precious reserves would flow unidirectionally with a constant drain on Citi which would soon be ruined.

Now divide the United States in half down the Mississippi River and apply the same principle: Eastern banks required to make good on their promises and pay up, but Western banks granted the privilege of refusing. Eastern U.S. banks would quickly be bankrupted and a major crisis would ensue in that half of the country, all precipitated by a sudden government-bestowed annulment of contracts.

Critics argue Scottish banks could have simply refused to accept Bank of England notes for deposit, but that would not have stopped the redemption of their own notes in the south and they would still have failed—although refusing English notes may have curbed the account balances of Scottish bank customers, reduced the prospects for domestic Scottish redemptions, and at best postponed the inevitable.

THE SUSPENSION'S EFFECTS

Despite being figuratively placed in a Parliamentary straitjacket and thrown into the water, the Scottish system still managed a heroic hold-out. In his 1802 classic *An Enquiry into the Nature and Effects of the Paper Credit of Great Britain*, English monetary theorist Henry Thornton recorded:

> "...the fear of an invasion took place, and it led to the sudden failure of some country banks in the north of England. Other parts felt the influence of the alarm, those in Scotland, in a great measure, excepted, where, through long use, the confidence of the people, even in paper money of a guinea value, is so great (a circumstance to which the peculiar respectability of the Scotch banks has contributed), that the distress for gold was little felt in that part of the island." [46]

Remarkably, Scotland's own citizens didn't feel compelled to withdraw gold coin even under such onerous circumstances.

Nevertheless the English suspension would ultimately persist for twenty-four years and Scottish banks could only brave through the southward gold drain for so long. Eventually the industry appealed to local leaders and the Scottish public for the right to suspend payment themselves, at least until Parliament's one-sided restrictions were lifted.

Ironically most everyday Scots supported their own banks' restriction and were relieved that the entire Scottish banking system would not be brought to ruin by London's capriciousness. In fact there is no record of a single attempt by any private Scot to sue a Scottish bank for gold payment even as such suits were filed in English courts.[47]

Parliament finally lifted the 1797 Restriction Act in 1821, six years after Napoleon's final defeat at Waterloo.

So the suspension lasted a very long time—over two decades. Business carried on normally throughout and, unlike in England, without a systemic crisis or waves of bank failures. But customers' contractual rights to banknote convertibility were undoubtedly violated. To this day it is still not referred to as a systemic crisis or panic by financial historians.

But it can't be overemphasized that the Scottish suspension did not betray some flaw in the free banking system itself for its cause was British Parliament's intervention. Far from what big government academics like to call "market failure," the 1797 suspension instead serves as yet another indictment of bad bank regulations.

April 11, 2021

PART THREE:
THE UNITED STATES

Number of Systemic Banking Crises Before Establishment of Bank of Canada (1935)

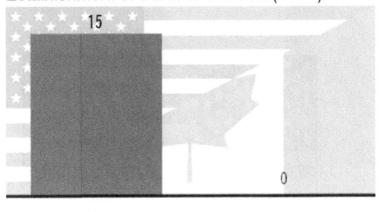

Chapter 10

Introduction to the United States and Canada

The Cautious Optimism Correspondent for Economic Affairs reopens his series on free versus regulated banking, this time focusing on the contrasting financial histories and banking systems of the United States and Canada.

Last year the Economics Correspondent posted several articles challenging the widely assumed view that very lightly regulated or even unregulated banking systems are inherently unstable and crisis-prone, while regulations and government interventions promote banking stability.

By "very lightly regulated" or "unregulated" banking the Correspondent means:

-No monopoly central bank
-No government-controlled fiat money
-No government price-fixing of interest rates
-No government-granted bank privileges
-No government backstops or bailout loans
-No government restrictions on banknote issuance
-No government restrictions on number of bank shareholders or partners
-No government restrictions on bank branching
-No government bondholding requirements
-No low-income lending mandates
-No government sponsored enterprises (GSE's) buying, repackaging, and guaranteeing private loans
-No compulsory government deposit insurance

As evidence the Economics Correspondent produced histories chronicling Scotland's nearly 100% deregulated "free banking" era of 1716-1845, under which that country experienced zero systemic crises, and England's heavily regulated system which included the privileged and later monopoly Bank of England and endured at least ten systemic crises during the same period.

Great Britain during Scottish free banking (1716-1845):

-English crises: 1721, 1745, 1763, 1772, 1793, 1797, 1810, 1815, 1825, 1837
-Scottish crises: None

(Readers interested in more details on the English and Scottish experiences can read Chapters 1-9)

Starting this January, we'll examine the parallel experience of North America when Canada, whose banking industry was very lightly regulated and had no central bank until 1935, experienced zero banking panics during its own "free banking" era of 1817-1935. Within the same period the United States, with a slew of perverse bank regulations and three central banks (1791-1811, 1816-1836, 1914-present), endured at least thirteen systemic crises.

North America during Canadian free banking (1817-1935):

-U.S. crises: 1819, 1837, 1839, 1857, 1873, 1884, 1890, 1893, 1896, 1907
                1930, 1931, 1933
-Canadian crises: None

Furthermore, prior to the 1817 establishment of Canada's first commercial bank, the Bank of Montreal, the United States suffered two more crises in 1792 and 1797 and has endured two more crises since 1933: the 1980's Savings and Loan Crisis and the 2008 Great Financial Crisis, bringing its total to seventeen.

Some economists argue the United States also suffered from banking crises in 1861, 1901, and 1921, but the impact of those disruptions on the financial system was more limited.

But surely, according to Paul Krugman of the New York Times and Modern Monetary Theorists such as Warren Mosler and Mike Norman, America's lousy record of banking panics can't be blamed on regulation. Rather the problem had to be that antiquated, unstable gold standard.

Well, aside from the problem that Canada and Scotland also operated on the gold standard during their crisis-free, free banking eras, the entire world has been far more unstable in the modern era of fiat money and government central banks than under gold.

During the classical gold standard era of 1875-1913, the most honest gold standard ever allowed by most governments, a total of four banking crises occurred worldwide (defined as industry losses > 1% of GDP).

In only three of the decades since the end of the Bretton Woods international gold standard (1978-2009), where fiat money has reigned supreme and governments and their central banks regulate financial systems more than ever before, the world has entered an unprecedented era of crisis with 140 banking crises globally (Calomiris, Columbia University).[48]

-Classical gold standard era (1875-1913): 4 bank crises

-Fiat money, central bank era (1978-2009): 140 banking crises

Finally, during the most tumultuous years of the Great Depression (1930-1933) the United States, with a regulatory lender of last resort central bank (the Federal Reserve System), was decimated by nearly 10,000 bank failures. In Canada, which had no central bank and scant few regulations and whose economy was hit just as hard as the United States, zero banks failed.

The United States and its banking history will be discussed first in forthcoming columns.

—————————

January 3, 2022

Free Versus Regulated Banking

	Branch Banking	Unit Banking
About	A bank that is connected to one or more other banks in an area or outside of it. Provides all the usual financial services but is backed and ultimately controlled by a larger financial institution.	Single, usually small bank that provides financial services to its local community. Does not have other bank branches elsewhere.
Stability	Typically very resilient, able to withstand local recessions (e.g., a bad harvest season in a farming community) thanks to the backing of other branches.	Extremely prone to failure when local economy struggles.
Operational Freedom	Less	More
Legal History	Restricted or prohibited for most of U.S. history. Allowed in all 50 states following the Riegle-Neal Interstate Banking and Branching Efficiency Act of 1994.	Preferred form of banking for most of U.S. history, despite its tendency to fail. Proponents were wary of branch banking's concentration of power and money.
Loans and advances	Loans and advances are based on merit, irrespective of the status.	Loans and advances can be influenced by authority and power.
Financial resources	Larger financial resources in each branch.	Larger financial resources in one branch
Decision-making	Delay in Decision-making as they have to depend on the head office.	Time is saved as Decision-making is in the same branch.
Funds	Funds are transferred from one branch to another; Underutilisation of funds by a branch would lead to regional imbalances	Funds are allocated in one branch and no support of other branches. During financial crisis, unit bank has to close down hence lead to regional imbalances or no balance growth
Cost of supervision	High	Less
Concentration of power in the hand of few people	Yes	No
Specialisation	Division of labour is possible and hence specialisation possible	Specialisation not possible due to lack of trained staff and knowledge
Competition	High competition with the branches	Less competition within the bank
Profits	Shared by the bank with its branches	Used for the development of the bank
Specialised knowledge of the local borrowers	Not possible and hence bad debits are high	Possible and less risk of bad debits
Distribution of Capital	Proper distribution of capital and power.	No proper distribution of capital and power.
Rate of interest	Rate of interest is uniformed and specified by the head office or based on instructions from RBI.	Rate of interest is not uniformed as the bank has its own policies and rates.

Chapter 11

Crippled by Unit Banking Regulations, Part 1

The Cautious Optimism Correspondent for Economic Affairs launches an analysis of the history and destructive impact of destabilizing regulations in American banking, starting at the nation's founding.

Since the 2008 financial crisis America's newspapers, news networks, and most elected officials and academics have cited the debacle as a reminder to the public: Deregulating banks leads to destabilization and panic while government regulation promotes smoothly functioning finance.

Aside from the problem that in the three decades prior to 2008 America's banks were subject to four new government regulations for every one removed or rewritten (Horwitz, Boettke-2010), the real fallacy from the experts is they seem completely unaware that the entire history of North American banking demonstrates precisely the opposite.

Namely, during the second half of the 19th and early 20th centuries the United States operated the industrialized world's most regulated banking system while its northern neighbor Canada possessed the second freest (1817-1844) and then most laissez-faire system (1845-1935).

The results were the opposite of what the "experts" causally assume: During Canada's 118-year "free banking" era the United States endured at least thirteen banking crises while Canada had zero.

History provides many firm and easily understood reasons for this contrast, but you'll never hear our politicians or the New York Times mention them. So read on to learn more about why America's most regulated banking system was also the world's most crisis prone.

AMERICAN BANKING: CONCEIVED IN CRONY CAPITALISM

> "At the start of the [20th] century, virtually all states maintained unit banking laws, which restricted banks from opening subsidiary offices called branches."
>
> -Russell Settle, "The Impact of Banking and Fiscal Policies on State-level Economic Growth" (1999)

In America's early days banking was an infantile industry. The U.S. Constitution didn't grant the federal government authority to charter banks, therefore that function fell to the states. Furthermore, there was no income tax and the Constitution granted exclusive power to levy tariffs to the federal governmen. From the very outset the states were pressed to find a reliable source of revenue.

These two constitutional restrictions led states to zero in on an obvious revenue target: banks. By the 1790's legislatures were imposing rules and restrictions on America's handful of banks to guarantee a flow of funds into their government coffers.

The first step was to demand financial favors from banks in exchange for permission to operate. To secure a new charter, banks paid handsome fees to state legislatures. Charters were also granted on a temporary basis by design. To renew a charter, banks had to pay a hefty fee or "bonus."

Banks also agreed to lend plentifully to state legislatures at reduced interest rates. One mechanism for realizing this arrangement was a common restriction that banks were prohibited from issuing paper currency unless fully backed by state government bonds—an arrangement the federal government would duplicate during the Civil War with truly disastrous results to be covered in a future article.

State governments also secured revenue by becoming bank shareholders. As legislatures were typically short of money they passed laws requiring banks to lend them investment capital which was plowed right back into shares of bank stock. The loan was then slowly repaid over time out of stock dividends.

By the 1830's the states were collectively receiving one-third of their revenue from these crony bank/government arrangements with Rhode Island and Massachusetts exceeding 70% and 80% respectively.[49]

These business-government partnerships may already sound like fertile ground for corruption and they were, but how did all these regulations lead to banking instability?

With the states' financial interests now aligned with those of the banks, legislatures had strong incentives to keep in-state banking highly profitable and free from competition.

Thus began the rise of interstate banking and unit banking restrictions.

Every state in the USA, from its early days to well into the mid-20th century, adopted interstate banking restrictions that prohibited any bank incorporated in one state from opening a branch office in another state.

The fiscal logic was sound: Why allow an out-of-state bank onto your turf? Their profits will be redirected to another state treasury. And the added competition will lower your own banks' profits and therefore your state treasury's as well.

Many states went further and restricted branching even within their own borders. Two venerable banks, both of which claim to be the nation's oldest still in operation—the Bank of New York (today Bank of New York Mellon Corporation) and the Bank of Massachusetts (today part of Bank of America)—opened in 1784 and were granted state-sanctioned monopolies within New York and Boston respectively.

A broader example is Pennsylvania's 1814 Omnibus Banking Act which divided the state into 27 regions and allowed 41 bank charters, each region being restricted to just one or two banks.[50]

From the politician's standpoint, why allow too much banking competition even inside your own state? It will only water down profits and deplete payments to your treasury.

But many states went even further than Pennsylvania and became "unit bank" states, meaning by law a bank could only operate one office with no branches whatsoever. Statutory language often specifically mandated "no more than one building" allowed for a bank's operations. Thus entire states were dotted with dozens and eventually hundreds of local bank monopolies.

Unit bankers liked this rent-seeking arrangement too. Why not pay the politicians off if they grant you a local monopoly? You never have to worry about another bank moving into your market and stealing your customers away.

Far from the laissez-faire mythology portrayed by today's media and uninformed intellectuals, American banking began as an exercise in mercantilism writ large, unsurprising considering it was during this same period that England was blocking its own banks from growing too large or branching. But as the U.S. was about to learn, unit banking comes with huge liabilities and downsides.

THE SCOURGE OF UNIT BANKING

The name "unit banking" may sound unexciting and fall short of inspiring great reader interest, but it's hard to understate the strain these laws inflicted upon the U.S. banking system for over 150 years. Unit banking's legal restrictions fomented multiple stability and commercial development problems for the nation.

In his study on the subject the Economics Correspondent has unveiled eleven in particular, although there could be more. Five promote instability and panics while six simply retard economic growth and work to the detriment of consumers.

To wrap up this column we'll discuss the five destabilizing problems and save the remainder for the next installment.

(1) No loan diversification.

This may be the most self-evident. If a bank has only one office in a local town and is forbidden from branching then its fate lies entirely with the local economy. Unit banks all across Iowa can easily fail if the price of corn plummets, banks on the Canadian border can fail if a new tariff reduces bilateral trade, or banks throughout mining towns can collapse if demand for the local ore falls.

In Canada, where unit banking restrictions didn't exist and banks quickly branched across the country, loan portfolios were highly diversified and risk was spread across geographic regions which in turn promoted systemic resilience.

(2) No deposits diversification.

A unit bank in a small town could be heavily dependent on one or two wealthy locals for its deposit base. During a downturn one large withdrawal could ruin the bank unless it held an oversized silver/gold reserve. And taking that precaution meant less lending and an underbanked community whose economic development was stunted.

Widely branched banks in Canada collected deposits from vastly more customers from across the country.

(3) Talent and regulators spread too thin.

In Marcus Nadler and Jules Bogen's *The Banking Crisis: The End of an Epoch*, unit banking is criticized as fundamentally lacking since...

> "No country boasts enough talented banking management to supply several thousand individual institutions with able direction." [51]

It's a lot harder to find competent presidents and executives for 20,000 banks than a few hundred banks or a few dozen.

Moreover, to the extent one supports government regulation of banks, unit banking makes that task extremely difficult. As Nadler and Bogen point out overseeing 20,000 unit banks...

> "...is in practice an impossible task for the regulatory authorities." [52]

Fraud and shenanigans are much more likely to be overlooked when regulators must track thousands of firms.

(4) Immobility of reserves during financial distress.

In times of turmoil unit banks experiencing deposit runs lived or died on their own reserve base, and frequently failed. But widely branched banks, which were common in Canada, could easily move reserves from a prosperous part of the country to a distressed one.

If depositors in Manitoba worried they might not be able to withdraw specie when the falling price of wheat and nonperforming farm loans stressed local banks, a nationally branched bank could transfer reserves from its branches in a booming shipping area like Nova Scotia. After a few days customers would notice withdrawals proceeding smoothly without bank closings, regain their confidence, and redeposit their money. A crisis was averted.

No such accommodation was possible under U.S. unit banking. Bank runs often led to bank failures or at minimum widespread suspension of convertibility.

(5) Lack of coordination between banks during financial distress.

Canada's smaller number of large, nationally branched banks participated in a mutual clearinghouse system and communicated regularly. If one bank experienced liquidity issues, other banks would often agree to make emergency loans or even acquire the bank. This was in all their interests to stem a wider panic, and if the troubled bank was still solvent such an emergency loan or buyout could even be profitable. Canadian banks also sometimes agreed to temporarily abstain from submitting each other's notes for redemption until systemwide deposits recovered.

Was interbank cooperation as good in the United States?

Consider that in 1914, coincident with the establishment of the Federal Reserve System, the United States had over 27,000 banks of which 95% had no branches (!) and the remainder had an average of only five branches (!), the outgrowth of unit banking regulations.[53]

Under such a fractured and divided system not only was it impossible to coordinate emergency lending among thousands of banks, buyouts and large-scale capital were also impeded from crossing state lines. It was virtually impossible for a larger, healthy commercial bank in New York City to rescue or acquire a small, distressed bank in Nebraska which in turn failed.

The best the U.S. could do was rely on investment bankers, who weren't bound to commercial bank rules, to coordinate what rescues and buyouts they could as J.P. Morgan famously did during the great Panics of 1893 and 1907.

However even J.P. Morgan couldn't coordinate rescues among 27,000 banks in times of distress. It was just too many institutions and sets of books to pore over in the heat of an emergency.

In the next installment we'll review the six remaining problems created by unit banking and its macroeconomic consequences.

January 6, 2022

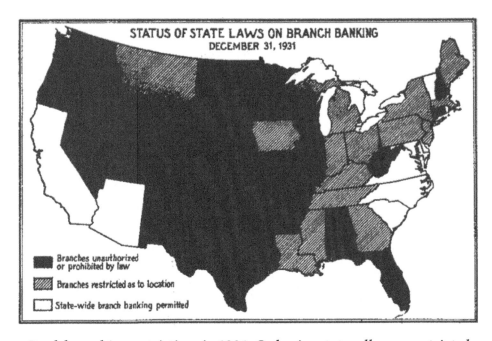

Bank branching restrictions in 1931: Only nine states allow unrestricted intrastate branching. Fifteen states restrict branching to only a small geographic area. Twenty-four more states prohibit branch banking entirely (i.e. unit banking). A nationwide ban on all interstate bank branching is codified by the 1927 McFadden Act.

Image from "Branch Banking in the United States," Federal Reserve Committee on Branch, Group, and Chain Banking (1932)

Chapter 12

Crippled by Unit Banking Regulations, Part 2

> "Practically every country in the world except the United States has recognized the utility, if not the absolute necessity, of the branch system of banking in handling commodities as liquid as money or credit. A bank system without branches is on par with a city without waterworks or a country without a railroad so far as an equable distribution of credit is concerned." [54]

> -E.L. Patterson, Canadian Bank of Commerce Superintendent— from his book *Banking Principles and Practice* (1917)

The Cautious Optimism Correspondent for Economic Affairs discusses more perverse consequences of legal restrictions on branch banking that plagued the United States economy for over 150 years.

In Part 1 we reviewed late 18th and early 19th century America's political origins of legal restrictions on interstate banking and the establishment of mandated "unit banks" which could only operate from a single office. As we left off, the Economics Correspondent discussed five negative consequences of unit banking laws, particularly those that fomented frequent financial crises and widespread failures.

To review go to Chapter 11.

In Part 2 we'll cover six anti-competitive, anti-consumer repercussions of bank branching restrictions and measure up its performance against Canada's unrestricted, nationally branched system.

While reading bear in mind this discussion takes place within the context of media and political accusations that U.S. banking was "laissez-faire" and "unregulated" during the 19th and early 20th centuries.

THE SCOURGE OF UNIT BANKING (cont.)

How did unit banking laws undermine the interests of borrowers and consumers?

(1) Lack of competition and underbanking.

It probably seems obvious that state governments drawing artificial lines around bank monopoly fiefdoms leads to less competition and it certainly did. However a specific example may illustrate just how underserved Americans were under such state restrictions.

In 1800 the four largest cities in America were New York, Philadelphia, Boston, and Baltimore with populations of roughly 72,000, 41,000, 27,000 and 25,000 each. Due to restrictive banking laws each of those cities had only two banks at the time.[55]

Canada had no commercial banks in 1800, but at the turn of the next century remote western Canada was spotted with tiny, disparate towns. The typical incorporated township of Alberta, Saskatchewan, Manitoba, or British Columbia averaged about 900 people. The same typical 900-resident township also averaged two competing bank branches (i.e. two banks) operating from large headquarters in Toronto or Montreal.[56]

Sadly for Americans, the average citizen of Medicine Hat, Alberta or Moose Jaw, Saskatchewan had as many banking choices in 1905 as Americans in New York City and Philadelphia in 1800, despite having only 2% or 3% of the population and even less commercial activity.

(2) Immobility of investment capital.

Depositors in Ohio may have been ardent savers, but due to interbank prohibitions their capital couldn't fund booming railroads in Missouri. The savings of consumers in one state frequently sat unused while promising enterprises in other states starved for capital.

The Correspondent hasn't found much material on this theory, but he suspects commercial interstate banking restrictions gave rise to investment banking and securities underwriting during the industrialized Gilded Age, making men like J.P. Morgan very wealthy.

How a Gilded Age icon like Bethlehem Steel could have grown so dominant from Scranton, Pennsylvania when even intrastate capital movements were so restricted suggests the company likely sought funding from outside the commercial banking sector.

(3) Geographically irregular interest rates.

Since large savings in one state were unavailable for industrial projects in other states the United States became a patchwork of inconsistent interest rates where bank customers of one state paid several percentage points more than their neighbors across the border.

Once again in Canada, where banks branched unrestricted throughout the entire country and capital moved freely to where it could earn the best return, interest rates were very comparable no matter what province the borrower lived in.

(4) An inefficient, high-cost business model.

Branch banking is a very efficient system where primary functions such as accounting, loan processing, and collections can be centralized at a home office. In the 19th century branch offices were cheap to operate, needing only some specie, till cash, a teller, and perhaps a lending officer.

Under U.S. unit banking every administrative function had to be duplicated across thousands of disparate unit banks. This high cost of decentralization led to higher interest rates and less credit for consumers.

(5) Depreciating private banknotes.

Under unit banking a small local bank in, say, Norfolk, VA would accept a gold or silver specie deposit and issue a banknote claim to its customer. As the banknote was spent, circulated through the economy, and moved further and further from Norfolk its value depreciated.

If the Bank of Norfolk's note was ultimately deposited at the Bank of St. Louis, the depositor might only get 90 cents on the dollar. The Bank of St. Louis had no idea if the Bank of Norfolk was a legitimate or even real institution, if it was still in business, if it had sufficient gold reserves to redeem the note, and there was a cost associated with sending the note back to Virginia and the gold coin in turn to Missouri.

Eventually innovative banknote gathering and redemption enterprises such as the New England-based Suffolk Bank sprang up, going around the country, collecting disparate banknotes for over 99 cents on the dollar, and returning them to their bank of issue for redemption.

But no Suffolk Bank was necessary in Canada where all banknotes were accepted virtually at par. A Bank of Toronto note issued in Ontario might find its way to deposit at the Bank of Halifax in Nova Scotia at which point it was accepted at 99 and more often 100 cents on the dollar.

Why so easy? Because the Bank of Toronto had a branch office in Halifax right across the street! And both banks had nationwide branch networks that allowed notes and reserves (both their own and their competitors') to move effortlessly throughout the country.

Large national branch networks made depositing even a Bank of Montreal note in Vancouver, BC no different from depositing it in Montreal, Quebec—much how we take effortlessly depositing a Bank of America check (headquartered in Charlotte, NC) at a Citibank branch in Los Angeles for granted in 2022.

(6) Finally, there's wildcat banking.

Wildcat banking is a favorite complaint of alleged deregulation for both New York Times columnist Paul Krugman and Joe Biden's Fed Vice Chair nominee Lael Brainard.

During a limited period of the 19th century new banks would spring up in more remote states and overissue notes, often sending their agents cross-country to eastern cities like New York and Boston to buy up assets. Wildcat bankers assumed, often correctly, that eastern banks wouldn't go through the trouble of shipping their notes across long distances to the remote middle of nowhere for redemption.

Overissuance by wildcat banks has been exaggerated as a problem given that scholarly estimates place the total number of wildcat banks at "as low as several dozen and no higher than 173" (Selgin-2021) out of some 2,450 banks chartered between 1790 and 1862.[57]

Furthermore "wildcat banking" only plagued five states, in each case for only a couple of years, and uncoincidentally all five states were highly restricted or unit banking states.

Which leads to the one of the strongest of the many counterarguments debunking the "endemic wildcat banking problem" thesis.

Far from being the consequence of deregulation it was precisely bad interstate banking legal restrictions that made wildcat banking so attractive to shady operators. Had New York and Boston banks been allowed to branch out of state any wildcat banknote they received would quickly find its way back to its origin demanding prompt redemption through their large branch networks.

Eventually the Suffolk Bank mitigated the wildcat banking problem, but as usual Krugman gets it completely backwards by blaming lack of government oversight. Deregulated Canada never had any meaningful wildcat banking problems. During most of its free banking era Canadian banks voluntarily agreed to accept each other's notes at par precisely because they knew other banks had wide branch networks. Any distant bank that considered engaging in wildcat practices was aware that none of its notes would stay far away for very long, thanks to the extensive branch networks of its competitors.

In Canada there were no anti-branching laws to prevent reputable banks from keeping disreputable ones in check.

UNIT BANKING'S DESTRUCTIVE RECORD

Unit banking reigned supreme in the United States from its founding, and the political alliance between local banks and state governments was a strong one for nearly two centuries. While it lasted it codified such a disparate and fragile system that the U.S. easily fell into panic during economic downturns—fifteen times from 1792 to 1933—while Canada never had a systemic crisis.

That's worth repeating. From 1792 to 1933 the United States, bogged down by restrictive unit banking laws that kept banks tiny, weak, undercapitalized, and undiversified, experienced fifteen banking panics. Canada, with no bank branching restrictions and the industrialized world's most deregulated system from 1845 to 1935, experienced no systemic panics.

By the dawn of the Great Depression politically powerful unit banking forces even convinced Congress to pass the 1927 McFadden Act which cemented the ban on interstate bank branching at the federal level.

In 1931 at least 39 of America's 48 states either restricted bank branching to a small, localized region or prohibited branch banking entirely, and banking across state lines was prohibited by both 100% of states and the federal government.

Therefore it's no surprise that the hardest hit states during the Great Depression were unit bank states. In California, a state that permitted unrestricted intrastate branching and the first state in the U.S. to reach more branches than bank companies, the incidence of failures among widely branched banks was less than one-fifth that of the entire country according to Carlson and Mitchener (2007).[58] George Selgin of the University of Georgia has argued there were no California bank failures in the early 1930's but the Economics Correspondent has not yet corroborated that conclusion.[59]

Also in the tumultuous early days of the Great Depression nearly 10,000 U.S. banks failed in the mother of all banking panics. Nearly all were unit banks and the tragedy occurred under the watch of America's central bank, the Federal Reserve.

In Canada, where full nationwide branching was always legal, no central bank existed yet, and the country was hit every bit as hard by the depression, zero banks failed.

That's also worth repeating:

> USA: Unit bank and interstate bank restrictions + monopoly
> central bank of issue = nearly 10,000 bank failures.

> Canada: Free, nearly laissez-fare deregulated banking industry
> and no central bank = zero bank failures.

In the next installment we'll wrap up with what became of unit banking regulations after the very Great Depression that they had such a large hand in creating.

_____

January 14, 2022

Table 1

STATE BRANCHING LAWS, SELECTED YEARS

Progressive loosening of state-level bank branching restrictions and unit banking laws throughout the mid-20th century.

Source: Federal Reserve Bank of Richmond[60]

	1910	29	39	61	79	90
Alabama		·	♦	♦	♦	♦
Alaska	–	–	–	■	■	■
Arizona	–	■	■	■	■	■
Arkansas		·	·	·	♦	♦
California	■	■	■	■	■	■
Colorado	·	·	·	·	·	·
Connecticut	·	·	■	■	■	■
Delaware	■	■	■	■	■	■
Florida	■	·	·	·	♦	■
Georgia	■	♦	♦	♦	♦	♦
Hawaii	–	–	–	■	■	■
Idaho		·	■	■	■	■
Illinois	·	·	·	·	·	♦
Indiana		·	♦	♦	♦	♦
Iowa		·	·	·	♦	♦
Kansas		·	·	·	·	■
Kentucky				♦	♦	♦
Louisiana	♦	♦	♦	♦	♦	■
Maine	♦	♦	■	■	■	■
Maryland		■	■	■	■	■
Massachusetts	·	♦	♦	♦	♦	■
Michigan		■	♦	♦	■	■
Minnesota	·	·	·	·	·	♦
Mississippi	·	♦	·	♦	♦	■
Missouri	·	·	·	·	·	♦
Montana		·	♦	♦	·	♦
Nebraska		·	·	·	·	♦
Nevada	·	·	■	■	■	■
New Hampshire					♦	■
New Jersey		♦	♦	♦	■	■
New Mexico	–	·	·	♦	♦	♦
New York	♦	♦	♦	♦	■	■
North Carolina		■	■	■	■	■
North Dakota			·	·	·	■
Ohio		♦	♦	♦	♦	■
Oklahoma				·	·	■
Oregon	■	·	■	■	■	■
Pennsylvania	·	♦	♦	♦	♦	■
Rhode Island	■	■	■	■	■	■
South Carolina		■	■	■	■	■
South Dakota		■	■	■	■	■
Tennessee	■	♦	♦	♦	♦	■
Texas	·	·	·	·	·	■
Utah		·	■	■	■	■
Vermont		■	■	■	■	■
Virginia		■	■	♦	■	■
Washington	■	·	■	■	■	■
West Virginia		·	·	·	·	■
Wisconsin	·	·	·	·	♦	♦
Wyoming					·	■

KEY
· Unit banking (branching prohibited)
♦ Branching limited geographically within state
■ Statewide branching
  No branching law
– Not yet a state

Sources: Chapman and Westerfield 1942; *Federal Reserve*

Henry Steagall (D-AL), powerful chairman of the House Committee on Banking and Currency, protected his state's unit banking interests by introducing anti-competitive provisions into the 1933 United States Banking Act (i.e. the Glass-Steagall Act)

Chapter 13

Crippled by Unit Banking Regulations, Part 3

The Cautious Optimism Correspondent for Economic Affairs closes his miniseries on legal branch banking restrictions that destabilized America's banking system, making it crisis-prone from the nation's founding through the Great Depression. In this last installment we'll find out what happened to those awful unit banking laws. (Hint: even the Great Depression wasn't lesson enough for politicians to repeal them)

UNIT BANKING DURING/AFTER THE GREAT DEPRESSION

In the aftermath of the unmitigated disaster of the early 1930's, virtually everyone in Congress knew that unit banking was a fatal weakness in America's broken and uniquely overregulated financial system.

However even as the U.S. economy lay in ruins unit banking forces were still strong enough to prevent meaningful reform. Instead of throwing out the destabilizing regulations, pro-unit bank politicians not only succeeded in preserving the broken framework but even managed to pass additional unit bank protections at the federal level.

Within the 1933 Glass-Steagall Act's many provisions unit bankers got Regulation Q passed which prohibited banks from paying interest on deposits.

The official rationale was that paying interest on deposits inclined banks to make higher yielding, riskier loans.

But the real impetus was limiting competition. Unit banks with monopolies in local areas were becoming more worried about competition as the automobile was replacing the horse, making it easier for customers to do regular business with other banks at greater distances. Unit banks wanted to make neighboring banks two towns away less attractive by prohibiting the competitive tactic of paying higher deposit rates to pick off customers.

More consequential was the establishment of federal deposit insurance, another provision of Glass-Steagall.

Instead of protecting depositors by legalizing unrestricted branching and greater loan diversification unit banks wished to avoid the prospect of new competition by preserving the fragile unit banking system but laying depositor risk at the feet of the government instead.

According to Charles Calomiris at Columbia University, between 1880 and 1933 there had already been 150 attempts in Congress to pass federal deposit insurance legislation, nearly always introduced by representatives from unit banking states.[61] Every past proposal had failed, but the crisis atmosphere of the Great Depression finally delivered unit banks the legislative victory they had unsuccessfully sought for fifty years.

Deposit insurance itself is a complicated proposition. Not only is deposit insurance unnecessary in an already stable, unrestricted system such as Canada's, it also introduces moral hazard since both banks and depositors can offload responsibility for taking bad risks onto the insurance fund. Indeed, Canada had no deposit insurance until 1967 yet had never experienced a banking crisis without it.

However, given the weaknesses created by legal restrictions on branching in the United States, combined with the destabilizing machinations of the Federal Reserve, post-1933 federal deposit insurance did go a long way towards stemming future bank runs from nervous depositors. Milton Friedman and Anna Schwartz commented in their treatise that:

> "Federal insurance of bank deposits was the most important structural change in the banking system to result from the 1933 panic, and, indeed in our view the structural change most conducive to monetary stability since state bank notes were taxed out of existence immediately after the Civil War." [62]

-A Monetary History of the United States, 1867-1960 (1963)

Unfortunately, although it was FDIC member banks that paid into the fund, not taxpayers, it was ultimately prudent banks that ended up subsidizing reckless banks when the latter failed. And the taxpayer was forced to fund unpaid deposit guarantees in the early 1990's when the FSLIC became insolvent during the Savings and Loan Crisis.

Therefore it should be no surprise to readers that the name Steagall in the Glass-Steagall Act belonged to Congressman Henry Steagall of Alabama, a unit banking state.

Steagall's primary interest when drawing up 1930's banking "reform" was protecting the revenue stream of his own state's legislature and protecting Alabama unit banks from outside and intrastate competition. From his powerful chairmanship on the House Committee on Banking and Currency he was able to not only save the unstable unit banking system, but bolster it as well with new anti-competitive and bailout measures.

Even Wikipedia understands Steagall's motives in its article on the 1933 Banking Act:

> "...the Glass bill passed the Senate in an overwhelming 54-9 vote on January 25, 1933... In the House of Representatives, Representative Steagall opposed even the revised strong bill with its limited permission for branch banking. Steagall wanted to protect unit banks, and bank depositors, by establishing federal deposit insurance..." [63]

LONG OVERDUE: UNIT BANKING'S EVENTUAL REPEAL

The dysfunctional unit banking system only began to fray slightly in the 1950's as large banks attempted to use holding companies as workarounds to bypass interstate branching regulations.

But once again unit banking political forces countered, getting the Bank Holding Act of 1956 passed which decreed bank holding companies headquartered in one state were banned from acquiring a bank in another state.

It was only in the inflation of the 1970's that the regime finally began to unravel. Unable to pay interest on deposits due to Regulation Q, banks began losing customers as inflation reached high single and double-digit levels. This was the age when banks compensated for lack of interest on deposits by promoting gifts like toasters to open a new account. Faced with an existential threat to the industry Regulation Q was finally repealed under the Depository Institutions Deregulation and Monetary Control Act of 1980.

The political power of unit banking forces also waned in the latter 20th century as the United States became more urbanized. City dwellers weren't as willing to put up with just one or two banks as rural residents, and the cities' voters were by now outnumbering the countryside's. At minimum more and more states were allowing wider intrastate competition (see progression from 1929 to 1990, p. 89).

The next nail in the coffin was ATM's. In 1983 when Buffalo-based Marine Midland Bank installed a grocery store ATM that participated in an interstate ATM network, the Independent Bankers Association recognized the nascent threat and filed suit claiming the ATM violated intrastate and interstate branch banking laws.

The case went to the Supreme Court which ruled, by a single vote, that an ATM was not a branch office and therefore legal.[64] Once ruled "not a branch," ATM's began popping up everywhere, dispensing cash and accepting deposits on behalf of banks all over the country.

During the S&L Crisis of the 1980's the federal government repealed certain interstate restrictions within the 1956 Bank Holding Act and states began allowing out-of-state banks to acquire their failing institutions via reciprocal interstate merging agreements. Between 1984 and 1988 thirty-eight states entered such agreements.

The writing was on the wall for unit banking as the states themselves, having long since enacted their own income taxes, were prioritizing saving their banks and S&L's over maintaining intrastate monopolies.

The last remaining vestiges of unit banking were finally repealed when the Riegle-Neal Interstate Banking and Branching Efficiency Act of 1994 was signed into law by President Bill Clinton, making nationwide branching fully legal.

However, in a cruel irony, buried within the legislation that finally closed the chapter on two centuries of destabilizing interstate banking restrictions lied a mandate that federally chartered banks must submit to Community Reinvestment Act (CRA) compliance reviews to receive permission to expand their branch networks or venture into other lines of business.

If federal regulators deemed a bank wasn't making enough loans in low-income areas or to low-income borrowers, it denied that bank's request to branch, effectively reverting back to the anti-branching arrangement they were supposed to end.

So Congress traded one destabilizing bank regulation for another destabilizing bank regulation, the latter being a major contributor to the 2008 financial crisis. By 2008 over $6 trillion in loan commitments were made by banks under Community Reinvestment Act mandates with over $1 trillion of actual money loaned out.

MORE TO COME

If you think unit banking was bad enough for America, brace yourself. It was only one of a plethora of state and federal regulatory restrictions that weakened the nation's banking industry.

Stay tuned for the next Free Versus Regulated Banking chapter where we'll discuss America's first two central banks—the abortive First and Second Banks of the United States—which spawned several banking panics themselves.

After that we'll examine the federal government's National Banking System of 1863-1914 which vaulted America into a dubious first place: the world's undisputed champion of banking crises.

Note: The Economics Correspondent credits Charles Calomiris and Steven Haber's 2014 book *Fragile by Design: The Political Origins of Banking Crises and Scarce Credit* for much of the material in the three chapters on unit banking.

January 20, 2022

Alexander Hamilton and Thomas Jefferson: Ideological adversaries whose differences included the question of a national bank

Chapter 14

The First Bank of the United States

> *Note: The Economics Correspondent is aware of Robert Morris'*
> *short-lived Bank of North America that operated under a*
> *privileged federal charter from 1782-1785 and which some*
> *consider to be the USA's first central bank. However, this series*
> *of articles considers the question of central banking only after the*
> *United States was established as a republic after the Constitution's*
> *ratification in 1788.*

The Cautious Optimism Correspondent for Economic Affairs had originally suspended his American banking history entries until news from Ukraine wound down, but given the continuing conflict after three weeks has decided to resume the series. Perhaps a little American history will be a welcome diversion from the constant barrage of Ukraine coverage.

Last month the Economics Correspondent reported on the two-hundred year history of "unit banking" laws that destabilized America's banking industry and precipitated multiple financial crises.

So unit bank laws were pretty much the extent of government's regulatory interference in our nation's banking system, right?

We haven't even gotten warmed up.

Not only was the early U.S. banking system not "deregulated"—as current day bureaucrats, journalists, and academics claim—it was also dominated by two government-connected central banks during forty of its first fifty years: the Bank of the United States (1791-1811) and Second

Bank of the United States (1816-1836). These two powerful institutions were themselves directly responsible for precipitating multiple financial crises.

THE ORIGINS OF THE FIRST BANK OF THE UNITED STATES

George Washington had barely begun his job as America's first president when a controversy erupted within his new cabinet. In a now-infamous debate Treasury Secretary Alexander Hamilton and Secretary of State Thomas Jefferson clashed over the question of establishing a government-connected central bank.

Alexander Hamilton, a brilliant polymath who was excellent on the issue of slavery (he was one of America's first abolitionists), and correctly foresaw that America's future lay in industry—not agriculture as Jefferson had predicted—had somewhat more dubious views on the subjects of government power and economics.

Hamilton was long an admirer of the English mercantilist system and wished to effectively recreate England's economy in America, including the Bank of England, only without a king. In lieu of a monarch Hamilton proposed that presidents and senators should serve for life at the 1787 Constitutional Convention. His motion obviously failed in the ratification vote.

Hamilton's economic outline proposed a large permanent national debt, a centralized federal taxing authority, and large government subsidies and protective tariffs for business, all based on the English system the colonies had just broken away from.

But the linchpin of his economic plan for America was the establishment of a national bank to act as the government's banker and lender, and which would create credit for the new republic in the name of promoting commerce and industry.

It was nearly a mirror image of the Bank of England.

A historical anecdote sheds some light on the thinking behind Hamilton's designs for the new country's economy:

In a 1791 dinner attended by Hamilton, Vice President John Adams, and Secretary of State Thomas Jefferson the discussion moved, as was often the case, to the proper roles and functions of government.

Adams opined:

> "Purge the British Constitution of its corruption, and give to its popular branch equality of representation, and it would be the most perfect constitution ever devised by the wit of man." [65]

Hamilton paused for a moment and then to Jefferson's shock, replied:

> "Purge it of its corruption, and give to its popular branch equality of representation, and it would become an impracticable government. As it stands at present, with all its supposed defects, it is the most perfect government that ever existed." [66]

Now before we portray Hamilton as a sleazy champion of blatant corruption let's make his more nuanced meaning clear.

Hamilton wanted the new, fledgling United States to succeed, and he believed the support of the elite aristocracy and moneyed classes was crucial for its survival. In his opinion the glue that would hold the fragile federation of states together was mercantilist self-interest. If the elites partnered with government and became conditioned to rely on state power to further their economic interests then they were more likely to throw their support behind the new republic.

In Hamilton's own words, the national bank was "a political machine, of the greatest importance to the state."

Thomas Jefferson, a prodigious polymath in his own right, couldn't have disagreed more.

As an intellectual product of the Scottish Enlightenment and reader of economists such as Adam Smith, Montesquieu, and Turgot, Jefferson was suspicious of centralized power and particularly central banks.

Jefferson viewed Hamilton's proposal as a dangerous financial tool of centralized government, a paper-money machine that would more easily enable war and enrich the connected moneyed classes at the expense of the general population.

He also believed a central bank would breed wanton corruption and financial instability, just as he already knew the French Banque Royale and Bank of England had induced crises and depressions during the notorious Mississippi Bubble of 1719 and South Sea Bubble of 1720.

Yet despite their sharp philosophical differences the final debate over the bank ultimately boiled down to legalities. Jefferson urged Washington to oppose a charter, arguing the Constitution provided no explicit authority for the federal government to charter banks let alone establish a national bank. Hamilton countered that the Constitution gave Congress the right to "coin money" (note: but not to "print" money), regulate its value, and regulate commerce between the states, and that federal authority to charter a national bank also existed under the Constitution's "necessary and proper" clause:

> "The Congress shall have Power... ...To make all Laws which shall be necessary and proper for carrying into Execution the foregoing Powers, and all other Powers vested by this Constitution in the Government of the United States, or in any Department or Officer thereof."

-Article 1, Section 8

Washington, never comfortable with matters of economics and finance, resolved the quarrel in his familiar fashion: a compromise. He would support the establishment of a national bank but its charter would only last twenty years after which a Congressional vote and presidential signing would be required for renewal.

Thus the Bank of the United States (BUS) opened in Philadelphia—uncoincidentally the U.S. capital at the time—on December 12, 1791. Although Alexander Hamilton was officially Treasury Secretary he unofficially ran the BUS as his personal project, making him the combined Janet Yellen and Jerome Powell of his day.

THE BANK OF THE UNITED STATES STRUCTURE

The Bank of the United States was given an exclusive federal charter, the exclusive right to branch across state lines, and became the exclusive steward of the federal government's deposits.

As Hamilton admired the Bank of England he used the same method to raise startup capital that the English bank directors had employed nearly a century earlier: a joint-stock share offering; in this case $10 million or five times the capitalization of every other U.S. bank combined and over double the federal government's annual revenues.[67]

After its successful share offering the BUS immediately loaned $2 million of its paid-in capital to the federal government which the Treasury returned to purchase a 20% stake back in the BUS. The government would then repay its loan to the BUS from future bank dividends.

As Hamilton had intended, partial ownership in the BUS quickly aligned the government's interests with the bank's.

Foreign investors also comprised a large share of the bank's equity ownership but were denied voting rights.

As soon as the BUS opened its doors Hamilton went to work inflating credit and the money supply by aggressively extending loans in the form of printed banknotes and deposits.

BUS notes were payable on demand in silver and gold specie, and the federal government's announcement that they were the only banknotes acceptable for payment of excise taxes (the government's primary source of revenue as there was no income tax at the time) gave them a quasi-legal tender status that guaranteed their acceptance and circulation.

Within just months of its opening the BUS had created over 2.5 million new dollars of money, a vast sum at the time, and price inflation was already taking hold in the young country. By Friedman and Schwartz's estimates (1968) the equivalent of U.S. M1 rose by nearly 20% during the longer 1791 to 1792 period. Rousseau and Sylla (2004) estimate closer to 33%.[68] This inflation is an important development and will be revisited in upcoming chapters.

We can see even early in George Washington's first term American banking was already far from laissez-faire.

In Part 2 we'll discuss Hamilton's success in using the BUS's power to finance the federal government's assumption of the states' Revolutionary War debts.

ps. The HBO Series *John Adams* does a fairly good job of portraying the Hamilton-Jefferson disagreement in a short two-minute dialogue (0:45-2:45) at:

https://www.youtube.com/watch?v=Vy7FJJ_ud84H

March 17, 2022

A depreciated Massachusetts Revolutionary War bond like those Alexander Hamilton's insiders bought for mere shillings on the pound

Chapter 15

The First Bank of the United States and the Revolutionary War Debt

The Cautious Optimism Correspondent for Economic Affairs pivots slightly away from financial instability to discuss Alexander Hamilton's first foray into managing America's national debt. Even readers with little interest in banking may be surprised at the level of political corruption endemic within U.S. government in 1791.

THE FEDERAL DEBT CONTROVERSY

In 1791 Alexander Hamilton directed his new central bank, the Bank of the United States (BUS), to invest heavily in U.S. Treasury debt, uncoincidentally since he was also the Secretary of the Treasury. The story surrounding Hamilton and the debt question is a fascinating one that we will examine here.

The Revolutionary War was funded partially from debts issued by the colonial state governments. At war's end it was clear that many states were struggling to fully repay their ballooning war debts and their bond prices fell dramatically.

Hamilton famously convinced President George Washington to use the powers of the U.S. Treasury to assume the states' debts and consolidate them into a single federal debt, again over the objections of Thomas Jefferson.

Hamilton believed a large national debt would establish the new government's credit in world markets and welcomed the resulting transfer of power from the states to the central government.

Furthermore he is known for calling the public debt "a national blessing."

103

In a 1781 letter to his financial colleague and mentor Robert Morris, the wealthiest man in America at the time, Hamilton had already signaled his plans to establish a national debt for the new United States:

> "A national debt if it is not excessive will be to us a national blessing; it will be powerful cement of our union. It will also create a necessity for keeping up taxation to a degree which without being oppressive, will be a spur to industry." [69]

-April 30, 1781

More controversially Hamilton convinced Washington to not only assume all state war debts, but to buy the bonds at par—full face value— even though many of the bonds traded at only 20 cents or even pennies on the dollar.

But where would the federal government find the money to buy up all these state bonds?

It would issue new federal bonds (i.e. a national debt) and Hamilton would ensure there was always a willing market to buy them using a two-pronged strategy:

(1) Although the BUS was legally prohibited from buying government debt directly, Hamilton's IPO terms required subscribers to buy their shares using only 25% in gold/silver specie payments and the other 75% with federal government bonds in three one-year installments, thereby creating an instant demand for U.S. Treasuries.

This share subscription rolled an enormous hoard of government bonds into the bank's coffers with interest payments profiting the BUS and its shareholders handsomely.

(2) Once Hamilton's central bank opened for business it would lend generously to his finance contacts in New York, Philadelphia, and Boston who in turn agreed to use the proceeds to buy more U.S. government bonds, pushing up securities prices and growing the large public debt Hamilton had coveted. The hapless U.S. taxpayer would then repay the government's debt plus interest.

It was precisely the arrangement Jefferson had warned about: the BUS acting as an instrument to enrich the moneyed classes at the expense of the general public.

HAMILTON'S INSIDERS PROSPER

Once Washington agreed to the assumption of state debts Hamilton's mentor Robert Morris and other political and finance associates got wind of the arrangement and immediately sent their agents up and down the Atlantic seaboard to buy up as many of the depressed state bonds as they could find.

Since word travelled very slowly using 1790's technology Morris and Hamilton's other colleagues were effectively armed with insider knowledge. Fully aware that the federal government would pay one hundred cents on the dollar, they bought up near-worthless state war bonds from anyone they could find including widows and war veterans, many of whom were permanently wounded or maimed, missing eyes, arms or legs.

As Claude Bowers' 1925 book *Jefferson and Hamilton* describes:

> "Expresses with very large sums of money on their way to North Carolina for purposes of speculation in certificates splashed and bumped over the wretched winter roads… Two fast sailing vessels, chartered by a member of Congress who had been an officer in the war, were ploughing the waters southward on a similar mission."

> "[War bonds] were coaxed from them [veterans] for five and even as low as two, shillings on the pound by speculators, including the leading members of Congress, who knew that provision for the redemption of the paper [at full value] had been made."

> "Everywhere men with capital… were feverishly pushing their advantage by preying on the ignorance of the poor." [70]

To pay off the federal bonds that financed the entire scheme Hamilton's first target was a tax on whiskey and distilled spirits which instigated the Whiskey Rebellion of 1794.

Most students of U.S. history are aware that Hamilton favored military force and arrests against angry corn and grain farmers and that he personally accompanied the militia army to western Pennsylvania.

Not only did the farmers feel singled out, but Pennsylvania was one of the few states that had successfully paid off its war debts and its citizens and government believed it was unfair they were now being taxed steeply to subsidize heavily indebted states like Massachusetts and South Carolina.

Hamilton also famously argued for the execution of rebelling farmers for treason but could only secure two hangings which Washington eventually canceled by presidential pardon.

Once Hamilton's Treasury Department purchased the depreciated state bonds at par, Morris and Hamilton's other friends made a fortune.

John Quincy Adams wrote to his father Vice President John Adams that...

> "Christopher Gore, the richest lawyer in Massachusetts, and one of the strongest Bay State members of Hamilton's machine, had made an independent fortune in speculation in public funds." (Bowers)[71]

And according to DiLorenzo (2009):

> "New York newspapers speculated that Robert Morris stood to make $18 million (more than $300 million in 2009 dollars), while Governor George Clinton of New York would pocket $5 million. Hamilton himself purchased some of the old bonds through his buying agents in Philadelphia and New York but insisted they were 'for his brother-in-law.'" [72]

The Economics Correspondent is a bit skeptical of the $18 million that New York newspapers speculated Robert Morris gained. Analyzing the total federal debt and federal revenues at the time, $18 million is barely mathematically possible, but as America's richest man Robert Morris undoubtedly profited to the tune of many millions of dollars. And there is no question that many of Hamilton's associates also made fortunes from the insider trading scheme.

Today Hamilton's assumption of the states' debts is lauded by liberal pundits as an unequivocal success, especially whenever the suggestion of the federal government bailing out bankrupt states and municipalities is floated (such as Detroit in 2013 and several financially distressed state governments in the post-2008 recession). No mention, of course, of the political corruption and profiteering that encompassed the bailout or the financial crisis it directly fostered.

More about that financial crisis in the next chapter.

It's no wonder the Broadway play *Hamilton* is such a success in large cities like New York and Los Angeles while Alexander Hamilton has recently become the favorite Founding Father among urban elites.

But what about banking panics? After all crisis and instability is the theme of the Economics Correspondent's series is it not? Aside from facilitating debt, inflation, cronyism, and corruption didn't the BUS also incite financial crises?

Absolutely. Stay tuned for the next column where we'll return to the subject of financial instability and review how Hamilton's dealings at the BUS precipitated America's first financial crisis: the Panic of 1792.

<hr />

March 23, 2022

William Duer: America's first Assistant Treasury Secretary
dies in debtors prison

Chapter 16

The First Bank of the United States and the Panic of 1792

The Cautious Optimism Correspondent for Economic Affairs continues with the history of America's heavily regulated and very crisis-prone banking system, this time examining how its first central bank—the Bank of the United States—precipitated the young nation's first financial crisis: the Panic of 1792.

As we discussed in a previous column, America's first Treasury Secretary Alexander Hamilton was a huge admirer of the British mercantilist economic system and wished to recreate it in the new United States.

After a fierce debate with Thomas Jefferson over the constitutionality of a government-connected central bank, Hamilton convinced President George Washington to sign a Congressional bill establishing the Bank of the United States (BUS) with a twenty-year charter.

Although Hamilton was Secretary of the Treasury, he unofficially ran the BUS out of its Philadelphia headquarters which was also the U.S. capital at the time—the equivalent of one man today serving both as Treasury Secretary and Federal Reserve Chairman.

In 1791 the BUS raised $10 million in a stock subscription, a huge sum at the time, and loaned out a multiple of its paid-in capital as BUS banknotes and deposits, its notes redeemable on demand in gold and silver coin (i.e. specie).

SUPPRORTING A NATIONAL DEBT

Although Hamilton preferred for the BUS to lend directly to the Treasury, Congress was still very suspicious of the central bank's capacity to directly monetize government debt. Many legislators remembered their own experiences fighting a British army funded by Bank of England credit, and they cautiously inserted a clause in the BUS charter prohibiting it from buying U.S. Treasury securities outright.

Nevertheless, Hamilton quickly employed methods to use the Bank's powers to support the national debt by indirect means.

First, under the terms of the BUS stock offering investors who bought initial shares at $400 apiece only had to pay the first $25 of their subscription in gold/silver specie and the rest in four deferred installments: $75 by December 1791, $100 by July 1792, $100 by December 1792, and the last $100 by July 1793.[73]

However, the last three payments—totaling $300 of the $400 share price—were to be made with U.S. Treasury bonds that paid 6% interest.

Investors accordingly rushed to buy Treasuries, extending credit to the U.S. government and bidding bond prices up while the BUS subsequently stockpiled millions of dollars of government securities in its portfolio. The U.S. taxpayer was now providing the interest payments that funded the Bank's profits.

Hamilton also used the BUS to lend heavily, mostly to his friends and contacts in the financial circles of New York, Philadelphia, and Boston. As we learned in Chapter 14 new BUS money inflated the M1 money supply measured by anywhere from 20% (Friedman, Schwartz-1968) to 33% (Rousseau, Sylla-2004) from 1791 to 1792.

But most importantly, Hamilton loaned selectively to financier friends who pledged to invest the proceeds into more U.S. Treasury securities. The entire BUS credit strategy supported Hamilton's scheme to finance a large national debt, establish the new country's credit, and provide the impetus for federal taxation.

"A national debt if it is not excessive will be to us a national blessing; it will be powerful cement of our union. It will also create a necessity for keeping up taxation to a degree which without being oppressive, will be a spur to industry." [74]

-Hamilton letter to financier Robert Morris, 1781

DUER, MACOMB, AND THE DEBT BUBBLE

Hamilton's plan to steer private investment into government debt was not a surprise to everyone. As previously mentioned, many of Hamilton's financial contacts in the large cities borrowed from the BUS on the condition they invest the proceeds in Treasury securities.

Of particular interest was Hamilton's associate and personal friend William Duer.

Duer was an attorney, speculator, and member of the first New York Legislature and the Continental Congress. Through their friendship and a Hamilton family connection he was appointed America's first Assistant Treasury Secretary in late 1789.

Upon learning of Hamilton's plans for the BUS to create a market for federal government debt Duer devised his own scheme to profit from his inside information. However, he was discovered trading in federal bonds (prohibited by Congress) and attempting to sell land in the American Northwest Territory that he technically didn't own. Duer was subsequently sued by the federal government, resigned in scandal and moved back to New York.

In New York he partnered with Alexander Macomb, a landowner and speculator rumored to be the wealthiest man in New York State. Still wise to Hamilton's plan, the two borrowed every dollar they could find— from banks, merchants, widows, family members and friends—investing in Treasury bonds and shares of the Bank of New York, a private bank founded by Alexander Hamilton in 1784.

Other financiers joined in the frenzy forming a clique known as the Six Percent Club, named such because U.S. bonds paid 6% interest. Armed with knowledge of the BUS's plan to divert vast sums of money into Treasuries they hoped to profit from their privileged information and even attempted to corner the entire government bond market.

Needless to say, this policy of deliberately shoehorning freshly printed BUS money into federal debt sent government bond prices soaring: from an index of 25 at the founding of the BUS to 129 by March of 1792. Shares of the BUS itself rose from an index of 530 in August 1791 to 712 by January 1792.

BUS "scrip" (not yet fully paid-in shares of stock) went on the wildest ride of all, rising from an index of 25 to 207 in the month of August 1791 alone.[75]

THE PANIC OF 1792

Unfortunately for the financial system Hamilton's knowledge of monetary economics left much to be desired and by the spring of 1792 redemption of the BUS's vast issuance of banknotes was draining its gold and silver reserves at an alarming rate.

Hamilton had loaned too much, too fast and issued too much paper money, inflating not only a sovereign debt and stock market bubble, but also outpacing the BUS's capacity to fulfill its redemption calls.

In just three months between December 1791 and March 1792 the BUS's metallic reserves plummeted by a precarious 34% and Hamilton quickly contracted credit.[76] He refused to renew short term loans and rapidly choked off the growth of the money supply, pricking America's first securities bubble.

As Treasury and stock prices collapsed the problem was further compounded by the BUS's sudden refusal to lend to businesses. Firms that had relied on revolving lines of credit from the BUS found the lending window promptly closed and were forced to sell what securities they held to raise cash, adding further downward pressure on bond prices.

The Panic of 1792 was underway.

With America in the throes of its first financial crisis Hamilton rushed to establish a federal emergency sinking fund—headed by himself, Vice President John Adams, Secretary of State Thomas Jefferson, Attorney General Edmund Randolph, and Chief Justice John Jay—to buy back $100,000 in government bonds in a bid to force prices back up.[77]

Jefferson, who had warned of the dangers of establishing the BUS just a year prior, was the only dissenting vote.

Hamilton urged the Bank of New York to lend $500,000 to private distressed banks collateralized by U.S. Treasuries. To convince the Bank of New York directors to lend into such uncertain markets he arranged federal government loan guarantees, promising to buy up to $500,000 of the collateral should the loans sour.

Hamilton also convinced the Bank of New York to engage in $150,000 of open market purchases and he guaranteed additional emergency lending support by the private Bank of Maryland.

Indeed, economic historians have credited Hamilton with anticipating Walter Bagehot's famous "lender of last resort" dictum a full 81 years before Bagehot wrote *Lombard Street* in 1873.

All the bailout loans, guarantees, and combined government/private open market purchases support worked. The panic was mitigated and the country suffered only a mild recession, most of the pain being felt in the financial sector.

If Hamilton's emergency lending and open market purchases facilities sound familiar, it's because he employed methods similar to those of the Federal Reserve during the 2008 financial crisis. It should come as no surprise then that modern day central bankers praise Hamilton for pioneering the rapid rescue of banks from the ravages of a major crisis.

What they rarely mention in their praise is that it was Hamilton and his central bank that created the crisis in the first place, much as we hear praise heaped upon the Federal Reserve for mitigating the 2008 Great Financial Crisis without mentioning the Fed's role in starting it.

Hence when the idea of removing Hamilton's portrait from the U.S. ten-dollar bill was floated in 2015, former Federal Reserve Chairman Ben Bernanke rushed to his defense, arguing:

> "Hamilton was without doubt the best and most foresighted economic policymaker in U.S. history... ...as Treasury Secretary Hamilton put in place the institutional basis for the modern U.S. economy. Critically, he helped put U.S. government finances on a sound footing, consolidating the debts of the states and setting up a strong federal fiscal system..."

> "...Importantly, over the objections of Thomas Jefferson and James Madison, Hamilton also oversaw the chartering in 1791 of the First Bank of the United States, which was to serve as a central bank and would be a precursor of the Federal Reserve System...
>
> ...As many have pointed out, a better solution is available: Replace Andrew Jackson, a man of many unattractive qualities and a poor president, on the twenty-dollar bill."
>
> -"Say it Ain't So, Jack," Ben Bernanke's Brookings Institute blog

Within a year of the recession the economy was growing again, but Hamilton evidently failed to learn lessons from the experience. He returned the BUS to even more spectacular lending and money creation in 1793 leading to another runup of speculation and prices that collapsed in the much larger Panic and Depression of 1797.

Hamilton's former Assistant Treasury Secretary William Duer, Alexander Macomb, and several members of the Six Percent Club were bankrupted by the Panic of 1792. Duer's losses are estimated at an astounding $3 million, four-fifths the entire federal government's revenues in 1792.[78]

He died in debtors' prison in 1799 at the age of 56.

April 2, 2022

The First Bank of the United States and the Panic of 1792

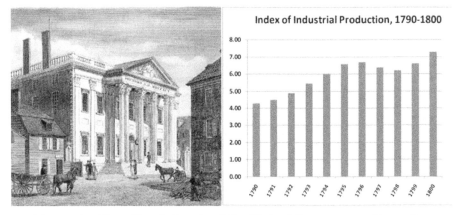

Alexander Hamilton's Bank of the United States sets off another banking panic and depression in 1797

Chapter 17

The First Bank of the United States and the Panic of 1797

"The [debtors'] prison is full of the most reputable merchants, and it is understood that the scene is not yet got to its height."

-Letter from Vice President Thomas Jefferson to President John Adams, 1798

The Cautious Optimism Correspondent for Economic Affairs continues with the history of America's very heavily regulated and very crisis-prone banking system, this time examining how its first privileged central bank—the Bank of the United States—precipitated the Panic of 1797.

As we discussed in the previous column on the Panic of 1792, U.S. Treasury Secretary Alexander Hamilton's Bank of the United States (BUS) opened for business in 1791 and immediately began aggressive lending and moneyprinting operations to support a large federal debt and spur industry.

The inflation created a major speculative bubble in U.S. Treasury bonds and shares of the BUS itself that collapsed in 1792, bankrupting many speculators and forcing Hamilton to use government money to prop up bond market prices, make emergency bailout loans to distressed institutions, and guarantee loans made by solvent banks.

The Panic of 1792 subsided quickly and the U.S. avoided a protracted recession with growth returning in 1793.

One would hope Hamilton would have learned lessons in 1792 about the dangers of aggressive money creation, but undeterred he returned to inflation in 1793, his BUS raising prices for several years and blowing another speculative asset bubble that burst in 1797.

117

THE DANGERS OF THE BUS' LEGAL PRIVILEGES

To understand how the BUS alone could wreak so much havoc upon the economy it's important to understand its unique structure at the time.

The BUS was not as powerful as modern central banks like the Federal Reserve. Under the nation's bimetallic silver and gold standard it lacked the ability to issue fiat money without limit. It still had to make good on its pledge to redeem its banknotes in specie, and it did not have a monopoly on paper currency since America's private banks were also issuers of banknotes.

But the BUS was by far the largest company in the country and its special connection to the federal government gave it more sway over the economy than any other private bank.

Not only was the government a 20% owner in the Bank itself—aligning their mutual interests as Hamilton intended—it also bestowed certain unique legal privileges upon the BUS that contributed to its outsized influence.

(1) Unlike other private banks the federal government announced it would only accept BUS banknotes for payment of excise taxes, thereby giving them a quasi-legal tender status and guaranteeing their ubiquitous circulation.

(2) The BUS was selected as the federal government's exclusive bank of deposit for Treasury funds, not surprising given Hamilton was Secretary of the Treasury. As caretaker of all federal funds the BUS was thus bestowed with outsized public prestige.

(3) As sole bank of deposit for federal funds the BUS gained an unofficial "too big to fail" status with the public. Everyone knew there was no way the federal government would allow its own bank to fail, taking its 20% stake and all federal deposits down with it. Hence the BUS attracted a large business for private retail and commercial deposits and secured enormous control over the nation's money supply and credit policy.

(4) Finally the BUS was given an exclusive monopoly on interstate branching. State-level unit banking laws, which we've discussed in previous articles on American banking, prohibited any private bank from branching outside its home state, and many states prohibited

118

branching outside a small region or forbade branching at all. The federal government allowed the BUS to branch anywhere it wanted, hence spreading its reach and influence nationwide.

Given the dominant and nationwide circulation of its currency alongside the prestige of being the government's bank of deposit, BUS banknotes were treated by private banks as a reserve asset themselves. Since a smaller share of its notes were submitted for redemption and instead held in reserve at other institutions, the BUS engaged in greater leverage and could issue far more currency than other private banks.

All these privileges granted to the BUS, and denied to competing private banks, made it an incredibly powerful institution posing an outsized risk to the economy.

In a free, competitive system with many private banks, if one bank errs and issues too much paper or deposit money it disproportionately suffers the consequences. But as we shall see Hamilton's mistakes during the mid-1790's inflicted injury upon the entire nation.

THE MID-1790's BOOM

Once the Panic of 1792 subsided Hamilton restarted his issuances of loans, printed vast quantities of new BUS banknotes and expanded demand deposits. The result was a multiyear price boom with consumer price index inflation reaching double digits in 1794 and 1795 (Officer-2010).

Wholesale prices rose 17-18% in 1793 and incredibly by over 50% in 1795[79] before collapsing in 1796 (U.S. Dept. of Commerce). Such inflation rates are astounding considering the U.S. was on a combined gold/silver standard at the time.

Furthermore BUS easy money and credit artificially drove down interest rates, fueling a craze of business startups and wild land speculation with many of the country's top financiers joining in the frenzy.

Hamilton's own mentor and former Bank of North America president Robert Morris raised $10 million with investment partners for business and land ventures, an enormous figure considering the federal government's annual budget was only $8 million in 1795.

A mania for transportation (canal and turnpike) companies began with firms popping up such as the Lancaster Turnpike Company and Robert Morris' Schuylkill & Susquehanna [Rivers] Company.

Hamilton's father-in-law, American Revolutionary War General and former New York Senator Philip Schuyler, used low-interest loans to found the Western Inland [Lock] Navigation and Northern Inland Lock Navigation Companies.[80]

Both Morris' and Schuyler's companies would go bankrupt in the ensuing depression.

And with so much easy money circulating a wave of new bank startups began. The number of private American banks is estimated to have nearly doubled from 12 in 1792 to 22 in 1796.[81]

Despite the dangerous buildup of asset bubbles everyday Americans viewed the mid 1790's as a benign boom period of riches, just as other central bank induced bubbles have cast similar illusions of perpetual prosperity. Real per capita GDP rose 5.7% annually from 1792 to 1795 and industrial production rose 8.1% per year.[82]

THE PANIC AND DEPRESSION OF 1797

Unsurprisingly the boom proved to be illusory when the BUS was forced to abruptly stop issuing credit in 1796. Not only were its notes overextended leading to increasing domestic calls for specie redemption, but price inflation also produced a gold drain from America to Europe via the price-specie flow mechanism.

Under an international gold standard, if the U.S. produces too many paper money claims and prices rise imports appear cheaper in gold terms and both its own and international consumers shift to buying cheaper overseas goods over inflated American ones. The inevitable result is a trade deficit for the U.S. producing net outflows of gold as the notes Americans use to buy imports are returned from abroad for gold redemption.

As the BUS saw its gold reserves dwindling due to overseas redemption calls it quickly halted new loans and called in existing ones to save itself, effectively contracting the money supply in a classic credit crunch. Starved of new money asset bubbles began to burst across the country, ruining speculators, many of whom had leveraged themselves to join in the investment schemes.

By 1796 deflation had set in. Businesses could not obtain new loans while their revenues fell in concert with prices and failures began en masse later that year. By early 1797 the United States was in full blown recession (called "depression" before World War II).

Incidentally some economists theorize that the Panic and Depression of 1797 were not endogenous events but rather the catalyst was the Bank of England's suspension of gold payments at the onset of the Napoleonic Wars.

Undoubtedly Great Britain calling in gold redemption and then hoarding gold from the world would have made the depression worse, but the Bank of England suspension began on February 27, 1797 while deflation and mass business failures already plagued America by late 1796. It's therefore difficult to see how America's 1797 slump could have originated with Britain's suspension of the gold standard.

Nevertheless the best historical records available indicate U.S. GDP turned decisively negative from 1796 to 1797.[83]

Retail CPI fell approximately 3% from 1796 to 1797 and again the following year.[84] Wholesale prices fell an astounding 30% from 1796 to 1797 reflecting a particularly harsh retrenchment in industry.

The index of industrial production fell approximately 7.3% from 1796 to 1798 which is somewhat comparable to the 8.3% decline America endured during the Paul Volcker Fed recession of 1981-82.[85]

On the ground widespread business foreclosures and factories that had sprung up only a few short years prior now lay empty ghost towns dotted throughout America's largest cities.

And speculators were ruined. Robert Morris and his partner John Nicholson—two of America's wealthiest men—went to debtors' prison.[86]

Supreme Court Justice James Wilson was brought down by bad land deals and spent time in debtors' prison. From jail he continued his legal duties as bad debts were not among the criteria listed for removal from the Court.

They were hardly alone as financiers across the nation lost fortunes. Vice President Thomas Jefferson noted in a 1798 letter to President John Adams that "the prison is full of the most reputable merchants, and it is understood that the scene is not yet got to its height."

In fact so many investors were ruined that the depression led to creation of the Federal Bankruptcy Act of 1800 to give petition to insolvent debtors.

1797 delivered the young republic its first truly nationwide depression, and its roots can be traced to the late 18th century version of what economists today recognize as a central bank-induced easy money speculative bubble.

Economic conditions bottomed out in 1798 and growth resumed late in the year. However, the damage to the BUS's reputation was already done. Americans adopted a suspicious view of the bank and the anguish of two financial panics in a single decade triggered the creation of a new political party, the Jeffersonian Democratic-Republican Party, serving as a counterweight to the power of the Hamiltonian Federalists.

It was, after all, Thomas Jefferson himself who opposed the Bank of the United States and warned of its dangers back in 1791.

Alexander Hamilton had already resigned as Treasury Secretary in 1795 to focus on private law and finance including BUS operations.[87] After weathering America's first political sex scandal in 1797 he attempted to exert influence during the John Adams presidency of 1797-1801 and was later killed in the famous duel with Aaron Burr.

His Bank of the United States would not get another chance to create more asset bubbles and depressions before failing to win renewal of its charter in 1811. The Senate vote deadlocked in a tie and Vice President George Clinton voted against renewal.

But the BUS would have a successor, the Second Bank of the United States, which picked up where Hamilton left off with a new charter in 1816.

April 12, 2022

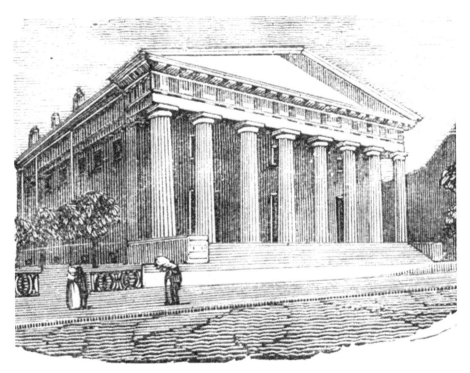

The Second Bank of the United States (1816-1836) building still stands today in Philadelphia across from Independence Hall

Chapter 18

The Second Bank of the United States and the Panic of 1819, Part 1

The Cautious Optimism Correspondent for Economic Affairs focuses on yet more federal intervention into America's banking affairs, this time with the nation's second central bank, the abortive Second Bank of the United States which directly precipitated the Panic of 1819.

WAR OF 1812 FINANCE

America's first central bank, Alexander Hamilton's First Bank of the United States, only survived for twenty years. Having spawned the Panic and Recession of 1792 and the Panic and Depression of 1797, its charter renewal died in 1811 by a single U.S. House and single Senate vote.

One year later the United States declared war on Great Britain, launching the War of 1812.

From the standpoint of government finance Congress' declaration of war might be history's worst-ever case of bad timing.

By the 19th century major powers were financing wars with plentiful central bank credit. British Parliament had relied on the Bank of England to provide generous funding for over a century and Napoleon had augmented his wartime tax revenues using the Bank of France.

The Economics Correspondent is not saying he necessarily agrees with the arrangement of central banks making vast wartime credit available to the very governments that grant them special privileges, only that the United States entered the War of 1812 without the central bank that Congress had just shuttered a year prior.

Pressed to find credit from somewhere, anywhere, to fight the world's most powerful military the states and eventually the federal government resorted to private inflation by temporarily suspending the obligation of state banks to redeem their notes in silver or gold specie—i.e. going off the silver/gold standard, also known as the bimetallic standard.

Under the bimetallic standard state-chartered private bank issuances of credit and paper banknotes were constrained by their stock of metallic reserves. If they overextended credit too many noteholders might demand banknote redemption at once and drain their silver/gold coin reserves (i.e. specie) leading to bankruptcy.

The bimetallic standard therefore acted as a market restraint on the amount of credit and paper money banks could issue, keeping inflation in check and preventing the formation of dangerous investment and speculation bubbles.

That all changed when the combined federal and state governments intervened and freed banks to renege on their contractual obligations to redeem notes in specie.

As intended, banks quickly went on a massive lending spree since, freed from the discipline of silver and gold, the more loans and paper banknotes they issued the more interest and profits they could earn.

Which was precisely the goal of Congress and the Madison administration: not only to free state banks to create vast amounts of credit and paper money, but also make much of it available to the Treasury for wartime financing, and with such a generous supply of credit available to lend it at favorable interest rates.

The strategy parallels Great Britain's when it suspended its gold standard in 1797 to fight Revolutionary France and Napoleon for the next eighteen years. The only difference was the British government received credit from its closely connected and highly privileged central bank whereas the United States government would rely on America's plethora of private state banks.

THE POSTWAR CENTRAL BANK

The War of 1812 ended with the Treaty of Ghent in early 1815, but the United States government was left with the problems of a large debt overhang and state banks which by now had printed far more paper money than they could credibly back with gold and silver coin.

Congress was fully aware that going back on the bimetallic standard too quickly could precipitate a large contraction of money and credit while placing enormous strain on the banking system. Hence debate reopened on the establishment of a central bank.

President Madison, who had previously opposed the First Bank of the United States' charter renewal, was convinced by Treasury Secretary Alexander J. Dallas of the necessity for a new central bank to facilitate the postwar transition from an unrestrained and highly inflated monetary system back to the more disciplined bimetallic standard.

Congress subsequently passed the charter establishing a second central bank, the Second Bank of the United States (SBUS), in April 1816. Headquartered again in Philadelphia the SBUS opened its doors for business in January 1817 under President William Jones.

Like its predecessor, the First Bank of the United States, the SBUS would operate on a twenty-year charter requiring renewal by Congressional voteand presidential approval.

Like the First Bank the SBUS raised its capital through a stock subscription. And like the First Bank it subscribed one-fifth of its shares to the federal government which became a minority owner.

Just as the First Bank had done 25 years prior the SBUS loaned the government's subscription capital to the U.S. Treasury which would repay the loan over many years from SBUS stock dividends.

Like the First Bank the SBUS acted as the Treasury's exclusive steward of federal deposits, giving it a "too big to fail" semblance as the public believed Congress would never allow its own bank of deposit to go bankrupt.

Like the First Bank the SBUS would accept deposits from the public and also extend loans to private businesses.

Like the First Bank the SBUS's notes were accepted for payment of federal taxes, giving them a quasi-legal tender status.

And like the First Bank the SBUS would be granted a monopoly by Congress: the exclusive right to open interstate branches and operate nationwide, giving it an outsized credit influence greater than any normal private bank.

Finally, as with the First Bank subscribers to the SBUS's stock offering would be allowed to purchase their shares with U.S. Treasury bonds, the objective being to support Treasuries prices while stuffing the Bank's portfolio with government bonds. Treasuries interest payments to the Bank and its shareholders would once again come courtesy of the hapless U.S. taxpayer.

On a side note, the plan for the SBUS to accept Treasury bonds as payment for bank shares was no coincidence, nor was the appointment of Philadelphia attorney Alexander J. Dallas as Madison's Treasury Secretary. Dallas' nomination had been lobbied for heavily by Philadelphia banker and merchant Stephen Girard, thought to be one of the two wealthiest men in America at the time.

Girard had personally bought the First Bank of the United States in 1811 when its privileged national charter expired. His by-then private bank served as the federal government's largest creditor during the War of 1812. Subsequently at war's end Girard found himself with enormous holdings of U.S. government bonds and was looking for a reliable buyer.

Murray Rothbard, for 57 years the only economist to have dedicated a book solely to the Panic of 1819, explains Girard's interests in the new national bank:

> "During the War of 1812 Girard became a very heavy investor in the war debt of the federal government. Both as a prospective large [SBUS] stockholder and as a way to unload his public debt, Girard began to agitate for a new Bank of the United States."

> "Dallas's appointment as Treasury Secretary in 1814 was successfully engineered by Dallas and his close friend, wealthy New York merchant and fur trader John Jacob Astor, also a heavy investor in war debt [and the second of the two richest men in the country]." [88]

We'll continue with the story of how the SBUS produced the Panic and Depression of 1819 in Part 2.

June 7, 2022

A Second Bank of the United States banknote

Chapter 19

The Second Bank of the United States and the Panic of 1819, Part 2

> "We are under the bank bubble, as England was under the South Sea bubble, France under the Mississippi bubble."
>
> -Thomas Jefferson letter to Charles Yancey (1816)

> "The Bank was saved, and the people were ruined."
>
> -American economist William Gouge (1833)

CORRUPTION, INFLATION, BOOM AND BUST AT THE SECOND BANK

Congress' strategy for chartering the Second Bank of the United States (SBUS) in 1816 was to use its prestigious banknotes to buy up excess private state banknotes which had been overissued in the wartime environment of irredeemable paper money.

The SBUS would then gradually demand specie redemption (gold or silver coin) from the state banks who would steadily retire their notes and the country could avoid a rapid contraction of the money supply.

At least that was the plan.

The SBUS did buy up state banknotes, but it never forced the issue of redemption, perhaps out of cowardice.

But also due to corruption. For the SBUS turned out to be riddled with fraud and corruption itself, particularly in its two largest branches: Philadelphia and Baltimore.

Of the SBUS's peak twenty-five nationwide branches, the Philadelphia and Baltimore offices issued a full three-fifths of the entire institution's loans.

Particularly guilty were Baltimore branch president and merchant James A. Buchanan (no relation to future President James Buchanan who voted against the SBUS's recharter) and branch cashier William McCulloch.

McCulloch had a habit of making large confidential loans to Buchanan and his merchant friends for undisclosed purposes "without any authority and without the knowledge of the board of that office, or of the parent bank." (William Graham Sumner-1896)[89]

In all $3 million of such secret loans were issued, over half of which was spent for personal reasons and most of which went unpaid, ultimately collapsing the Baltimore office when the ruse was later discovered.

But together the SBUS's hoard of government securities, refusal to call in state banknotes, and fraud and corruption posed insignificant risk to the U.S. economy when compared to its greatest blunder of all: inflation.

From the late Professor Murray Rothbard, for 57 years the only economist to have written a book exclusively on the Panic of 1819:

> "From its inception, the Second Bank launched a spectacular in-flation of money and credit... ...At the peak of its initial expansion, in July 1818, the Bank of the United States's specie totaled $2.36 million, and its aggregate notes and deposits totaled $21.8 million. Thus in a scant year and a half of operation, the Second Bank of the United States had added a net of $19.2 million to the nation's money supply... ...The huge expansion of money and credit impelled a full-scale inflationary boom throughout the country." [90]

Citing J. Van Festermaker's estimates (1965), the "total money supply in the nation rose from $67.3 million in 1816 to $94.7 million in 1818, a rise of 40.7 percent in two years." [91]

Rothbard also provides a sketch of how enormous the resulting price and speculative booms became:

"The index of export staples in Charleston rose from 105 to 160 [from 1815 to 1818]; the prices of Louisiana staples rose from 178 to 224 in the same period… exports rose from $81 million in 1815 to a peak of $116 million in 1818. Prices rose greatly in real estate, land, farm improvement, and slaves, much of it fueled by the use of bank credit for speculation. There was a boom in turnpike construction, furthered by vast federal expenditures on turnpikes." [92]

Frontier land values also surged in remote western states like Tennessee, Kentucky, Ohio, Indiana, and Alabama.

Stock prices soared too. Trading activity on the outside curbs of Wall Street ballooned so much that traders were forced to open the nation's first indoor stock exchange, the NYSE, in March of 1817.[93]

And all the new cheap SBUS money in circulation…

"…impelled a further inflationary expansion of state banks on top of the spectacular enlargement of the central bank. Thus the number of incorporated state banks rose from 232 in 1816 to 338 in 1818 (+45.7%). Kentucky alone chartered 40 new banks in the 1817-1818 legislative session." [94]

But the cheap-money speculative mania was not lost on everyone. Thomas Jefferson, himself a student of economic history who was keen to past central bank-induced bubbles in France (1719), England (1721, 1772) and the United States (1791, 1797) warned in a letter to his friend Colonel Charles Yancey that:

"The American mind is now in that state of fever which the world has so often seen in the history of other nations. We are under the bank bubble, as England was under the South Sea bubble, France under the Mississippi bubble."

CONTRACTION, PANIC, AND DEPRESSION

By 1818 the Second Bank realized it was in deep trouble. Late 1818 and early 1819 marked the final maturity dates for America to repay its Louisiana Purchase debt. Not only was the U.S. Treasury scheduled to repay over $4 million but the terms of the original 1803 agreement obliged payment in gold or silver coin only—no paper notes.

As the SBUS was the federal government's banker the Treasury was poised to withdraw a massive $4 million in specie within months, but the Second Bank had only $2.36 million of specie backing $21.8 million of paper liabilities. The SBUS was in real danger of bankruptcy.

Therefore the Bank resorted to the only course of action available: It stopped lending and aggressively called in loans from all corners of the country. In a desperate attempt to raise coinage and save itself the Second Bank launched a massive contraction of money and credit just as spectacular as the expansion it had just inflated. According to Rothbard:

> "Contraction of money and credit by the Second Bank of the United States was almost unbelievable, total notes and deposits falling from $21.9 million in June 1818 to $11.5 million only a year later (-47.2%)." [95]

Starved of new money to fuel speculation, asset bubbles in land and business ventures quickly popped, setting off widespread bankruptcies and bank failures. The latter, whose notes and deposits became worthless, led to further contraction of the money supply.

> Rothbard: "We get the following estimated total money supply [of the United States]: in 1818, $103.5 million; in 1819, $74.2 million, a contraction in one year of 28.3 percent." [96]

To put this deflation in perspective, the Great Depression is largely blamed on a 30% contraction of the nation's money supply over three-and-a-half years. The slightly smaller 1819 contraction was compressed into one year.

America quickly fell into a full-fledged national depression.

The number of bank failures lends credence to the name "Panic of 1819." From 1819 to 1822, over 20% of America's incorporated banks failed, reduced from 341 to 267.

Former President Thomas Jefferson wrote to former President John Adams in late 1819 that ...

"The paper bubble is then burst. This is what you and I, and every reasoning man, seduced by no obliquity of mind, or interest, have long foreseen."

And there was more bloodletting. From Rothbard:

"The index of export staples fell from 158 in November 1818 to 77 in June 1819, an annualized drop of 87.9%... ...imports fell from $122 million in 1818 to $87 million the year later [-29%]... ...Bankruptcies abounded, and one observer estimated that $100 million of mercantile debts to Europe were liquidated by bankruptcy during the crisis." [97]

Lastly, falling wages and widespread unemployment plagued the country. The estimated wage for agricultural workers rose from 60 cents a day in 1811 to $1.50 in 1818, but one year later it fell to 53 cents.[98]

Nationwide unemployment estimates are difficult to calculate for 1819 when the government didn't keep official statistics. However, manufacturing in cities was hard hit and one telling statistic from Philadelphia reveals that of the 9,700 employed in branches of manufacturing in 1815 only 2,100 remained by the fall of 1819.[99]

By 1821 the economy bottomed out. With the process of debt liquidation and monetary contraction cleared a recovery began. However the Second Bank had done itself no favors ingratiating itself to the public which largely blamed it for the economic pain and suffering inflicted upon the country. 19th century Americans appear to have been far more educated in matters of economic causality than their 21st century descendants.

To end with a synopsis from Rothbard:

"In the dramatic summing up of hard-money economist and historian William Gouge, by its precipitous and dramatic contraction 'the Bank was saved, and the people were ruined.'"

June 9, 2022

Andrew Jackson and Nicholas Biddle: Two presidents and arch-nemeses in the famous "Bank War"

Chapter 20

Andrew Jackson, Nicholas Biddle, and the Bank War

"The Bank is trying to kill me, but I will kill it."

-Andrew Jackson on the Second Bank of the United States

The Cautious Optimism Correspondent for Economic Affairs continues with his series on financial regulation throughout American and Canadian history.

The Panic of 1819 did the Second Bank of the United States (SBUS) no favors with the American public who largely blamed it for the financial crisis and resulting depression.

Bank President William Jones stepped down in 1819 and after a short tenure by replacement Langdon Cheves the presidency was assumed in 1823 by the brilliant but controversial 36-year-old financier and statesman Nicholas Biddle.

Just two months later a mercurial, argumentative Tennessee politician nicknamed "Old Hickory"—the future President Andrew Jackson—began his first full term in the U.S. Senate. The Democratic Jackson, whose ideology was based on Thomas Jefferson's vision of limited government and agrarian populism, strongly opposed central banks, the SBUS, or any suggestion of an extension of its charter.

The two men quickly found themselves on a political collision course, dubbed by historians as the "Bank War," and best encapsulated by Jackson's famous quip to his Vice President Martin van Buren:

"The Bank is trying to kill me, but I will kill it."

-July 4, 1832

THE BANK AND JACKSON'S PRESIDENTIAL ELECTIONS

The details of the Bank War are many and the politics lurid. For a digestible version the Correspondent can recommend Robert Remini's *Andrew Jackson and the Bank War*. However, here's the basic picture in a five-minute read:

Andrew Jackson lost his run for the presidency in 1824 to John Quincy Adams in what historians title The Corrupt Bargain of 1824.

Although Jackson won a plurality of both electoral and popular votes in a four-way race, the lack of a majority winner sent the decision to the House of Representatives. From there House Speaker and Jackson nemesis Henry Clay used his influence to garner a majority of votes for Adams who reciprocated by appointing Clay as his Secretary of State.

Jackson believed the Second Bank had interfered in the election, pouring money and political support behind his opposition. Although he never found any evidence to corroborate his suspicions in 1824, the Bank made things easy for him by giving him all the evidence he needed several years later in another presidential election.

Jackson ran again in 1828, this time successfully, loudly criticizing the SBUS on the campaign trail and promising to oppose its recharter.

Bank President Nicholas Biddle, described even by the present-day Minneapolis Federal Reserve as "arrogant, hypersensitive to criticism and unschooled in politics," was none too pleased at Jackson's anti-SBUS rhetoric and decided to engage in open political warfare.[100]

Biddle's first move was to apply for the Bank's charter renewal four years early in 1832, signaling to Jackson that he opposed the charter at his own reelection year risk.

Historian Stephen Campbell records that Biddle recruited...

> "...an impressive array of branch officers, state bankers, lawmakers, intellectuals, vote counters, lawyers, and confidential agents... ...to transmit pro-BUS ideas through articles, essays, pamphlets, philosophical treatises, stockholders' reports, congressional debates, and petitions, all in a standardized campaign message." [101]

Campbell also notes that Biddle's reach extended to politicians, sending...

> "...confidential agents into the state legislatures in Pennsylvania and New York, in some cases equipped with bribe money, to persuade undecided lawmakers and secure pro-BUS resolutions." [102]

Biddle is estimated to have spent $100,000 of SBUS money, loaned another $100,000 to newspaper editors, and another $150,000-$200,000 directly to Congressmen for their support.[103] In 2022 dollars that's roughly $10-$11 million; higher when adjusting for number of states, state legislators, newspapers, and U.S. senators and representatives.

And Congress reciprocated, giving Biddle his coveted renewal by a vote of 28-20 in the Senate and 107-85 in the House.

But Jackson vetoed the bill and pro-Bank forces did not have the numbers to override him (a key passage from Jackson's veto appears at the end of this article).

Beaten but not deterred, Biddle focused on his next strategy: pouring more money and political influence into newspapers and other media to bolster Jackson's 1832 presidential campaign opponent Henry Clay.

Reports of Biddle's heavy involvement gave Jackson confirmation that the Bank was indeed interfering in the political process.

Biddle had been warned by colleagues and Washington insiders that attempting to intervene in a presidential election might backfire, and backfire it did. Jackson seized upon reports of the Second Bank's newspaper payoffs and subsequently campaigned as a champion of the average citizen, fighting against the corrupt financial elites who were trying to buy their way into power.

JACKSON WEAKENS THE BANK, WAR ENSUES

Jackson won reelection by a landslide, garnering 219 electoral votes to Clay's 49.

Still angry at Biddle's attempts to destroy him politically, Jackson moved to reduce the Bank's power and directed his Treasury Secretary to cease using the SBUS as the federal government's banker, to withdraw federal funds from the Bank, and to deposit them across nineteen private state banks, dubbed "pet banks" by historians.

Mainstream economic historians criticize Jackson for this move, but ironically the U.S. Treasury has maintained deposit accounts at thousands of private banks since 1979 (known as Treasury Tax and Loan or TT&L accounts).

TT&L accounts make processing tax payments and refunds easier since most taxpayers make payments or receive refunds through their private bank accounts anyway, not through the Treasury's deposit account at the Federal Reserve—the Treasury General Account (TGA).

The TT&L program was largely suspended during the 2008 financial crisis due to concerns about possible bank failures, but the point is for what establishment historians today call a terrible policy decision Jackson's transfer of deposits from the central bank to private "pet banks," was adopted by the U.S. Treasury in the late 20th century.

Biddle, now unhappy about losing the political battle over rechartering, losing in the 1832 presidential election, and losing the federal government's deposits, contracted credit and withdrew large quantities of SBUS banknotes from circulation, creating a small financial panic and recession in 1833.

There is renewed debate among historians whether Biddle did this deliberately to discredit Jackson, some of it rekindled in recent years since Donald Trump named Andrew Jackson his favorite president and placed his portrait in the Oval Office, prompting academics to launch a new campaign to tear down Jackson's reputation.

But there's no debate in the Economics Correspondent's opinion: the contraction was a deliberate political attack and vintage exhibit of the dangers of concentrated power in the hands of a central banker.

Remini records (in 1965, long before the arrival of Trump Derangement Syndrome) that...

> "Biddle considered it his duty to strike back—and the harder the better. If he brought enough pressure and agony to the money market, perhaps he could force the President to restore the deposits." [104]

And even Biddle-sympathizing historian George Rogers Taylor writes in 1924 that:

> "In 1833-34 Biddle used the tremendous power of the Bank against the general good to force a disastrous contraction on the business community in his effort to win his personal war with President Jackson."

> "By this display of power he [Biddle] ruined whatever chances the Bank may have had for recharter... ...Biddle had demonstrated what his enemies had charged: the ability of the Bank to affect the whole course of business of the country and his willingness to use that power to the public detriment and his own personal advantage." [105]

At first the public did blame Jackson for the recession, but by 1834 the economy had recovered nicely—due in part to an international inflow of silver which we will discuss in the next chapter—and public sentiment turned again against the SBUS for causing the 1833 slump.

Without its renewed charter the SBUS lost its special government-granted privileges in 1836 and became just another ordinary, albeit very large, private commercial bank.

But once again Americans of the 19th century proved far more adept at identifying the causes of financial and economic turmoil than their 21st century descendants.

July 15, 2022

Postscript: Passage from Jackson's 1832 Bank veto message:

"It is to be regretted that the rich and powerful too often bend the acts of government to their selfish purposes... In the full enjoyment of the gifts of Heaven and the fruits of superior industry, economy, and virtue, every man is equally entitled to protection by law; but when the laws undertake to add to these natural and just advantages artificial distinctions, to grant titles, gratuities, and special privileges, to make the rich richer and the potent more powerful, the humble members of society—the farmers, mechanics, and laborers—who have neither the time nor the means of securing like favors for themselves, have a right to complain of the injustice of their Government... ...In the act before me there seems to be a wide and unnecessary departure from... ... just principles." [106]

Andrew Jackson, Nicholas Biddle, and the Bank War

Caricature of hard times in 1837

Chapter 21

The American Panic of 1837

As part of his ongoing series on banking regulation the Cautious Optimism Correspondent for Economic Affairs writes in unavoidably wonkish detail about one of the worst and most complicated financial crises in American history: the Panic of 1837.

Once the Second Bank of the United States (SBUS) lost its monopoly privileges in 1836 it began to operate as just another private bank, now renamed the United States Bank of Pennsylvania (USBP).

That same year Andrew Jackson enacted the Specie Circular, an executive order mandating that all purchases of western public lands must be paid in gold or silver coin—no paper notes—in an attempt to rein in a speculative boom in land investments.

Combined with a massive inflow of silver coinage from Mexico and simultaneous Bank of England malfeasance, the Panic of 1837 struck two months after Jackson left office followed by the smaller Panic of 1839.

THE PANIC ITSELF

The Panic of 1837 was one of the worst economic crises in American history. Of America's over 800 private state-chartered banks, nearly 400 failed, many of them having only opened in the previous year. Total assets held by banks fell by over 40%. After the smaller Panic of 1839 the price level fell by over 40%, a steeper decline than that of the notorious 1929-33 Great Contraction.

The resulting depression, while long, was not as severe as the panic. Real GDP barely fell albeit in part due to America's rapidly growing population. Real GDP per-capita fell by 3.2 points.[107]

Unemployment plagued mostly the urban areas and full employment was not achieved until 1844, five years after the 1839 panic and interestingly still two years faster than the post-2008 "Obama recovery."

But in terms of determining proximate causes the Economics Correspondent considers the Panic of 1837 among the most complicated and difficult to ascertain of any financial crisis in U.S. history, hence a longer explanation.

Mainstream economic historians place the blame squarely on Andrew Jackson's shoulders for shuttering the SBUS and signing the 1836 Specie Circular.

A great deal of the Jackson blame has been revived only in the last few years ever since Donald Trump stated Andrew Jackson is his favorite president, sending academics and journalists scouring to produce as much Jackson-denigrating material as possible in a rush to smear Trump by extension.

However blaming Jackson ignores other, larger proximate causes such as the destabilizing effect of unit banking laws, a massive inflow of silver coinage from Mexico, and the effects of Bank of England mismanagement.

The mainstream historian fable goes as follows: The Second Bank of the United States competently managed the nation's money supply and regulated state banks, restraining their tendency to overissue loans and banknotes. When Andrew Jackson killed the SBUS's recharter, state banks went on a wild cheap-money ride, overissuing notes and deposits far beyond any credible ratio to their tangible gold and silver reserves.

Furthermore, many historians say, Jackson's order of the Specie Circular required federal government land sales to be paid for in metallic coinage, precipitating a major withdrawal of gold/silver reserves which forced the banking system to sharply contract credit and produce a banking panic and depression.

Supporting the mainstream thesis is data confirming the U.S money supply did indeed rise sharply: by 12% in 1836, the year that the SBUS ceased operations as a central bank.

MEXICO AND ENGLAND

But data from former MIT Economics Chair Peter Temin, a Keynesian economist and hardly sympathetic to free banking, completely contradicts the "undisciplined state banks" thesis.

Temin's book *The Jacksonian Economy*, written over a half-century ago and still a classic today, provides strong evidence that the expansion of the money supply was spurred by neither irresponsible banks nor the absence of some mythical restraining central bank.

Temin's research confirms that the money supply did rise by 12% the year before the 1837 crisis. But the data also reveal the money supply had already increased another 64% in the three years prior to the central bank's closure (17.9% annualized).

U.S. MONEY SUPPLY
1832 - $150 million
1833 - $168 million
1834 - $172 million
1835 - $246 million
1836 - $276 million (SBUS loses central bank status)

Source: Van Fenstermaker and U.S. Treasury[108]

Contrary to what columnists at the New York Times and Washington Post might say, the SBUS was either doing a lousy job of restraining state banks for those three years or some other factor was responsible for the monetary inflation. Indeed, Temin records that it wasn't just bank paper that expanded. U.S. gold and silver coinage reserves rose by an incredible 129% in the same four years prior to 1837.

U.S. GOLD/SILVER SPECIE
1832 - $31 million
1833 - $41 million
1834 - $51 million
1835 - $65 million
1836 - $71 million

Source: U.S. Office of the Comptroller of the Currency[109]

With so much base metal deposited into the system, reserve ratios at the nation's banks actually *increased* in the years leading up to the panic, the opposite of what happens when banks irresponsibly produce too much paper money.

So where did the vast imports of silver and gold come from?

Mostly from prodigious silver mines in Mexico and gold from England, both slightly offset by silver outflows to China for its growing opium purchases.

The largest driving force was Mexico's General Santa Anna, who in 1833 had just assumed the first of what would be many of his career presidencies. Financing his government with debased copper coinage, Santa Anna declared copper compulsory legal tender at par with traditional silver coins (Rockoff-1971).[110]

Through an age-old economic mechanism known as Gresham's Law—sometimes phrased as "bad money drives out good"—Santa Anna's edict drove the undervalued metal (silver) out of Mexico to the United States where it created a bona fide hard-money inflation.

(The Economics Correspondent will write a fuller explanation of Gresham's Law in a future column)

To a lesser extent, the Bank of England pushed interest rates far too low for several years, sending gold overseas to its primary trading partners which included the United States.

These two international monetary phenomena were not trivial events. To put their historic scale into perspective, a 129% increase in the United States' stock of gold and silver specie in four years is probably a record. The Economics Correspondent has only seen tables for the first half of the 19th century and entire 20th century and nothing else comes close, not even the smaller increase during the California Gold Rush (1848-1856) which took twice as long at eight years.

The impact of the Bank of England's monetary policy during the mid-1830's can't be understated either. Its insistence on keeping interest rates at rock bottom, even as gold left the country in droves, was condemned as the worst example of the Bank's incompetence in its history-to-date by Scottish economist Henry Dunning Macleod who wrote: "Of all the acts of mismanagement in the whole history of the Bank, this is probably the most astonishing." [111]

In late 1836 the Bank of England directors finally realized their gold reserves were in danger of being depleted and responded by rapidly raising interest rates, sparking the English Crisis of 1837 which is considered the trigger point for the American panic in May of 1837.

Another rapid hike of England's interest rates in 1839, an attempt to quickly stem another outflow of gold, promptly reversed the flow of metal back from the U.S. again, worsening another panic that had already begun in March. By 1839 the Bank of England's gold position was so desperate that the directors were forced to plead for a humiliating bailout loan from the Bank of France.[112]

And in the United States, what started that second panic in March of 1839?

Nicholas Biddle's bank, now the private but still outsized United States Bank of Pennsylvania, found itself unable to redeem its notes in specie and suspended payment. Although the USBP survived the 1839 suspension it ultimately failed and closed its doors in 1841.

Civil suits hounded Biddle the short remainder of his life. He was arrested, indicted for fraud, and forced to pay creditors from his personal estate. The fraud charges were later dropped and Biddle died in 1844 at the age of 58, but his wife's family was forced to bear the cost of ongoing civil lawsuits related to the USBP's failure.

WHERE TO BLAME?

So how much of the complicated Panic of 1837's origins can be blamed on government and how much on free market forces?

For once the Second Bank of the United States, which had closed its doors over a year before the panic began, can't be blamed.

The evidence points to the largest factor by far being the massive inflows of silver from Mexico and, to a lesser degree, gold inflows from Britain.

And were those inflows free market phenomena?

Absolutely not. Rather they were the direct result of policies enacted by the governments of Mexico and Great Britain—the former absurdly declaring copper to be legal tender on par with silver and the latter granting a near-monopoly to its privileged central bank to mismanage interest rates and international gold flows through incompetence.

And one more critical factor that can't be ignored: legal restrictions on U.S. interstate branch banking and unit banking laws that persisted throughout the entire 19th century and into most of the 20th, making the entire U.S. banking system weak, fragile, and that much more crisis-prone when disruptive shocks appeared. The Panic of 1837 would have been much milder, or perhaps not even a systemic crisis at all, had American banks been allowed to branch freely across the country.

Scotland, with its large and nationally branched banks, watched as crisis engulfed England in 1837. Yet sitting on its beleaguered neighbor's northern border and sharing a common currency Scotland felt virtually none of the crisis' effects.

As economist Robert Bell recorded in 1838 "While England, during the last year, has suffered in almost every branch of her national industry, Scotland has passed paratively uninjured through the late monetary crisis." And economic historian William Graham noted in 1911 that "In the heavy losses and banking failures [of 1837] which ensued, Scotland had little share."

And Canada, allowing its banks unrestricted branching while simultaneously suffering from the Patriots War and Upper Canada Rebellion (both 1837-1838), witnessed stress on some Ontario banks but avoided a systemic crisis.

And what of Jackson himself? Does he play a role in the Panic of 1837?

Mainstream historians and academics, recently campaigning to attack all things Jacksonian, have laid blame on his Specie Circular since it led to the withdrawal of large balances of specie from the nation's private state banks.

Jackson's Specie Circular did induce Americans to withdraw specie from banks for public land purchases in western states, then pay the federal government which in turn redeposited coinage right back into the private "pet banks," mostly in eastern states.

According to Temin the Specie Circular circulated gold and silver, albeit unevenly, within the U.S. banking system but the Bank of England drove a net loss of gold from the United States.[113]

It would therefore be a mistake to argue the Specie Circular played no role whatsoever in the Panic since it caused monetary disruption, not so much in the national supply of specie as much as reshuffling the disposition of reserves.

However the main impetus for the asset bubbles preceding the Panic, a massive influx of overseas gold and silver coinage and resulting inflation of the money supply, had already occurred for several years before the Specie Circular. Some economists even argue the Specie Circular played a positive role by stopping the speculative frenzy before it could grow even larger and cause more damage, but such a position implicitly concedes that Jackson's policies—alongside those of the Bank of England—played at least a partial role in pricking the unsustainable asset bubble.

———————

July 20, 2022

RUN ON THE SEAMEN'S SAVINGS' BANK DURING THE PANIC.

The Panic of 1857

Chapter 22

The "Free Banking Era" of 1837-1862

The Cautious Optimism Correspondent for Economic Affairs examines U.S. banking in the quarter-century before the Civil War, a chapter when the federal government withdrew from regulating banks but state governments filled the gap. Accordingly, the period has been misnamed the "free banking era" by many economists who present it as proof that "laissez-faire" and "deregulation" in American banking have already been tried and failed.

After the Second Bank of the United States was shuttered and the Panic of 1837 passed the federal government backed away from intervening in the American monetary system. For the next 25 years its only contribution to money and banking was at the U.S. Treasury which accepted newly mined gold and silver from the public and minted it into coins.

For this reason the quarter century from 1837 to 1862 has been named the "free banking era" by many economists and historians.

But even without federal intervention the period was hardly free from government interference. Washington might have temporarily bowed out, but the states still played a disruptive role in the regulation of banks and in fact increased their interference. Legislatures ratcheted up control over the industry with a slew of new and also misnamed "free banking" laws.

Unfortunately, the free banking misnomer has stuck with the mainstream economics and journalism communities—in the Correspondent's opinion, deliberately—and the problems that sprang from the era's regulations have been blamed on a nonexistent "deregulation" and "laissez-faire" of the time (some examples appear at the end of this article).

153

FAMILIAR PROBLEMS

Why wasn't the free banking era really free?

First, state unit banking regulations hadn't gone anywhere. The lion's share of U.S. banks were still made artificially weak and fragile by anti-branching regulations dating back to the nation's founding. No bank anywhere in the USA was permitted to branch outside its home state. Many states restricted intrastate banking to just one or a few counties while others forbade branching entirely, mandating that a bank could literally be only one building (i.e. a "unit bank").

Unable to branch, banks couldn't diversify their loan portfolios or depositors, couldn't shift capital from healthy branches to distressed ones experiencing elevated customer withdrawals, and endured a host of other regulation-induced problems.

The Economics Correspondent has previously written in detail on the problems of branch banking restrictions and you can revisit the topic in Chapters 11-13.

Adding atop old problems were new and widespread state "free banking" laws that introduced more mechanisms for failure.

Prior to 1837 it took a lot for a prospective banker to get a charter from his state legislature. To open a new bank one often had to lend to state governments so that legislatures could in turn buy ownership stakes in the bank itself, using dividend payments as a revenue source.

Banks also had to pay hefty fees to secure a charter and the charters usually came with rapid expiration dates, meaning banks had to return only a few years later and pay another "fee" to renew. Often "fees" implicitly meant flat out paying bribes to legislators for a charter vote and was sometimes euphemistically called a "bonus."

When the federal government backed away from bank regulation in 1837 there was an outcry in many states against these onerous and sometimes downright corrupt charter provisions, both from the public and the bankers themselves. Many states responded by altering the rules to make it easier—more "free," if you will—to open a bank.

And one of the first problems with the characterization of "free banking" is that free banking states required banks applying for new charters to operate as unit banks (Calomiris, Haber-2014). [114]

Yes, securing a "free banking" charter explicitly prohibited operating branch offices. Already the historical fable of laissez-faire under this system is undermined, but we're only getting started.

YOU MUST BUY OUR BONDS

Yet free banking laws went much further with their regulatory interventions. For they not only expanded the onerous unit banking mandate but layered another problem upon it: the bond deposit requirement for issuing paper currency.

It's important to remember that in 1837 there was no monopoly central bank issuing paper currency. Instead private banks, which accepted gold and silver deposits from customers, issued banknotes which were payable on demand in the dollar's defined weight of specie: 24.75 grains of pure gold or 371.25 grains of silver. And like nearly every other country at the time America relied on private banks to provide paper currency.

Unhappy to leave well enough alone, the free banking states fastened a new condition for banks to supply private currency: banknote issuances had to be 100% backed by bonds.

And just what kind of bonds? The state government's itself of course.

Why state government bonds and how did this rule breed financial instability?

The political rationale marketed to the public was "If your bank fails what better asset to back your banknote than a government bond that is repaid with the power of the state's taxing authority?"

But the real impetus was that state legislatures wanted a generous source of revenue for "infrastructure" spending.

In the 1830's, 40's, and 50's the U.S. was engulfed in an infrastructure craze. Steamboats, canals, railroads, bridges, and turnpikes were all the rage being built up everywhere.

While building an advanced infrastructure for a country is generally a good thing, state governments weren't content letting private industry handle the work. Many states decided to get in on the party themselves and borrowed heavily to do so.

And if you want to borrow a lot of money quickly and easily what better place to find it than banks? Banks are concentrated money centers and it's far easier to borrow from a handful of banks than to solicit thousands of private households or wealthy widows to lend you money in small, disparate amounts.

Hence the state bond mandate. If banks wanted to issue paper currency they were forced by free banking laws to lend the same amount to their state governments and hold the bonds on their balance sheets.

BAD BONDS = BAD BUSINESS

Even given the misnomer of "free banking," one can already see how this state/bank arrangement provided opportunities for waste and corruption, or what many call crony capitalism today. Unfortunately, it also led to unnecessary bank failures and one significant financial crisis in 1857.

Most "free banking" state governments proved to be incompetent, if not completely corrupt, when it came to building infrastructure. Their borrowed funds were often wasted or simply disappeared. States commonly squandered their budgets before projects had even begun, the coffers running dry before the first bridge girder was installed, the first mile of turnpike was paved, or the first foot of railroad track was laid.

On a side note, does any of this sound familiar today? Like the hundreds of billions of dollars in federal "stimulus" money from 2009 that promised to fix America's infrastructure yet largely evaporated?

Unsurprisingly most free banking states had difficulty servicing their bonds and many of them defaulted. As the value of their bonds plummeted, often reaching zero, banks found themselves unable to issue paper currency since by statute the value of notes outstanding was limited to the value of their state bond holdings, much of which was now worthless.

Prohibited from issuing cash, banks were faced with angry customers who demanded something they could use to conduct hand-to-hand transactions, so depositors withdrew the only remaining option: gold or silver coin. The loss of gold and silver reserves forced banks to contract credit and a monetary crunch then ensued.

Worsening the strain was the impact of lousy bonds on bank balance sheets. State bonds were added to the assets side of bank ledgers, but when bonds depreciated or became worthless the bank's adjusted assets took a large haircut. When word got out a bank was now technically insolvent its depositors rushed for the exits, lining up to withdraw their gold and silver coin in a classic bank run.

And all because state governments forced banks to serve as a tool of fiscal policy, mandating they lend heavily to legislatures which in turn misspent the proceeds.

As monetary economist George Selgin points out "Careful economic historians have shown that [depreciating state government bonds] was the main cause of free bank failures in the antebellum United States."

THE FINAL TALLY

At its peak how prevalent was free banking in the United States?

Selgin places the number of states at "a great many," at least thirteen states with Michigan starting in 1837, followed by New York and Georgia in 1838.[115]

Chris Surro (UCLA, 2015) numbers free banking states at eighteen by 1860 when there were thirty-three states (55%).[116]

And prolific economic historian Hugh Rockoff (Rutgers, 1975) provides the most comprehensive list so far, confirming eighteen states in 1860 including their dates of adoption.[117]

Michigan (1837, again in 1857)
New York (1838)
Georgia (1838)
Alabama (1849)
New Jersey (1850)
Massachusetts (1851)
Vermont (1851)
Ohio (1851)
Illinois (1851)
Connecticut (1852)

Tennessee (1852)
Indiana (1852)
Wisconsin (1852)
Florida (1853)
Louisiana (1853)
Iowa (1858)
Minnesota (1858)
Pennsylvania (1860)

Three more states—Virginia, Kentucky, and Missouri—forced the bondholding requirement on their banks without passing comprehensive free banking laws, bringing the total number of states requiring bond purchases to twenty-one of thirty-three (64%).[118]

Yet despite eighteen of thirty-three states forcing their banks to become non-branching unit banks and twenty-one states compelling banks to buy their mostly lousy government securities, the absence of the additional layer of federal regulation still made the so-called "free banking" era one of the quieter periods in terms of America's banking panics.

Only one substantial crisis, the Panic of 1857, struck during the quarter century and the country was able to rebound fairly quickly from the ensuing recession. This stands in contrast to the two panics of the First Bank of the United States era (1791-1811) and the highly destructive Panic of 1819 under stewardship of the Second Bank of the United States (1816-1836) followed shortly by the Panic of 1837.

None of which stops many academics and the press from depicting free banking era disruptions as failures of "deregulation" and "laissez-faire."

The free banking era ended in 1863 but only because the Civil War Union government returned to regulating banks with a vengeance.

In our next column we'll visit the 51-year long "National Banking System" era (1863-1914) which produced the worst run of banking crises in the nation's history.

July 26, 2022

Postscript: A few quotes from academics and/or the U.S. press regarding the "free banking" and Gilded Age eras:

(1) "Andrew Jackson had famously allowed the charter of the Second Bank of the United States to expire in the 1830s. With only loose regulation, the financial system was decentralized and rudderless...
...so the industrializing United States suffered a continual spate of financial panics, bank runs, money shortages and, indeed, full-blown depressions."

–Daniel Gross, "The Horsetrading that gave birth to the Federal Reserve," *Washington Post*

(2) "...for most of the 19th century and into the 20th century, laissez faire attitudes and minimal state regulations led to a succession of financial panics."

-Jon Talton, "Trump's reshaped Fed won't reveal itself until the next crisis," *Seattle Times*

(3) 'We've had periods when banking was relatively free of regulation. Those periods were characterized by one crisis after another... ...In much of the 19th century, when banking regulation was virtually nonexistent, financial panics and bank failures were commonplace."

-Robert Bennett, "A Banking Puzzle," *New York Times*

(4) "History tells us that banking is subject to occasional destructive 'panics' that can wreak havoc with the economy... ...Gilded Age America — a land with minimal government and no Fed — was subject to panics roughly once every six years."

-Paul Krugman, "Why We Regulate," *New York Times*

Chapter 23

The U.S. National Banking System of 1863-1914, Part 1

The Cautious Optimism Correspondent for Economic Affairs continues his series on American banking history with an analysis of the pivotal National Banking System of 1863-1914, a regime of federal codes and rules that inflicted sufficient pain and agony on the American financial system for the country to acquiesce to the adoption of the Federal Reserve System.

As everyone knows the U.S. Civil War broke out in 1861. After 25 years of federal non-intervention in banking the Union government found itself pitted against the Confederacy.

Just as with the War of 1812 Washington, DC found itself with an expensive conflict to pay for but no central bank to finance it.

Thus the Lincoln administration decided to fund the war effort in three ways: a new income tax (later struck down by the Supreme Court), the issuance of U.S. Treasury "greenback" paper notes, and an expansion of credit under the new National Banking System (NBS).

Greenbacks are an easy concept to grasp. In 1862 the Treasury simply began printing its own money. As black and white photography had newly arrived the Treasury chose green ink to preempt counterfeiting.

Greenbacks were not redeemable in gold or silver but the Treasury made a vague promise to do so at some unspecified date after war's end, a promise that the federal government ultimately kept beginning in 1879. They were also declared legal tender, but several western states defied the mandate so greenbacks depreciated against private gold and silver-backed money wherever the edict was challenged.

THE NATIONAL BANKING SYSTEM

The National Banking System was somewhat more complicated and its creation would drag the United States into a half century of larger, increasingly frequent, and more destructive banking panics.

Prior to the Civil War all private banks, with the exceptions of the Bank of the United States and Second Bank of the United States, were chartered by state governments and required to comply with state regulations to open and remain in business.

In 1863 the federal government decided to create a parallel system for chartering national banks that would abide by federal rules.

Nationally chartered banks would issue uniform currency and each would be legally compelled to accept notes from every other. But insidiously, and in a manner eerily similar to the previous "free banking" era of 1837-1862, national banks were only allowed to issue paper currency if backed 111% by U.S. government bonds.[119] Once again a government—this time the federal government—forced banks to lend generously to its treasury for the right to issue paper currency.

Surveying the National Banking System and all its restrictions most banks said "no thank you" and elected to remain state chartered.

So in 1864 Congress added a greater incentive to join the national system by slapping every state-chartered bank with a 10% tax against the face value of all banknotes issued, effectively taxing them out of existence.[120] State banks were forced to either join the National Banking System (which most did) or give up their lucrative note-issuing operations and consolidate into banks of deposit only.

PROBLEMS ARISE

As of 1864 America found itself with a radically different banking structure. All paper money was now issued exclusively by nationally chartered banks which were forced to hold one dollar in U.S. government bonds for every 90 cents of private currency issued (111% backing). Clearly this was a revenue measure to finance the Civil War and it worked for a while, performing far better than the Confederacy's direct issuance of government "grayback" currency. While prices roughly doubled in the

Union during the course of the war the South was wrecked by hyperinflation.

However major problems began to appear after the war, problems that generated larger and more frequent financial crises than at any time before.

In the years after the war successive Republican administrations frequently ran fiscal budget surpluses and (brace yourselves for a shock) steadily paid down the national war debt. From 1865 to 1893 the national debt fell from $2.8 billion to $1.5 billion, and as a share of the rapidly growing economy it fell even faster; from 33% of GDP to just 10%.

But the National Banking System regulations didn't change. Banks were still required to back their currency 111% by U.S. government bonds, bonds that were disappearing as the Treasury retired them one after another.

So even as the U.S. economy boomed during the Gilded Age the nation's stock of cash was shrinking. For half a century outdated wartime regulations handtied banks' ability to issue cash in a rapidly growing economy, and the scarcity of banknotes increasingly translated into outright crisis when demand for cash rose; namely during harvest seasons.

Hence we reach the primary, although not exclusive, NBS mechanism that triggered major financial crises in 1873, 1893, and 1907 with incipient crises in 1884, 1890, and 1896.

When farmers paid hired hands to help with harvests they needed cash (most farm laborers didn't have checking accounts) and visited their local bank to convert some of their deposit balances into tangible banknotes.

But under NBS rules many banks were forced to refuse, explaining to customers "I'm sorry, there aren't enough federal bonds available for me to issue notes. I'm not allowed to give you cash."

Given that farmers had to pay their hired hands with some hand-to-hand instrument they demanded the only other option available to them: gold coin. And as large balances of gold coin were withdrawn from national banks the entire system lost reserves, forcing a general contraction of credit. Banks abruptly stopped lending, called in loans, and interest rates surged.

Further illustrating this mechanism, the Economics Correspondent recently completed Edwin Hoyt's 1965 biography on the life of John Pierpont Morgan. Describing the famous Panic of 1907 Hoyt writes:

> "It was the usual problem: the shortage of cash in the marketplace with the Western harvests in progress and much cash needed." [121]

Hoyt doesn't explain in detail *why* shortages of cash were so frequent but now CO Nation knows: the bondholding requirement mandated by the National Banking System which in turn provided the primary regulatory trigger that destabilized the financial system.

All it took was a slightly disruptive event to occur anywhere in the world and, combined with NBS-inspired gold withdrawals, the U.S. found itself in full blown panic, again and again.

It's no coincidence that of the six panics recorded during the 1863-1914 National Banking Era—1873, 1884, 1890, 1893, 1896, 1907 and possibly a seventh smaller one, the Northern Securities Crisis of 1901—all but one occurred in the autumn months.

THE UNITED STATES VS CANADA

The Economics Correspondent has provided a visual aid (next page) that illustrates the regulatory kneecapping of American banks' ability to issue paper currency.

In the chart we see the quantity of banknotes circulating—not the entire money supply, just the cash component—in both the regulated United States and very lightly regulated Canada. The American line is smooth and steadily declining for the first dozen years or so. The jagged, sawtooth Canadian line steadily rises for three decades.

United States: Already we see one major problem in the U.S. graph. Currency declines by nearly 50% during the most rapid period of economic growth in the nation's history, a completely upside-down correlation that was forced upon the country by the Treasury bond deposit mandates of the National Banking System.

By the early 1890's Congress recognized there was a problem and issued more bonds, but the quantity was still inadequate as banknotes outstanding only increased by 100% from 1880 to 1910 whereas nominal GDP grew by 223% during the same period.[122]

Canada: The Canadian supply of banknotes rises and falls in a sawtooth pattern reflecting seasonal demands for cash. Banknotes in circulation expand reliably every fall and decline by winter as paid hands spend their cash, merchants deposit the cash into the banking system, and notes are converted back into deposit balances.

Unlike in the United States the deregulated Canadian banks were allowed to accommodate the market's seasonal demands for cash. American cash balances were held rigid and inflexible by National Banking System rules. Hence during the Gilded Age while the U.S. suffered from at least six banking panics, three of them major, Canada experienced none.

The American graph also reflects the so-called "inelastic currency" that modern-day economists accuse the pre-Fed banking system of and hail the newly formed Federal Reserve System for then fixing.

They're correct to call the pre-Fed era currency inelastic, but what they nearly always fail to mention is the inelasticity was imposed completely by federal banking regulations that the Federal Reserve was never held to.

A final note: As monetary economist George Selgin has pointed out, if you show the Canadian graph to today's typical government or Keynesian economist they will likely applaud "Look at the banking system issuing cash in accordance with the seasonal demands of the economy."

Followed by: "What omniscient central banker was managing the supply of currency for the banks so effectively all those years?" [123]

They might be shocked at the answer: None.

Canada didn't have a central bank until 1935. In fact, Canada imposed very few regulations on its banks at all. From 1845 to 1935 Canada operated the industrialized world's most deregulated banking system, a horrifying prospect for Keynesian economists who would undoubtedly howl "laissez-faire" were anyone to suggest resurrecting it today.

But the "omniscient central banker" of 19th century Canada was in

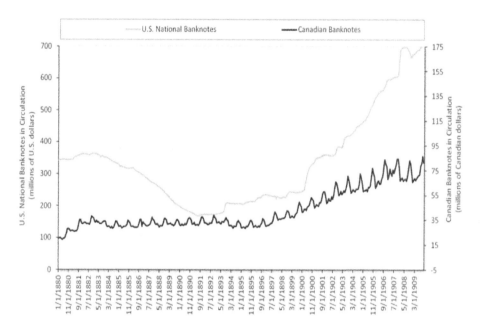

***U.S. National Banknotes (grey) in circulation vs
Canadian Banknotes (black), 1880-1910*** [124]

fact the free market: every private bank satisfying the cash demands of its customers, unimpeded by the perverse legal restrictions that afflicted the United States.

Stay tuned for Part 2 where we'll discuss even more crisis-breeding provisions of the National Banking System and the politicized decision to seek resolution with the Federal Reserve.

October 7, 2022

THE CURRENCY QUESTION

How Canada Has Solved It with Fair Success.

MUCH FLEXIBILITY SECURED

Circulation Rises with Crop Demands — Some Interesting Comparisons with Our System.

New York Times, January 14, 1906

Bygone era of reason at the New York Times:
"Congressman [Charles] Fowler's [R-NJ] currency bill...
...embodies many of the features of the system to which the
currency of Canada owes its admirable quality of elasticity"

166

Chapter 24

The U.S. National Banking System of 1863-1914, Part 2

The Cautious Optimism Correspondent for Economic Affairs concludes his analysis of the dysfunctional U.S. National Banking System of 1863-1914, discussing more backwards regulations that bred multiple financial crises—ultimately leading to Congressional horse trading that replaced the NBS with the Federal Reserve System.

As we discussed in the last chapter, America's National Banking System (NBS) regulations prohibited federally chartered banks from issuing paper currency unless backed 111% by U.S. government bonds.

As the Civil War national debt was paid down, national banks found it impossible to secure sufficient bonds to satisfy seasonal demands for cash. In lieu of paper currency farmers demanded gold coin to pay harvest season workers, precipitating several credit crunches and general monetary panics.

Combined with state-level unit banking laws that had already weakened American banks going back to the nation's founding, National Banking System regulations precipitated severe banking panics in 1873, 1893, and 1907 with incipient panics in 1884, 1890, and 1896.

RESERVE BANKS

But there was another provision within the National Banking Acts that not only made financial crises worse and more frequent but also entrenched the system politically, making it harder to reform.

In the pre-NBS era of 1837-1862, state-chartered banks issued banknotes and deposits backed by their own gold and silver coin reserves and (problematically) state government bonds.

Under the NBS, federally chartered banks were no longer required to hold as large a gold or silver reserve. For reasons we'll discuss in a moment the National Banking Acts divided banks up into three tiers and loosened the reserve requirements for them all.[125]

The three tiers, from smallest to largest, were:

(1) Country banks: Thousands of tiny banks, usually unit banks with no branches, that were scattered throughout rural areas.

(2) Reserve city banks: Larger banks in regional metro centers like Chicago, St. Louis, or Atlanta.

(3) Central reserve city banks: A handful of large Wall Street banks.

Whereas prior to the NBS *all* banks' reserves were comprised of gold and silver coin, the new system significantly expanded the list of what qualified as a reserve holding.

Country banks' legal reserves were changed to smaller gold and silver holdings, U.S. Treasury greenbacks—which were essentially unbacked paper money—and most notably deposit accounts at reserve city banks.

Reserve city banks' reserves were reduced under similar terms, the only difference being the amount of gold, silver, and greenbacks they were required to hold was reduced more gradually than the country banks. A large share of reserve city banks' reserves were also deposit accounts at central reserve city (i.e. Wall Street) banks.

Finally central reserve city (i.e. Wall Street) banks were also allowed to reduce their gold and silver holdings and back their obligations with greenbacks.

The NBS multi-tier system redesigned the entire industry to inflate more credit and paper money upon the same base of gold and silver reserves, replacing hard money with paper greenbacks and IOU's from banks in larger cities.

This was after all the whole idea as the Union sought inflation and ample bank credit to finance the war effort. And state banks that declined to participate in the NBS system were taxed out of existence in 1864 with a 10% federal tax on every private banknote issued.

Which brings us at last to the destabilizing element.

When the system was stressed by farmers withdrawing gold coin from their country banks the highly inflated system tended to collapse on itself, exacerbating the crisis.

When farmers asked their country banks for gold coin to pay hired hands, not only did the country banks lose reserves, contract credit and raise interest rates, they also had to tell their customers (in technical parlance) "Actually we don't have enough gold physically in our vaults. We have to withdraw gold from our reserve city bank in St. Louis."

As thousands of regional country banks descended upon reserve cities like St. Louis for gold coin, the reserve city banks offered the same response: their physical gold stocks were limited, typically more than half of their reserves being deposit claims on gold in New York banks.

And as reserve city banks from across the country descended upon a handful of Wall Street central reserve city banks for gold coin, Wall Street banks responded: "Actually we don't have enough gold physically in our vaults and can't pay."

There was no higher tier for Wall Street banks to petition for help. They were the last level of reserve bank. In each panic what started as withdrawals from small rural banks quickly grew into systemwide bank runs which produced widespread failures and nationwide suspensions of gold payment.[126]

CALLS FOR REFORM

After the enormous Panic of 1907 America's financial system was so shaken that Congress acknowledged the need for reform. The National Monetary Commission was established in 1908 to study alternatives, headed by powerful Senate Finance Committee Chairman Nelson W. Aldrich (R-RI).

Two lobbying camps quickly assembled and attempted to exert their influence on the commission. The first was a bona fide "free banking" lobby that wished to replicate the Canadian banking system.

To both the free banking lobby and Canadian bankers themselves the key to Canada's soundness was no secret. Canada had no central bank to stir up asset bubbles and crises as the First Bank of the United States and Second Bank of the United States had done during the Panics of 1792, 1797, and 1819.

Canada also had no government bondholding mandate that prevented banks from issuing currency as the National Banking System had required since 1863.

And Canada never had any unit banking laws that made branching illegal. From the very beginning Canada's banks branched nationwide and were allowed to hold diversified loans from all corners and industries of the country. As Charles Calomiris of Columbia University points out, Canadian bankers at the turn of the century were literally laughing at the stupidity of the American system.

But the free banking lobby was opposed by a more powerful alliance of special interests who comprised the "central banking" lobby. State governments, small unit banks, Wall Street banks, and Senator Aldrich himself didn't want many of the foregoing restrictions lifted since they had vested interests in seeing the NBS system preserved.

State governments and their unit banks didn't want unit banking ended because they feared competition—both intrastate and interstate— would water down their monopoly profits, profits that state legislatures often reaped as shareholders in unit banks themselves.

Wall Street banks didn't want to see the multi-tiered National Banking System ended either. Even though it precipitated bank runs, crises, and suspensions, it was also good business as banks from all over the country deposited more of their reserves in New York City.

And Nelson Aldrich himself was seduced by the panacea of central banking. Aldrich had toured Europe on a National Monetary Commission assignment to study other banking systems and was highly impressed; not only by what he viewed as the sophisticated operations of institutions like the Bank of England, Bank of France, and German Reichsbank, but also by the elevated culture, architecture, and artistic worldliness of the European capitals in contrast to the provincial backwardness of the young United States.[127]

NO REAL REFORM: A CENTRAL BANK ATOP AN ALREADY LOUSY SYSTEM

Hence Aldrich returned to America with his mind already made up. The National Monetary Commission would search for a solution that it had already chosen, the inquiry simply being a staged façade to "discover" its own preordained recommendation.

In the end, instead of allowing banks to branch freely throughout their states and the country, and instead of ending the centralization of gold reserves at large regional reserve banks and Wall Street banks, the lousy National Banking System was mostly preserved with all its flaws only now with a central bank—the Federal Reserve System—placed atop it.

For as the Commission ultimately concluded, the American banking system was hampered by an "inelastic currency" which required a central bank. Never mind the inelasticity was the direct result of federal regulations that had governed the industry for the previous half century.

The Federal Reserve Act was passed on a near party-line vote—Democrats for, Republicans against—in both houses of Congress and signed into law by President Woodrow Wilson on the evening of December 23, 1913.

Aside from preserving unit banking and most National Banking System provisions there were only a few superficial changes:

(1) Gold reserves would be even more centralized, held mostly at the twelve regional Federal Reserve banks.

(2) To solve the "inelastic currency" problem the Federal Reserve would replace private banks as new monopoly issuer of paper currency and enjoy an exemption from bondholding mandates.

(3) Most importantly to the unit bank lobby, if systemic liquidity stresses occurred the regional Federal Reserve banks would act as lender of last resort, making short-term cash loans to solvent firms on good collateral.

And as history has recorded, the establishment of the Federal Reserve hardly quelled banking panics. The greatest financial crisis in American history, the Great Depression Panics of 1930, 1931, and especially 1933, occurred under the watch of the Fed just sixteen years after its founding. Only with the introduction of federal deposit insurance in 1934 did the U.S. system finally find some semblance of stability.

Incidentally, Canada didn't have deposit insurance either as its far less regulated and far more stable system had never experienced a crisis and therefore never needed it.

However Canada finally adopted deposit insurance in 1967.

October 13, 2022

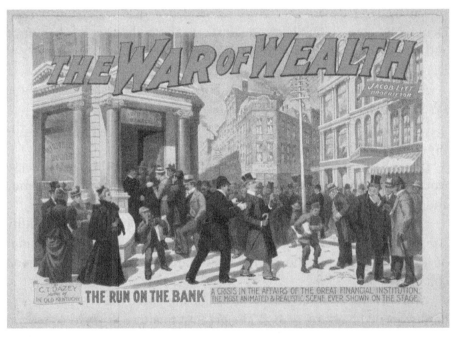

Contemporary portrayal of the Panic of 1893

Chapter 25

The U.S. National Banking System and the Panic of 1893

The Cautious Optimism Correspondent for Economic Affairs explains how a heap of government regulations and a botched return to a silver standard induced the Panic and Depression of 1893, arguably the second worst economic downturn in U.S. history—or what Americans dubbed "The Great Depression" for a generation before the arrival of the 1930's.

Although the National Banking System (NBS) of 1863-1914 produced multiple large and incipient banking panics throughout its tenure, one NBS-era crisis stands head and shoulders above the rest.

The Panic of 1893 and resulting depression were so disruptive that Americans called it "The Great Depression" for nearly 40 years. It was only when the 1929 stock market crash morphed into the more famous calamity that the 1930's disaster inherited that title.

The Panic of 1893's severity is no coincidence as it was caused by a confluence of regulatory factors that outmatched all financial crises before it: the simultaneous merging of three destabilizing legal regimes that came together to create the mother of all depressions in American history to-date.

First, as we've already reviewed in previous chapters, there were the two ever-present problems of state unit banking laws which forbade or severely restricted branch banking, and federal regulations from the Civil War-era National Banking Acts that plagued the industry for a half century until the establishment of the Federal Reserve System in 1914. These two problems were enough to precipitate plenty of crises on their own in 1873, 1880, 1884, 1890, and 1907.

More details on unit banking laws can be found in Chapters 11-13 and the National Banking System in Chapters 23 and 24.

However during the early 1890's Congress and President Benjamin Harrison added a third layer of regulatory dysfunction atop the others: the remonetization of silver at an absurdly overvalued rate.

BIMETALLIC RATIOS AND GRESHAM'S LAW

Countries that attempted to define their currencies simultaneously as weights of both gold and silver had struggled for centuries to avoid the unwanted effects of Gresham's Law, the disappearance of one metal from circulation when its value vis-à-vis the other metal falls below the fixed ratios defined by governments.

The Coinage Act of 1792 defined the U.S. dollar as approximately 1/20th of an ounce of gold and approximately 15 times that weight in silver—a 15-to-1 ratio which was nearly identical to the going market ratio between the two metals at the time.

Over the next few decades prodigious output from Latin American mines boosted world silver supplies, lowering that metal's market value against the more scarce gold. With the U.S. 15-to-1 ratio still in effect any American would have been a fool to pay for goods and services with undervalued gold dollars which began to disappear from circulation, either hoarded or shipped overseas where they fetched a more honest price.

In 1834 Congress recognized the need to adjust the ratios and the silver dollar was revalued at 16 times the weight of a gold dollar.

Silver continued to fall steadily in world markets until the California Gold Rush expanded world gold supplies, restabilizing the ratio around 16-to-1 again.

But in the 1870's silver took a global nosedive against gold. The industrialized nations of Europe began adopting the less erratic monometallic gold standard—Britain having been first going de facto gold in 1717 (also the result of Gresham's Law) and de jure in 1821. The German Empire joined in 1873 followed by the Latin Monetary Union of France, Switzerland, Italy, and Belgium, then Scandinavia and the Netherlands in 1875 with the U.S. joining last in 1879.

In less than a decade global demand for silver plummeted due to widespread demonetization and its world market value fell to 32-to-1 against gold. It would have fallen even further had China, India, and several Spanish colonies not remained on a silver standard.

America's decision to join the international gold standard was domestically controversial from the start, and under it a mild deflation set in with prices falling about 0.5% a year (1879-1900).

By the 1880's two major political camps were agitating for a return to inflation: western silver miners and debtors, many of whom were farmers. The former sought to revitalize demand for their trade while the latter wanted debts that were easier to pay back with less valuable dollars. Together they rallied around their slogan to return the country to "free silver at 16-to-1."

POLITICS AND CRISIS

By the 1880's the Republican Party was mostly pro-silver and pro-inflation while the Democratic Party tended to support the gold standard.

(Their roles completely reversed in the 1896 presidential election between pro-silver populist Democrat William Jennings Bryan and pro-gold establishment Republican William McKinley)

True to partisan form Republican President Benjamin Harrison signed the 1890 Sherman Silver Purchase Act which mandated the United States government act as world's largest silver buyer, the Treasury's purchases set roughly equivalent to the entire U.S. silver mining industry's annual output.

To purchase so much silver the federal government—not a central bank—would print new paper money, unceremoniously dubbed "Treasury Notes," that were redeemable upon demand in either silver or gold (more on that added mistake in a moment).

This new government currency delivered the inflation that miners and silver-movement farmers had sought but that wasn't its only effect.

It's important to stress there's nothing inherently wrong with returning to silver and bimetallism. But what went horribly wrong in 1893 was Congress' reckless error of granting a grossly overvalued silver currency to pro-inflation constituents in exchange for political support.

In 1890 the world market value of silver vis-à-vis gold was still roughly 32-to-1, reflecting low global demand. Given silver's relatively low value, the resources required to mine a new ounce cost more than the silver ounce itself making its production a moneylosing enterprise. Therefore Congress threw an additional political bone to silver miners by valuing the silver dollar at the old 1834 ratio of 16-to-1, a 100% premium over its world market price.

Once again in 1890 and more than ever, only a fool would pay for anything with gold dollars or ever redeem Treasury Notes in silver.

Gresham's Law quickly took hold and gold rapidly disappeared from U.S. circulation with overvalued silver inundating the money supply.

But most critical of all was the impact of this overvaluation on foreign investment. America's economic and industrial upsurge of the 1870's and 1880's was financed largely by European capital. But the new, unbalanced bimetallic monetary regime triggered a severe capital flight somewhat like the 1997 Financial Crisis when several Asian countries sharply devalued their own currencies.

For a British bank converting gold pounds to dollars to invest in an American enterprise wasn't thrilled at the prospect of being repaid with the same number of silver dollars (plus interest) which only fetched half the price in Europe—all because U.S. Congress was foolish enough to overvalue the silver dollar by 100%.

Foreign speculators could also make easy profits by capitalizing on the government-introduced arbitrage. A European investor could sell one gold ounce for the market price of 32 silver ounces overseas, ship the 32 silver ounces to the United States where by legal tender decree it could be traded for two gold ounces, and double his money (minus shipping costs).

The foreseeable consequence of these incentives was a domestic outflow of gold with overvalued silver pouring into the country, aka. Gresham's Law.

Thus the rapid withdrawal of foreign investment, compounded by unit banking and NBS regulations, produced one of the worst banking panics in American history.

600 banks failed in 1893 alone with hundreds more avoiding failure only by suspending redemption of cash into metallic coin. About 75

bank clearinghouses also suspended operations and 16,000 businesses failed that same year.

Unemployment reached 18.4% in 1894 (Lebergott) before improving in 1895, but spiked again when another incipient panic struck in 1896 pushing joblessness back up to 14.5% in 1897.

It wasn't until 1900 that the country finally restored full employment of 5.0%, the same year the Gold Standard Act of 1900 was passed placing the dollar on the unambiguous monometallic gold standard.

And as remains the case to this day without exception there was no financial crisis in Canada, although Canada did contract the effects of recession from its larger neighbor.

J.P. MORGAN SAVES THE TREASURY

President Grover Cleveland, the last Democratic president to ever embrace anything resembling laissez-faire capitalism, was inaugurated only a few months before the Panic of 1893 struck. He (correctly) blamed the Sherman Silver Purchase Act for the crisis. Congress successfully repealed the law in 1893 and the issuance of new Treasury Notes was halted.

However Cleveland faced another crisis in 1895 due to the lingering byproduct of the original 1890 Act: the near-bankruptcy of the U.S. Treasury itself. With silver preposterously overvalued no one in their right mind would redeem the previously issued notes in silver and the Treasury was overwhelming by demands for gold. By 1895 the Treasury's gold stocks were precariously low and noteholders the world over were losing confidence in the United States government's capacity to honor the pledge written on its own money.

Investment banker John Pierpont (J.P.) Morgan was aware of the Treasury's plight and organized a cabal of bankers to offer a gold loan to the government. However, Cleveland, a strong proponent of separation of economy and state, strove to solve the problem without private help.

But the writing was on the wall. The Treasury's mistake was too great and without help the government was headed towards bankruptcy.

Morgan secretly took a train to Washington D.C. and waited for the president's inevitable call from a friend's house, away from hotels and by extension the prying eyes of journalists. Several days passed before the White House, in desperate straits with the Treasury literally one day away from exhausting its gold reserves, called on Morgan and reluctantly agreed to the $65 million gold loan.[128]

The gold drain stopped as confidence resumed and the Treasury bought the time needed to replenish its gold stocks with tax payments.

But amidst today's complaints about the federal government bailing out private banks few Americans are aware of the 19th century role reversal: that J.P. Morgan and the private banking industry bailed out the federal government.

October 20, 2022

The U.S. National Banking System and the Panic of 1893

President Benjamin Harrison: Authorized the issuance of paper U.S. "Treasury Notes," died of natural causes in retirement

Chapter 26

The Panic of 1893 Retires a Banker Conspiracy Theory

A brief critique of a single banking conspiracy theory from the Cautious Optimism Correspondent for Economic Affairs.

Two days ago the Economics Correspondent posted the story of the U.S. Panic of 1893, possibly the worst banking crisis and depression in American history after only the Great Depression. The sordid details involve the remonetization of silver at an absurdly overvalued rate against the then gold dollar, authorized by Congress and signed by President Benjamin Harrison in 1890.

But the Panic of 1893's story also lampoons one of what are many, many conspiracy theories floating around the subject of money, banking, and central banking of which the Economics Correspondent has heard more than his share.

Although a tiny handful of such conspiracy theories are occasionally rooted in truth—such as the famous Jekyll Island, Georgia duck hunting meeting of central bank architects in 1910—most are untenable myths.

One of the less convincing conspiracy stories claims to uncover the assassinations of American presidents by evil, shadowy bankers whose demands for exclusive rights to print the nation's money were backed up with political violence.

A linchpin of supporting evidence is the assassinations of Abraham Lincoln and John F. Kennedy, the only two presidents to authorize the federal government to print its own paper money instead of relying on private commercial banks or the privately owned, but state-privileged, Federal Reserve System.

A kernel of truth in the "evidence" is that Abraham Lincoln did authorize printing of substantial quantities of government "greenback" notes during the Civil War, something the Economics Correspondent wrote about in a recent entry on the Civil War-era National Banking System.

John F. Kennedy also authorized a limited quantity of "silver certificate" Treasury notes to facilitate the eventual transition to a purely Federal Reserve currency regime.

Both paid for crossing the bankster star chamber with their lives, or so the story goes.

But aside from the fact that private, decentralized, deregulated banks have historically done a much better job of producing money than governments, one huge problem already exists in the story of the Panic of 1893: namely that President Benjamin Harrison signed the Sherman Silver Purchase Act of 1890 authorizing the Treasury to print vast amounts of government notes to serve as circulating money.

For this supposed disobedience Harrison was not assassinated nor were there any attempts on his life.

Other presidents have also authorized the printing of federal paper currency: Chester Arthur and Franklin Roosevelt.

Furthermore, so-called "silver certificates" go back to the Bland-Allison Act of 1878, and such federal government paper currency was repeatedly issued under the presidencies of Rutherford B. Hayes, Grover Cleveland, William McKinley, Theodore Roosevelt, Calvin Coolidge, Herbert Hoover, and Dwight D. Eisenhower.

Numismatists and currency enthusiasts can search online for images of federal note issuances from 1878, the 1890 Sherman Silver Purchase Act, 1899, 1908, 1923, 1928, 1934, and 1953.

So of the ten presidents outside Lincoln and Kennedy who authorized or oversaw the federal printing of public money, only one was assassinated (McKinley) and amateurish failed attempts were made on the lives of two (Theodore and Franklin Roosevelt).

Which means seven of ten were wholly "allowed" to finish their terms and their natural lives with one dying in office (FDR)—a record hardly consistent with an all-powerful conspiracy of globalist bankers pulling the planet's puppet strings of political power and eliminating any president who impedes on their currency monopoly.

The Economics Correspondent's verdict? International bankster cartel acquitted.

October 22, 2022

1890 series banknote issued by the U.S. Treasury

PART FOUR: CANADA

Canada's first bank, est. 1817

Chapter 27

A Glancing History of Canadian Banking

For some time the Cautious Optimism Correspondent for Economic Affairs has posted on the contrasting regulatory frameworks governing historically unstable banking systems in England (17 bank panics in 194 years) and the United States (17 panics in 216 years) against the nearly laissez-faire deregulated system of Scotland (zero panics in 129 years).

Now the Economics Correspondent begins the last chapter of the series with a final handful of articles on the exceptional performance and stability of Canada's 118-year free banking era.

So far the Economics Correspondent has devoted a great deal of writing to explain the many destructive, perverse, and downright bad American bank regulations that contributed to its roughly seventeen bank panics going back to 1792.

By contrast Canada, which had the most deregulated banking system in the industrialized world from 1845 to 1935 (and second-most deregulated from 1817 to 1845) experienced no panics at all during its "free banking" period.

Much less penmanship is required to explain Canada's success, for describing what Canada didn't do (tie its banks' hands in destructive ways) doesn't take as long as dissecting the United States' long chain of pernicious and destabilizing regulations or the chronologies of its multiple financial crises.

Because Canada had very little of the first and none of the second.

Nevertheless, a very simplified overview of Canada's banking industry and history does provide some insights.

THE BANK OF MONTREAL

During Canada's early years of French colonization (1534-1763) money was a vague and undefined commodity. Aside from barter, attempts at a common medium of exchange included wheat, wampum (shell beads), beaver pelts, and moose skins.[129]

These attempts at functioning monies were generally unsatisfactory since wheat and shell beads are not uniform, homogenous, or durable, and beaver pelts and moose skins are not divisible or uniform. French traders even famously tried using playing cards as money with equally unsatisfactory results.[130]

As was the case in other western societies coins minted from rarer metals eventually found their way into Canada, mostly higher denomination French coins from the West Indies, Spanish silver dollars minted in Mexico, and copper coins for low denomination transactions.

The French crown briefly authorized the colonial government to issue currency "cards" that could be traded for bills of exchange which in turn were redeemed for silver in France. [131]

The new card money was initially successful, but the colonial government soon began printing "Treasury notes" alongside the cards. Upon entering the French-Indian War with Great Britain (1754-1763) the government quickly ended convertibility and overissued the notes, leading to inflation.[132]

At the war's conclusion Quebec changed hands to become the British Province of Quebec, later "British North America," and by the early 19th century commerce in cities and towns was being conducted with an inconsistent hodgepodge of gold, silver, and copper coins of varying weights from different countries.[133]

It was at this point that a group of nine merchants met in Montreal to discuss the idea of a bank of deposit and issue that could supply uniform paper currency to the local region.

The idea was not novel. By then a few hundred banks in the independent United States were already accepting gold and silver coin deposits, issuing paper banknotes, and even crediting deposit accounts to make commercial exchange less cumbersome, all instruments we take for granted today (except gold convertibility). And commercial banking with private note issuance had already been conducted in Great Britain for well over a century.

The merchants petitioned the Parliament of Lower Canada for a bank charter. The charter was slow in coming so the merchants decided to open without one in 1817, signing the Articles of Association founding the Bank of Montreal in a rented house.[134]

Of the nine founding directors, a majority (five) were Scottish or of Scottish descent including John Richardson, known as the "Father of Canadian Banking." A majority of Scots was no coincidence, something we will revisit in a later column. The other four included one Frenchman, two Americans, and one Englishman.[135]

Hence the Bank of Montreal, Canada's first commercial bank and still operating today, issued the country's first private banknotes in 1817. A charter for incorporation followed in 1822.

The bank accepted deposits in gold and silver coin, issued banknotes and deposit accounts in exchange, extended interest-bearing loans in the form of its own banknotes and deposits, and discounted securities.

The arrival of uniform cash made conducting commerce in Montreal and surrounding areas much easier, and large commercial transactions could now be handled at the bank instead of through schlep; the cumbersome process of hauling heavy bags of coins across town to make a large payment.

OTHER EARLY BANKS

Word of the Bank of Montreal's success quickly spread, spurring a small wave of new bank startups. In a few short years several new banks were opened, many of whose names have been forgotten—either by failure or more commonly by acquisition—including:

- The Bank of Quebec (Quebec City, 1818)
- The Bank of Canada (Montreal, 1818), not to be confused with Canada's central bank established in 1935
- The Bank of Upper Canada (Kingston, 1819)
- The Bank of New Brunswick (St. John, 1820)
- The Second Bank of Upper Canada (York–later Toronto, 1822)

But of particular note was the creation of a new bank in Halifax, Nova Scotia.

The privately owned Halifax Banking Company was founded in 1825, but with only a handful of private partners to finance its startup capital its regional benefit was limited.

The Legislative Assembly of Nova Scotia felt a larger public bank, funded by shares sold to the public, would better serve the colony and was amenable to providing the bank a charter, but the company's directors insisted on a government-granted provincial monopoly.

In a key difference between the early days of American and Canadian banking the Nova Scotia Assembly refused to grant a monopoly and the Halifax Banking Company continued as a limited private partnership.[136]

This stands in stark contrast to the American states of the 1800's which granted literally hundreds of local bank monopolies in exchange for bank favors, or to the U.S. federal government that bestowed an interstate branching monopoly upon its two antebellum central banks—the Bank of the United States and Second Bank of the United States—to carry out Washington, D.C.'s monetary and fiscal policy.

Nova Scotia still lacked a large regional bank, but a few years later a group of merchants founded the Bank of Nova Scotia which opened as a publicly owned bank, issuing shares of stock via the 1832 equivalent of an IPO. The Bank of Nova Scotia's directors didn't ask for a government monopoly so its charter was granted, and a new, more heavily-capitalized competitor emerged in the Canadian market.

The Bank of Montreal and Bank of Nova Scotia remain two of Canada's largest banks today, known to Canadians as BMO ("bee-mo") and Scotiabank.

The story of Scotiabank's founding is informative for it serves as example of a pattern that was to follow for decades to come: All through the early period of Canada's bank startups no special government privileges were granted to Canadian banks nor were their business activities handtied by onerous regulations—although a few regulations policing fraud and insider conflicts of interest were applied.

Another difference was branching. While in the United States state governments universally prohibited the branching of any bank into any state other than its home state, and frequently restricting branching to only two or three counties or no branches at all, Canadian banks were free to open branches wherever they chose. It wasn't long before most Canadian townships were served by competing bank branches operating from headquarters in Halifax, Montreal, or Toronto.

Around the time of Canadian confederation (1867), when Canada was granted self-government by Great Britain as an independent Dominion country, a few other notable banks were founded.

In 1867 the Canadian Bank of Commerce was chartered as was the Imperial Bank of Canada in 1875. After a series of acquisitions the two large banks merged in 1961 to create the Canadian Imperial Bank of Commerce or CIBC.

In 1864 the Royal Bank of Canada was chartered which, through organic growth and acquisitions, grew into what has until recently been Canada's largest bank.

Two more banks, the Bank of Toronto and the Dominion Bank, were founded in 1855 and 1869 respectively and merged in 1955 to form the Toronto-Dominion Bank which has recently overtaken Royal Bank as Canada's largest.

TODAY

Today Canada's five largest banks by assets (popularly branded as) are:

-Toronto-Dominion Bank (TD)
-Royal Bank of Canada (RBC)
-Bank of Nova Scotia (Scotiabank)
-Bank of Montreal (BMO)
-Canadian Imperial Bank of Commerce (CIBC)

(Note: RBC and TD have been leapfrogging over one another for the #1 position for the last few years, depending on whether one measures rank by assets, deposits, market capitalization, etc...)

East coast and midwestern Americans may have noticed the presence of Canadian banking expansion into the U.S. market in recent years as RBC and TD branch offices have cropped up along the Atlantic coast states and southeast while BMO Harris has a large Midwest presence.

BMO has also recently acquired Bank of the West from French supernational BNP Paribas, so BMO's U.S. presence will soon expand significantly into the western United States.

Scotiabank has a tradition of expansion into Latin America while CIBC has remained a predominantly domestic operation.

Lastly, Canada's "Big Five" combined assets are estimated at 42% the combined value of the USA's "Big Four":

-JPMorgan Chase
-Bank of America
-Citigroup
-Wells Fargo

...and number five U.S. Bancorp

However, considering Canada only has 11.3% the population of the United States and 7.9% the gross domestic product, the relative size of its banks but absence of any banking crises is yet more testament to the stability and success of the industry.

In Part 2 we will look closely at more regulations Canadian banks were never subjected to (and American banks were) which helped them completely avoid banking panics throughout the industry's 205-year history.

———————————

November 29, 2022

Two capitals, two very different approaches to banking

Chapter 28

Canada's Free Banking Era: Deregulation and Stability

The Cautious Optimism Correspondent for Economic Affairs continues with his analysis of Canada's remarkably stable 205 years of commercial banking. This time we examine the greatest single reason for its success: U.S. regulations that Canadians never adopted.

TOO BIG TO FAIL?

Consolidation of market share into a few large banks has been a hallmark of the Canadian banking industry for over 140 years (more on why in the next column).

Today Canada's banking sector is dominated by the "Big Five" of RBC, Toronto-Dominion, Scotiabank, Bank of Montreal, and CIBC who collectively control over 80% of the country's banking assets. That's far more concentration than the USA's "Big Four" of JPMorgan Chase, Bank of America, Citigroup, and Wells Fargo who control closer to 45%.

Yet politicians tell us "too big to fail" is an unacceptable risk to the U.S. banking system, just tempting another financial crisis shoe to drop, and that large American banks simply must be broken up for the greater good of the country.

But Canada has had "much too bigger to fail" for over a century and never experienced a banking panic, including for the last 65 years of its largely deregulated "free banking era" (1870-1935) when the industry was also highly concentrated.

How on the one hand can politicians allege America's few large banks are a recipe for disaster while the far more concentrated banking industry of Canada has never experienced a single financial crisis?

The answer is Canada's lack of onerous, perverse, and I shall include "dumb" regulations that have plagued the United States since its founding.

UNIT BANKING

Market share, concentration, and deregulation have never been the problem in the United States; bad regulations have.

The first, which we've touched on previously, is unit banking.

During the 19th and early 20th centuries most American state governments legally prohibited their banks from branching, leaving the country dotted with thousands of tiny banks that were often just single buildings in a town or countryside acting as localized government-sanctioned monopolies.

Unit banking made it impossible for American banks to diversify their loan portfolios, diversify their depositors, move capital from one region of the country to another, equalize interstate interest rates, or cooperate during times of financial stress.

But Canada never had any branching restrictions and its banks rapidly spread across the country. Once Canadian banking had matured shortly after Confederation (1867) most Canadian banks were large, well-capitalized, and competing fiercely in nearly every township.

By comparison in 1914 the USA had over 27,000 banks, 95% of which had no branches (!) and the remaining 5% of which had an average of only five branches.[137]

Around that same time Canada had roughly twenty large banks, each well-capitalized with several hundred branches, a few dozen more thrifts, and even a handful of credit unions. Even the average tiny township of 900 people in western provinces like Alberta or Saskatchewan averaged two branches from competing banks—more than most Americans got.

Note: If twenty banks doesn't sound like many, keep in mind that in 1914 Canada's population was about 8 million or roughly the size of

Oregon. If twenty banks and several dozen thrifts, all competing in every city and town in Oregon with even tiny townships of 900 people getting at least two bank branches sounds competitive enough it's because it was. Twenty Canadian banks free to go anywhere also provided a far more competitive system than America's 27,000 mostly local monopoly unit banks.

This fatal flaw in the U.S. system had long been recognized by Canadian bankers. Canadian Bank of Commerce superintendent E.L. Patterson wrote in 1917 that:

> "Practically every country in the world except the United States has recognized the utility, if not the absolute necessity, of the branch system of banking in handling commodities as liquid as money or credit. A bank system without branches is on par with a city without waterworks or a country without a railroad so far as an equable distribution of credit is concerned." [138]

-Banking Principles and Practice

One more point about branches: During the Great Depression nearly 10,000 American banks failed in the years 1929 to 1933.

In Canada zero banks failed.

The Federal Reserve System played a large role in the American banking disaster, but so did unit banking. Over 95% of American banks were still unbranched in the 1930's, leaving their loan portfolios completely undiversified and vulnerable to failure with the downturn of a single crop, local factory, or the local economy.

While over 95% of U.S. banks had zero branches, Canada—which by 1931 had grown to over 10 million people, about the population of North Carolina—employed large branch networks.[139]

-Royal Bank of Canada: 805 branches
-Bank of Montreal: 624 branches
-Bank of Nova Scotia: 307 branches
-Canadian Bank of Commerce: 758 branches
-Banque Canadienne Nationale: 591 branches
-Bank of Toronto: 190 branches
-Dominion Bank of Canada: 137 branches

A 1932 Federal Reserve report on branch banking tallied Canada's total branch office count at 3,970. On a population-per-bank office basis the estimated 2,613 Canadians per branch was more favorable than the USA's 5,457 and even better than today's ratio of 4,320 Americans per FDIC-insured bank branch.[140]

In most respects Canada was hit harder by the Great Depression than the United States. Yet Canada's banking system—with no central bank until 1935 and no deposit insurance until 1967, but unhampered by onerous regulations and allowed to diversify assets, deposits, and customers—held up.

In fact during the global crisis years of the early 1930's, the freest, most unregulated banking system in the industrialized world also proved the best performing and most resilient.

THE NATIONAL BANKING SYSTEM

For half a century after the Civil War (1863-1914) American banks were governed by another set of pernicious regulations, this time from Washington, D.C.: the National Banking Acts.

The National Banking System's regulations were many and gruesome, but a simplified explanation is its rules made it illegal for commercial banks to issue paper currency unless they secured their note issuances with U.S. government bonds.

This may not have been so problematic if not for the fact that after the Civil War government bonds began to disappear as the federal debt was paid down, so the law in effect made it illegal to issue paper currency at a time when commercial banks were the country's primary source of paper currency.

One can imagine the havoc wreaked upon a rapidly growing economy when its banks weren't allowed to provide cash, and the problem frequently manifested itself as a credit crunch during fall harvest season.

When farmers asked banks to convert some of their account balances to cash to pay hired hands, banks were forced by regulation to say no. Thus farmers withdrew gold coin (i.e. bank reserves in the days of the gold standard) forcing banks to contract credit and raise interest rates. This system produced major banking panics in 1873, 1893, and 1907 with incipient panics in 1884, 1890, and 1896.

By the early 20th century proponents of central banking were accusing the private banking system of failing the country due to an "inelastic currency."

But in fact it was bad regulations that made the currency inelastic.

Across the border the deregulated Canadian banks were free to issue currency without any government bond deposit requirement (more detail on that in the next chapter). So during the 50-year U.S. National Banking Era Canadian banks operated crisis-free while America faced a crisis roughly every seven years.

Modern day Fed apologists make similar claims about the Gilded Age's banking failures: that before the Federal Reserve's establishment the country experienced frequent shortages of cash and repeated banking panics that finally ended when the Fed came along to fix things.

(That's actually false, the panics got even worse for the first quarter-century after the Fed's establishment)

Of course Fed officials and their allies say nothing about the regulations that caused the pre-Fed cash shortages and panics to begin with, leaving it to the reader to fill in the blanks with assumptions that it must have been laissez-faire's fault or yet another "market failure." But if only the market had really been allowed to work America would have avoided many of the NBS-era panics, although unit banking would still have remained a lingering problem.

CENTRAL BANKS

There is one regulatory exception in the modern era: central banks.

The United States twice attempted to establish central banks in its early days: the First Bank of the United States (BUS: 1791-1811) and Second Bank of the United States (SBUS: 1816-1836).

Canada had no central bank until 1935.

The American BUS and SBUS both engaged in cheap money policies that inflated nationwide asset bubbles—one in Treasury securities, one in inland and transportation companies, and another in land and stocks— all of which burst followed by the Panics of 1792, 1797, and 1819.

Later the Federal Reserve System deliberately inflated the asset bubbles of the late Roaring Twenties leading to the Recession of 1929. The Fed then transformed that recession into the Great Depression in the early 1930's by abstaining from the lender of last resort role it had nationalized from the private bank clearinghouse system.

In Canada there was no central bank at all during its free banking era of 1817-1935.

Modern day mainstream and left-leaning economists tell us without a central bank a country's financial system will be vulnerable to shocks and powerless to prevent frequent and devastating banking crises. Yet the experience of Canada proves the exact opposite: no central bank corresponded to no crises, while the USA's experience also proves the opposite: central banks corresponded to (indeed caused) many crises.

The same dichotomy existed in 18th and 19th century Great Britain. The Bank of England monopoly produced seventeen banking crises in two centuries. Scotland, with no central bank, suffered no crises during 129 years of free banking that were fully encompassed within those same two centuries.

So what's Canada's central bank "exception?"

Even after the establishment of the Bank of Canada in 1935, Canada has still avoided any bank panics for 87 years up to the present day. And the Economics Correspondent will explain the reasons behind Canadian banking's exceptional performance—even with a monopoly central bank—in an upcoming column.

———————————

December 7, 2022

John Richardson, M.P., J.P., "Father of Canadian Banking,"
Bank of Montreal cofounder, Scotsman from Banffshire

Chapter 29

Did Canadian Free Banking Have Any Regulations? Part 1

After reviewing how Canada's two centuries of banking have been crisis-free while the United States has experienced at least seventeen banking panics, the Cautious Optimism Correspondent for Economic Affairs explains next why Canada resisted adopting the USA's awful, destabilizing bank regulations and what few regulations Canada did enact.

In our previous columns we reviewed how Canada has avoided even a single financial crisis during its 205 years of commercial banking despite having the industrialized world's most unregulated banking system from 1845 to 1935 and the second most unregulated system (after Scotland) from 1817 to 1845.

We also contrasted Canada to the United States, which had the industrialized world's most regulated banking system from 1863 to at least 1933, and was neck and neck with England for most regulated from 1784 to 1862.

During those 149 years the United States suffered from fifteen systemic banking panics.

The case for the superiority of Canada's free banking system over America's badly regulated one is strong, but a logical question readers may ask is: "From 1817 to 1935 were there literally no bank regulations in Canada at all?"

The answer is a decisive no. There are no cases in history of 100% laissez-faire banking going back to at least the Scottish Enlightenment.

203

SCOTLAND

But there are cases of "almost laissez-faire" systems such as Scotland: (1716-1845) and "very lightly regulated" Canada (1817-1935).

In fact, it's no coincidence that Canada's embryonic banking industry developed along such deregulated lines starting with the Bank of Montreal which opened in 1817. Because early 19th century Canada was a period of massive Scottish immigration.

Hence when the Bank of Montreal's original nine founders—five of whom were Scottish including John Richardson, named "the father of Canadian banking"—opened for business they relied heavily on Scottish banking as their model, just as the founders of other early Canadian banks did.

Being Scottish settlers, the harebrained regulations being enacted in the United States—like making bank branching illegal, establishing privileged monopoly central banks, or forcing banks to back their paper note issuances with lousy state government bonds or scarce federal government bonds—never crossed their minds.

Incidentally, if you doubt the impact of Scottish immigration on Canada's development, just observe all the Scottish, "Mc" and "Mac" figures in Canadian history. A few include:

-John Macdonald, Canada's first Prime Minister.
-Alexander Mackenzie, Canada's second Prime Minister.
-James McGill, founder of Canada's prestigious McGill University.
-George Stephen, first President of the Canadian Pacific Railway.
-William Lyon Mackenzie King, Canadian Prime Minister for 21 years including during the critical periods of the Great Depression and World War II.
-Sarah McLachlan: Pop singer and founder of Lilith Fair.

OK, the Economics Correspondent will strike Sarah McLachlan off the list of historically important Canucks. But the point is Scots and Scottish heritage are still prevalent in Canada even today.

By the 1880's fifty percent of Canada's business leaders were of Scottish descent, and skim through any other record of Canadian history and you'll lose track of all the Mc's and Mac's although admittedly a small number of them are Irish.

But back to the Scottish banking model.

Not only was Scotland operating under its own free banking system in the early 19th century, but 1800-1845 is considered the golden age of Scottish free banking, a time when Scottish banks were also large, publicly traded, heavily capitalized, and had already established nationwide branch networks.

So sound were Scottish banks that in the 1820's British Parliament urged reform of the English banking system—which had suffered from at least ten crises in the previous 130 years—along the Scottish model which had experienced none.

However, there is one key difference between Scottish and Canadian free banking.

The Canadian free banking period (1817-1935) took place about a century after Scotland's, and by the turn of the 20th century western governments everywhere were imposing more progressive and interventionist measures on their economies. Canada's free system—lightly controlled as it may have been—was still a product of the times and subject to a few more regulations.

We'll examine the most important few here.

EARLY DAYS

Even in the earliest days of Canadian banking there were still a few regulations common to the various provinces. However they virtually all involved policing fraud and insider conflicts of interest. And few were outright edicts of government but instead usually conditions of receiving a charter.

And none of them mirrored the foolhardy U.S. regulations that prohibited branching, forced banks to buy lousy government bonds for permission to issue currency, or established central banks that blew multiple asset bubbles that crashed into financial panics.

For example, in exchange for a charter Canadian banks had to agree to open their finances to their shareholders.

Limits were also placed on the size of loans banks could make to their own directors, and banks were prohibited from using shares of their own stock as borrowing collateral.[141]

Beginning in 1836 the Gore Bank of Hamilton's charter established double liability for bank owners in the event of failure. Written into the charter was a clause declaring:

> "The shareholders of said bank shall be respectively liable for the engagements of the company to the extent of twice the amount of their subscribed shares, including the amount of said stock held as aforesaid." [142]

The double liability system seems to have worked, still providing painful enough consequences for insolvency to focus on sound credit quality, but not unlimited to the point of bankrupting all the owners.

Such conditions would offend few aside from the most purist libertarians, and if anyone were to propose they become today's new U.S. banking regulatory regime we would surely hear cries of "irresponsible laissez-faire!" from all corners of government, academia, and the media.

There was also a common clause that chartered banks must accept the notes of other chartered banks at par to keep the currency uniform, but this requirement quickly proved unnecessary as nationwide branch banking and the establishment of private clearinghouses made accepting, verifying, and redeeming competing banks' notes at par universal and virtually effortless.

Nevertheless, Canadian banking was an infantile industry in the 1820's and 1830's and, not having yet accrued vast experience, there were initially several isolated bank failures, something that became much rarer around the time of Confederation.

In fact the closest Canada ever came to a systemic banking crisis was also in its early days: the 1837-1839 period.

During this time, the effects of two panics in the United States had spread to Canada (the Panics of 1837 and 1839), but compounding matters were two major insurrections known as the Patriot War (1837-38) and the Canada Rebellions (1837-38).

Some historians liken these two rebellions to bordering on civil war (that may be a slight exaggeration), but chaos, violence, and civil unrest did force several Ontario banks to suspend specie payment although only one bank in the entire country failed (the Agricultural Bank) due to heavy withdrawals from the United States.[143] Breckenridge (1895) confirms one failure and none attributable to the national violence.[144]

The 1837-1839 period is not considered a systemic banking crisis by monetary historians even as Canada endured the effects of two major financial panics in the larger, neighboring USA while coping with two domestic rebellions of its own that produced a commercial depression.

These results, compared to hundreds of banks failing in the older, more mature and more developed U.S. market between 1837 and 1839, demonstrate greater resilience within the Canadian system even in its infancy.

Part 2 on Canadian regulations after Confederation to follow shortly.

December 13, 2022

An odd-denomination private banknote; the unintended
consequence of early Canadian banknote regulations

Chapter 30

Did Canadian Free Banking Have Any Regulations? Part 2

The Cautious Optimism Correspondent for Economic Affairs discusses the Canadian government's early experiments with banking regulation in the latter decades of its lightly regulated "free banking" era.

CONFEDERATION

In Part 1 of Canadian banking regulation we reviewed the handful of provincial rules imposed on colonial banks before Confederation.

When Canada became a self-governing Dominion of the British Empire in 1867 the new Canadian Parliament took a longer look at the question of banking legislation.

One of Parliament's seminal regulatory initiatives was the Banking Act of 1871 which imposed federal rules in lieu of provincial ones and established Parliament would revisit the subject of banking regulation once every decade.

(If only U.S. Congress would wait for a decade before drumming up new bank regulations!)

However the first federal regulations weren't much different from their colonial predecessors–once again mostly precluding fraud and conflicts of interest.

New federal laws required banks to open their finances to shareholders and the federal government every six months, and banks agreed to comply with surprise government inspector audits. Ironically, no surprise audits took place for decades.

However one new edict in the 1871 Act authorized Canadian Parliament to intervene in the note-issuing business.

Unsurprisingly the results were negative.

First, low denomination private banknotes–which had been banned even in Scotland in 1765–were not only prohibited in 1871, but Parliament took the further step of getting into the low denomination banknote printing business for itself.

Private banks were prohibited from issuing notes in denominations under four dollars which became the exclusive monopoly domain of the Department of Finance.

The government's newly dubbed "Dominion notes" had to be backed 20% by gold, but they still served as a major revenue source for Parliament.[145] The federal government could hold, say, $1 million in gold but print $5 million in Dominion notes to pay for its expenses.

The edict led to bizarre albeit not crisis-inducing outcomes.

Canadians may now have been forced to conduct $1 and $2 transactions using government Dominion notes, but they didn't always have to use Dominion notes for larger odd payments.

For Canada's private banks responded with their own workaround: issuing odd-denomination notes with face values of $4, $6, and $7.[146]

A consumer could make a $17 purchase and pay with a combination of private $10 and $7 banknotes instead of needing two $1 Dominion government notes.

In 1880 Parliament countered, raising the minimum private denomination to $5 and banning the issuance of private notes in anything but multiples of $5, thereby forcing Canadians to use Dominion notes to facilitate all odd payments going forward.[147]

Soon after the establishment of the Bank of Canada in 1935, which marked the end of the free banking era, the central bank was granted a legal monopoly on all banknote issuance and private banknotes disappeared from circulation (the Bank of Canada was nationalized in 1938).

Still, the old private odd-denomination notes are sought after by collectors for their numismatic value.

CONSOLIDATION

Finally, we reach the two most consequential regulations of the free banking era: greater barriers to entry and capital requirements on note issuance.

Beginning in the late 1880's Parliament raised the paid-in capital requirement for new banks to receive charters. In 1890 the minimum was upped to $500,000, a significant sum at the time, with a precondition that the entire capital subscription be completed within one year of the charter's approval.[148]

The government's objective was clear: to prevent too many new competitors from entering the market.

The long-term effects were also quite predictable: a multi-decade period of bank consolidation with mergers and acquisitions reducing the number of institutions but scant few new entrants to offset the decline.

Many financial historians believe there has long since been an unspoken agreement between Canadian banks and Parliament: the government will keep the number of banks relatively small in exchange for increased competition and stability via nationwide branching.[149]

Whether or not that was the original intent the result turned out exactly that way.

By the 1910's Canada was served by about twenty major banks plus another few dozen thrifts—all for a country of 8 million (about the population of Oregon). Yet despite the smaller number of banks, Canadian consumers enjoyed greater competition, smaller lending/deposit interest rate spreads, more access to credit, and far greater banking stability than Americans with 27,000 banks!

The reason was unbridled access to markets via branches. Canadian banks could branch anywhere—and did. In the United States, most towns only had a single unit bank which was granted a local monopoly by its state legislature.

Thus Parliament's higher barriers to entry were hardly an example of laissez-faire and almost certainly unnecessary, but the legislation did not lead to banking crises the same way that American restrictions on branching did.

MORE SEVERE PRIVATE BANKNOTE RESTRICTIONS

Lastly we examine the closest thing to a destabilizing regulation during the Canadian free banking period: the paid-in capital requirement for banknote issuance.

In the United States banks were only legally allowed to issue currency if backed 111% by U.S. government bonds.

Canadian Parliament placed a similar restriction on its banks, limiting the allowable quantity of banknotes issued to 100% of the bank's paid-in capital, a measure to secure the value of the notes should the bank fail.

For the most part the Canadian version of the banknote restriction was trouble-free for reasons we'll explain in a few paragraphs, but it did produce industry stresses in one year: 1907.

During that year the effects of America's seminal crisis, the Panic of 1907, spread into Canada. But unlike previous U.S. panics, Canadian farmers and depositors asking to withdraw cash this time were told, much like Americans, "sorry, no cash available" if bankers lacked sufficient paid-in capital to legally issue more notes.

For that reason 1907 proved to be the worst year in Canadian history for bank failures. Hold onto your seats...

Three smaller banks failed.[150]

Parliament examined the problem shortly after and simply upped the banknote limit during crop-moving season from 100% of a bank's paid-in capital to 115%.[151]

The problem never occurred again and, unlike in the United States, 1907 wasn't severe enough to be considered a Canadian banking crisis by anyone then or ever since.

The United States took a radically different course: Congress adopted the Federal Reserve System to impose a monopoly over note-issuance and act as lender of last resort.

But the paid-in capital requirement serves as an example of Canada inching towards a financial crisis as it flirted with more and more intrusive bank regulations... just before stepping back from the brink.

Incidentally the Canadian paid-in capital requirement was always less onerous than America's federal bondholding equivalent, hence why Canada had just one instance of industry duress while the USA suffered from at least six banking panics during the 1863-1914 National Banking era.

Why were U.S. banknote restrictions less flexible?

The quantity of U.S. government bonds required to back private banks' note issuances was limited by the national debt, debt that was declining during the law's first thirty years and later, even when new bonds were floated, was still inadequate to meet the demands of the public.

But the Canadian paid-in capital requirement was far more flexible. If a Canadian banker noticed customer demand for banknotes was nearing his paid-in capital limit he could always go to the equity markets and raise more capital to up his note issuance allowance.

A U.S. banker had no such recourse since the supply of U.S. Treasury bonds was under exclusive control of the federal government.

In the next installment we'll discuss a few criticisms and praises of the free banking system from the handful of academics even aware of its existence.

_____

December 20, 2022

Canadian post-Keynesian economist Marc Lavoie

Chapter 31

Present-Day Criticism and the Post-Keynesian School, Part 1

The Cautious Optimism Correspondent for Economic Affairs pivots to addressing a few criticisms of Canada's free banking story from very left-leaning economists.

Up to now we've examined Canada's vastly superior track record of banking stability vis-à-vis the United States, established that Canada had none of the highly destructive laws that America imposed on its banks, and discussed the handful of mostly inconsequential regulations that existed during Canadian banking's 19th and early 20th centuries.

Canadian banking's successful history is largely unknown—or deliberately concealed—by mainstream economists and the American media, and its lack of major financial regulations is even more unknown. The idea that a largely deregulated system could be so successful is such an anathema to government policymakers and mainstream academics that the subject has been largely stricken from the history books.

However there are a handful of intellectuals who have kept the history alive. The subject is still well known among Canada's economists and financial historians, and outside of Canada the story is still preserved by the modern free banking economics school and economic historians dedicated largely to banking—the largest cluster at Rutgers University starting with Milton Friedman understudy Michael Bordo, then Hugh Rockoff, and more recently Eugene White.

Example: "Why Didn't Canada Have a Banking Crisis in 2008 (or in 1930, or 1907, or ...)?"

-Michael Bordo, Angela Redish, Hugh Rockoff: NBER, 2011

Of those few economists who are even aware of Canada's free banking story, most praise its record of stability and success.

However over the years the Economics Correspondent has discovered some dissident criticisms.

POST-KEYNESIANS DISLIKE FREE BANKING

The first comes from Marc Lavoie at the University of Ottawa, a leading post-Keynesian economist.

But before we get into Lavoie's critique, a word for those who haven't heard of post-Keynesian economics.

The heterodox post-Keynesians tend to view the larger, more mainstream New Keynesian school—which largely controls the liberal wings of governments around the world—as betrayers of the original ideas and spirit of British economist John Maynard Keynes' book *The General Theory of Employment, Interest, and Money.*

In the post-Keynesian worldview, New Keynesians such as Paul Krugman, Larry Summers, Janet Yellen, and Ben Bernanke have "sold out" Keynes' ideas to the free-market crowd and don't go nearly far enough pressing for greater government control of the economy.

Post-Keynesians call for far more central bank money creation, far larger government deficits, and much tighter regulation to manage effective demand and properly steer the economy away from its inherent (in their view) instability towards technically-managed full employment.

If any of this sounds familiar it's worth noting that post-Keynesians consider themselves natural allies with Modern Monetary Theory economics. Read nearly any interview with a post-Keynesian and you'll hear at minimum qualified, although more commonly highly enthusiastic support for MMT.

Since post-Keynesians and MMT'ers think banking systems are inherently crisis-prone and must by tightly controlled by authorities, it follows that any evidence of free banking systems being historically resilient and stable doesn't sit very well with them.

Another example: "Against Free Banking: The Liability Side Isn't The Place For Market Discipline"

-Warren Mosler (MMT)

LAVOIE AND THE GREAT DEPRESSION

Which brings us back to Lavoie.

His criticism of Canadian free banking? That its reputation for stability is a myth—at least in the 1930's.

In a podcast interview with George Mason economist David Beckworth, Lavoie disagreed with Beckworth's characterization that no Canadian banks failed during the Great Depression.

Lavoie: "During the Great Depression in Canada, the belief is that many, perhaps all of our banks, were insolvent, but because nobody ever said anything, then they just keep on going until things got better, and they became solvent again."[152]

So free banking, in Lavoie's view, was not a success but a failure, but Canadian banks concealed their many failures from the public.

Unfortunately that was the end of discussion on the Canadian banking subject and the two moved on to talking about central bank floor operating systems. No evidence was offered nor were any sources provided.

However the Economics Correspondent considers the claim that "many, perhaps all of our [Canadian] banks were insolvent" (but all successfully hid their bankruptcy by saying nothing) quite incredible.

A few problems with Lavoie's theory:

(1) Keep in mind ever since the Banking Act of 1871 Canadian banks were required to open their financial books to both federal government officials and shareholders several times a year.

Lavoie must therefore believe that most or all Canadian banks successfully committed blatant fraud and doctored their books–accounting deceptions that still have not been uncovered to this day–or that banks, government officials, and shareholders were all aware of but conspired to conceal their problems from depositors.

(2) Another problem. The biggest culprit behind the nearly 10,000 bank failures in the United States during the 1930's was illiquidity, not insolvency.

American banks were unable to diversify their portfolios due to unit banking laws. Yet most, while distressed, were not yet insolvent when they failed. Rather as the public realized certain banks were experiencing difficulty they ran to withdraw cash, precipitating failures due to illiquidity. And once the banking crises of the early 1930's ended, a full 60%+ were still operating with solvent balance sheets.

Thus it's even more unbelievable that "most or all" Canadian banks, which unlike American banks were allowed to diversify their loans and depositors nationally, were insolvent while at least 60% of their legally handtied American counterparts were not.

(3) All of Canada's major banks paid uninterrupted shareholder dividends throughout the 1930's. A simple online check of the histories of Canada's "Big Five" banks confirms that RBC, Bank of Montreal, Scotiabank, and the original predecessors to Toronto-Dominion and the Canadian Imperial Bank of Commerce have all paid uninterrupted dividends going back to the late 19th century.

That's a neat trick for allegedly bankrupt banks: to not only go about financing their day-to-day operations, making loans, paying out for withdrawals, and hiding their insolvency, but also pay regular dividends to shareholders. While it's not technically impossible for an insolvent bank to hold just enough liquid cash to temporarily meet immediate depositor and shareholder dividend demands, for "most or all" Canadian banks to successfully walk that tightrope every day for nearly a decade does seem unbelievable.

(4) History has consistently demonstrated that it's incredibly difficult for even a single bank to hide financial distress, let alone insolvency, from the public and its depositors who nearly always run for the exits. Word of financial difficulty has always found a way of getting out and depositors have always sniffed out problems and lined up to withdraw their money. The United States was no exception.

Yet somehow we're to believe the customers of Canadian banks, which were huge and branched everywhere during the 1930's, were somehow more stupid than depositors in virtually every other country on earth.

Evidently Canadians never had the slightest clue that most or even all their banks were bankrupt and putting up a façade of solvency every day, year after year, even as Canadian newspapers routinely reported American banks were failing by the thousands next door.

Lavoie's claim is a tall order to believe, but it would be interesting to see if he's written a paper with credible evidence backing his claim.

Finally, keep in mind that during Canada's free banking era (1817-1935) there were thirteen systemic banking panics in the United States: in 1819, 1837, 1839, 1857, 1873, 1884, 1890, 1893, 1896, 1907, 1930, 1931, and 1933.

Lavoie argues Canadian banks were insolvent in the 1930's but doesn't produce any claims of financial crises being concealed at any other time during the 118-year free banking era.

It's a strange argument that Canadian banks, which for over a century had done such a pristine job of managing their loan portfolios and avoided the bad credit pitfalls that had plagued American banks, suddenly became insolvent in the 1930's at a far greater rate than even their failure-prone U.S. counterparts.

But even in the unlikely event Lavoie's incredible claim about the Great Depression is true, Canada's very lightly regulated system would still have only produced a single panic during a period when the USA's much more heavily regulated system, with a central bank for 40 of those 118 years, endured thirteen.

We'll address a more formidable set of challenges to Canadian free banking in the next installment.

January 4, 2023

Chapter 32

Present-Day Criticism and the Post-Keynesian School, Part 2

The Cautious Optimism Correspondent for Economic Affairs apologizes for the length of this latest entry, but an intelligent post-Keynesian blogger has made formidable criticisms of Canada's successful, lightly regulated banking history which requires a thorough response and (as CO himself says) everything is better when presented as a numbered list.

In Part 1 we addressed a single criticism of the Canadian free banking story by University of Ottawa professor Marc Lavoie, a post-Keynesian economist.

We also discussed post-Keynesianism's similarity to Modern Monetary Theory (MMT) and their shared enthusiasm for heavier government regulation of the financial sector and economy as a whole, and shared dislike of any idea of bank deregulation let alone stories of its success.

"LORD KEYNES"

In Part 2 we examine a much more comprehensive list of objections from a more formidable critic: a self-described "Left socialist... ... post-Keynesian in economics" blogger named "Lord Keynes" whose website is titled *Social Democracy for the 21st Century: A Realist Alternative to the Modern Left.*

Lord Keynes' writing is proficient enough that the Correspondent believes he could very well be an economist by training. He also has a prolific body of work on his blog and provides plenty of academic sources.

In his post titled "Canada's Banking Stability in the Early 20th Century and the 1930's," Lord Keynes criticizes what he calls "Austrian, libertarian and free banking myths."

We'll analyze it here, but you can read the entire column yourself at:

https://socialdemocracy21stcentury.blogspot.com/2013/12/canadas-banking-stability-in-early-20th.html

Lord Keynes' chief complaint is that Canada's banking system was not regulation-free during the early 20th century and he proceeds to list several examples of regulations he argues saved the system from what would otherwise have been systemic crisis or even collapse during the 1920's and 1930's.

There are a lot of objections in his article, and we'll try to address them one-by-one.

LORD KEYNES' LIST

Lord Keynes' criticisms, in nine parts, include:

(1) Free bankers claim Canada did not have a lender of last resort (such as Selgin-1996), but in fact it did.

Lord Keynes points out that during the 1930's some smaller Canadian banks that were short on liquidity received short-term cash loans from the Bank of Montreal, the largest bank in Canada at the time.

But Selgin's "lender of last resort" commentary was, within the his very same sentence about Canada, referring to the United States Federal Reserve, a government-privileged central bank which failed in its role miserably during the 1930's leading to nearly 10,000 American bank failures.

While it's true that the Bank of Montreal did act as a private-sector lender of last resort on several occasions, if anything its experience demonstrates the private banking system of Canada performed that function far better than the U.S. Federal Reserve did. And the Canadian system was also effective without the downside of a government-privileged central bank inflating multiple crisis-inducing asset bubbles as the U.S. Federal Reserve and Bank of England have done so many times throughout history.

Score one for free banking.

(2) Lord Keynes immediately follows up his lender of last resort critique with

> "Nor was it true that Canada's banking system was unregulated."

This is tearing down a straw man. The Economics Correspondent knows of no pro-free banking academic, Selgin included, who has written that Canada's or any other free banking system was 100% laissez-faire. Rather free bankers have argued that Canada's lightly regulated regime was neither harmful enough to precipitate financial crises (one possible exception below) nor did it rescue Canadian banks from some impending panic of their own alleged free-market creation.

(3) Lord Keynes concedes that the nationwide branch banking system, which was legally prohibited in the USA, did make Canadian banks more resilient to crisis.

But he counters that...

> "The number of branches dropped from 4049 to 3640 between 1929 and 1933, loans and deposits fell, and bank-stock prices dropped. The interwar period showed a trend towards fewer and larger banks."

To which the Economics Correspondent replies: "So what if some branches closed?"

There was, after all, a Great Depression taking place in Canada.

If the worst thing that happened during the Great Depression was that 10% of bank branches closed, loans fell, and the prices of bank shares fell—but not a single bank failed and there was no financial crisis while in the USA nearly 10,000 banks failed—the Economics Correspondent calls that a very positive outcome and endorsement, not indictment, of the Canadian system. Besides, what reasonable standard of stability

*Blogger "Lord Keynes'"
online avatar*

requires a banking industry to expand and its share prices to rise in the middle of a Great Depression?

(4) Lord Keynes revisits regulations and argues:

> "Chartered banks in Canada even in the 1920s and 1930s were 'heavily regulated' by the Bank Act of 1871 and subsequent revisions of that act, which 'specified (among other things) audits, capital requirements, directors' qualifications, and loan restrictions...'"

We've covered this territory before. The Economics Correspondent already wrote previously about these specific restrictions in the articles where he stated:

> "Even in the earliest days of Canadian banking there were still a few regulations common to the various provinces. However, they virtually all involved policing fraud and insider conflicts of interest... ...limits were placed on the size of loans banks could make to their own directors, and banks were prohibited from using shares of their own stock as borrowing collateral."

And such restrictions hardly amounted to "heavily regulated." As the Correspondent has also pointed out:

> "None of them [Canadian laws] mirrored the foolhardy U.S. regulations that prohibited branching, forced banks to buy lousy government bonds for permission to issue currency, or established central banks that blew multiple asset bubbles which ultimately crashed into financial panics."

(Previous commentary on light regulations in Chapter 29)

(5) Lord Keynes argues that the government actually did save the Canadian banking system from crises because:

> "The 'Canadian Bankers Association' [formed in 1891] – which in 1900 became a public corporation – also provided stability by organising bank mergers to deal with insolvent banks."

But the CBA was always a private association, making it yet another example of the private sector, not regulations, more effectively addressing industry difficulties.

By calling the CBA a "public corporation," Lord Keynes is referring to (from the CBA's own website): "[CBA was] incorporated by a special act of Parliament in 1900." [153]

Receiving a charter for incorporation as a publicly owned company does not make one a government agency nor is it an example of a stabilizing regulation. General Electric and Apple are also publicly owned and incorporated by filings with the government of Delaware.

(6) Lord Keynes suggests Canadian depositors didn't inflict runs on their banks because some implied form of government deposit insurance existed—even though Canada didn't adopt federal deposit insurance until 1967.

> "There is some evidence that successive Canadian governments from the 1920s made public statements and implicit promises to protect depositors in failed private banks, at least to some extent…"

Well that's a bit thin.

"Some evidence" of...
"public statements" [i.e. not legislation, regulation, or policy] and...
"implicit promises" during the 1920's...
"at least to some extent"

...is a pretty weak case that depositors held firm in the turmoil of the Great Depression because they had unshakeable confidence in deposit insurance that didn't really exist.

(7) His attempt at a slightly more forceful argument for "implied deposit insurance," which ultimately undermines his case, is:

"Governments did pay to reimburse or protect depositors: when in August 1923 the Home Bank of Canada failed, the Canadian government in June 1925 passed legislation which eventually resulted in the government paying 22.3% of average depositors' claims."

Lord Keynes omits a lot from the story here, the details of which are in the very paper he cites as a source (Carr, Mathewson & Quigley-1995).

The missing facts are:

When the Home Bank failed depositors, who were not insured, argued the government should make up their losses due to what they claimed was the state's failure to adequately investigate allegations of bank fraud from years prior.

A suit was filed, a Royal Commission was established to hear the arguments, and the claims languished in hearings for two years before the House of Commons finally agreed to reimburse depositors.

However, the Senate held up the ruling and eventually lowered the compensation to just 22% of depositor's claims.[154]

And two years later the Bank Act of 1927 settled the matter for good when it "...made clear that the government was not responsible for losses to depositors, shareholders, or creditors to the banks."[155] [156]

This evidence effectively demolishes all the "implied deposit insurance" arguments as well.

Whatever "public statements" or "implied protections" may have been floated in the 1920's, weak as they may have been, the 1927 *law* proclaimed there will be no depositor reimbursements coming from the government, squashing any implied expectations.

And a last word on the Home Bank story.

Even if the 1927 law had never been passed it's unbelievable that depositors of the 1930's, unnerved by the Great Depression and ready to run on Canadian banks, chose to leave their money on deposit because they were thinking...

Depositor: "I'm not worried. If my bank fails, first I can hope it was due to fraud and that someone had previously complained to the government years ago."

"Then I just need to organize a petition with other depositors, file a suit, hope that a Royal Commission is set up to listen to arguments for two years, and then let the Senate water down my compensation to just 22% of my money which I might get a few years later if I'm lucky."

With iron-clad guarantees like that, why would any depositor ever consider withdrawing 100% of their money during a major depression?

(8) Lord Keynes' most compelling arguments involve Dominion notes. He points out that:

> "In 1907 the Canadian government lent $5 million in Dominion
> notes to the private sector banks during a banking panic, which
> averted a serious financial crisis."

There are several problems here, starting with the fact that no economic historian considers 1907 "a banking panic" in Canada.

However, it is true that Canada's banks were short of paper currency in 1907, and the shortage did create duress in the industry that led to the failure of three small banks.

However, as the Economics Correspondent has already pointed out in an earlier column, the shortage of cash itself was the result of government regulations—the worst, most damaging regulations Canadian Parliament had attempted to that date.

Canadian banks were legally forbidden from issuing private bank-notes beyond 100% of their paid-in capital. When customer demand exceeded that limit depositors withdrew gold coin as a hand currency substitute leading to a national credit contraction.

History records that, in the middle of a problem of its own creation, Parliament loaned liquid Dominion notes to make up for a shortfall that its own regulations, not free banking, had induced.

(9) In his last Dominion notes objection Lord Keynes points out that banks repeatedly borrowed Dominion notes from the federal government throughout the 1920's, so it can be assumed these borrowing facilities saved the banking industry in the 1930's.

> "More important was the Finance Act of 1914. This allowed Dominion banks to borrow notes directly from the Canadian Department of Finance: such notes were issued at the request of the banks with no gold-reserve requirement..."

> "The Finance Act (1914) allowed the Canadian government the power to expand the money supply by creating dominion notes...
> ... Moreover, the use of this system continued long after the war...
> ...this mechanism had extensive use during the 1920's."

Once again Lord Keynes leaves out important details that undermine his thesis.

First, the 1914 Act wasn't a stabilizing "regulation" but rather a wartime inflation measure. At the outbreak of World War I the Dominion government, like every member of the empire coming to Great Britain's aid, suspended the gold standard, declared its own notes a legal gold reserve substitute, and inflated the money supply to finance its own war expenditures.

Also, as the Economics Correspondent has already written about, in 1880 the federal government granted itself a monopoly on the issuance of banknotes under $5 and restricted the issuance of private banknotes to multiples of $5 only.

Hence from 1880 onwards federal law forced Canadian banks to become completely dependent on the central government for low denomination notes since they were forbidden from supplying any of their own under $5.

Although Lord Keynes doesn't offer evidence that Canadian banks made healthy use of the discount window in the 1930's, only:

> "...one can posit that the heaviest use... was in the crisis years from 1929–1933"

...to do so would prove nothing; least of all that a deregulated Canadian system got itself into crisis and was only saved by government assistance.

Banks experiencing higher than normal cash withdrawals during the turmoil of the 1930's would logically notice that demand for low denomination notes was also higher than usual—not only to satisfy depositors, but also for merchants needing more low denomination "small change" bills to accommodate the greater national share of commerce that shifted to hand-to-hand currency. Since the 1880 restriction prohibited banks from supplying their own low denomination notes to the public, it follows that of course they would approach the only source legally available—the federal government—for more.

In fact, the history of central banking is largely a story of all governments eventually granting banknote monopolies to their central banks which in turn set up cash facilities which private banks draw upon, going back to the first note monopoly bestowed upon the Bank of England by the Peel Act of 1844. In the case of Canada in 1914-1935 a minor difference is the issuance of low denomination notes was administered exclusively by the Department of Finance instead of a central bank, but it operated as a government monopoly nonetheless.

The federal government's Dominion notes facility and monopoly is another example of Canada flirting with bank regulations that made the industry less flexible and forced Canadian banks to come begging on knee to the government to fix a currency shortage that Parliament itself had created.

The Economics Correspondent has written in more detail about Parliament's private banknote restrictions and the problems they caused in Chapter 30.

January 11, 2023

Present-Day Criticism and the Post-Keynesian School, Part 2

Canadian banking: A Hamiltonian framework (or not)?

Chapter 33

Present-Day Praise and Debate

The Cautious Optimism Correspondent for Economic Affairs continues analyzing the historically successful and stable Canadian banking system with the academic question of Alexander Hamilton's influence on its original blueprint.

ACADEMIC PRAISE AND AGREEMENT

Although the story of Canadian banking's success under very light regulation has been largely stricken from history books, there are a few intellectuals who have kept the history alive.

As one might expect the story is more widely known in Canada where many monetary economists and historians still study the subject. Some the Economics Correspondent has read or followed include Angela Redish (University of British Columbia), James Darroch (York University) and Joe Martin (University of Toronto).

In the United States the modern free banking school of economics writes extensively on Canada's experience, notably George Selgin (Professor Emeritus, University of Georgia), Lawrence White (George Mason University), and Kurt Schuler (Johns Hopkins, George Mason, and most recently the U.S. Treasury Department).

Several scholars at Rutgers University's unique economics department have written on the Canadian experience such as Michael Bordo and Hugh Rockoff.

And Charles Calomiris of Columbia University, now at the United States Office of the Comptroller of the Currency, has written much on Canada's banking success.

What all these academics agree on is that Canada's nationwide branch banking networks made its industry far more resistant to crisis than the United States where state laws prohibited interstate branching and often banned branching of any kind whatsoever from 1787 to as late as the 1990's.

U.S. economists, also having naturally studied problems in the American system, have cited problems with the U.S. National Banking System (1863-1914), noticeably absent in Canada, and even the mainstream economics community is acutely aware of massive failures by the U.S. Federal Reserve during the Great Depression.

SPLIT ON HAMILTON

Where opinions differ concerns the original blueprint for the Canadian system.

Many Canadian economists, along with Calomiris, argue the original authors of Canada's 1871 Bank Act borrowed Alexander Hamilton's vision of banking which in turn planted the seeds of success for over 150 years.

The free banking school economists disagree with this characterization and the Economics Correspondent hasn't yet found a position from the Rutgers economists.

But first let's clarify what is meant by a "Hamiltonian" framework.

American founding father Alexander Hamilton advocated for a much stronger central government than his political nemesis Thomas Jefferson. Among their many disagreements Hamilton wanted the federal government to charter private banks and pressed for the establishment of a privileged national central bank in the mold of the Bank of England.

Jefferson, who distrusted centralized government power, consistently argued that the federal government had no constitutional authority to either charter banks or establish a central bank.

Hamilton won out on the issue of a central bank. Congress and two presidents approved the First (1791-1811) and Second Bank of the

United States (1816-1836), both of which were 20% owned by the federal government itself.

But Hamilton lost on the question of chartering which was left to the individual states. From the nation's founding to the Civil War, all private banks other than the First and Second Bank of the United States were chartered exclusively by state governments.

The Economics Correspondent has already discussed the aftereffects: state governments largely traded bank favors for charters and became shareholders in the banks themselves. To maximize bank profits and state government revenue streams, legislatures granted monopoly privileges to thousands of banks by making them "unit banks" that were forbidden from branching, but by extension enjoyed exclusive banking rights in their own townships.

The vulnerability in this arrangement was unit banking made it impossible for banks to diversify lending beyond their local towns and the result was waves of bank failures and frequent banking panics when the prices of certain crops fell in farming regions or when imports or exports declined in trading cities.

One more criticism leveled at the Jeffersonian model is lack of a central regulator.

Initially individual states regulated their own banks. Later at the outset of the Civil War the federal National Banking Acts established the Office of the Comptroller of the Currency to regulate new nationally chartered banks.

After 1914 the Federal Reserve was tasked with regulating its member banks. And once the FDIC was created in the 1930's it too took on regulatory responsibilities since it was liable for depositor claims in the event of bank failures.

But in Canada, which granted chartering and oversight powers to the central government shortly after Confederation, a single national agency regulates banks: OSFI or the Office of the Superintendent of Financial Institutions, although its origins go back to embryonic predecessors in 1925.

Hence another argument for the success of adopting a Hamiltonian model arises: the splintered American system led to four agencies capriciously regulating different and often overlapping groups of banks while the Canadian system has been more straightforward with a single national entity applying one consistent set of rules.

MOSTLY MISTAKEN?

In the Economics Correspondent's opinion, the "stable Hamiltonian vision" argument is mostly, albeit not entirely, mistaken. The free banking school shares skepticism towards the Hamiltonian hypothesis.

But first let's start with what's right about the Hamiltonian theory.

It's true that had Hamilton gotten his way and American banks were all required to obtain national charters then it's very unlikely the states would have been able to engineer the fractured unit banking system that dominated American finance for over 150 years.

This is not an inconsequential argument. Unit banking was a major contributor to banking crises in the United States from the late 18th century through the Great Depression although it wasn't alone; part of a trio comprised of central banks and bondholding mandates, state and federal, that share the blame.

Also, to the extent one wants governments regulating banks, it is indeed simpler for one national agency to consistently apply rules than assigning oversight responsibilities to separate state regulatory agencies, the OCC, the Federal Reserve, and the FDIC all at once.

However the Hamiltonian argument falters on several fronts.

(1) Hamilton championed a government-connected central bank.

Not only did Canada not have a central bank during the first 118 years of its banking history—a very un-Hamiltonian framework—but it was precisely the absence of a central bank that contributed heavily to financial stability.

By contrast Alexander Hamilton's central banks produced horrendous results. The First Bank of the United States (1791-1811) and its successor, the Second Bank of the United States (1816-1836), inflated three different asset bubbles, all of which burst and set off banking panics in 1792, 1797, and 1819 with the last two hatching major depressions.

America's modern central bank, the Federal Reserve System is largely blamed for transforming the Recession of 1929 into the Great Depression, and the Economics Correspondent has written in detail on the Fed's inflation of stock market and real estate bubbles during the late 1920's that started the whole catastrophe (see Chapters 38-40).

There's more anguish associated with central banks. Since the United States went off the international gold standard in 1971 central banks have dominated the global monetary system, spawning an unprecedented 140 financial crises globally including the United States; namely the U.S. Savings and Loan Crisis and 2008 Great Financial Crisis.[157]

Thus in at least one major respect Canada absolutely did not model its banking system on Hamilton's vision and subsequently avoided a lot of pain and suffering.

(2) Per Hamilton's design America's antebellum central banks were 20% owned by the federal government, his objective being to align the interests of the State with those of the bank.

To further align their interests Hamilton deliberately packed the Bank of the United States' coffers with U.S. Treasury bonds, and he required subscribers to the Bank's shares to pay with Treasuries in a scheme to inflate demand for sovereign debt thereby lowering the government's borrowing costs.

The outcome was a bubble in Treasury securities that burst in 1792, instigating the young United States' first banking panic.

But the Canadian Bank Acts were not Hamiltonian in the sense they contained no such crony provisions. Hence the new Dominion of Canada averted the government securities bubble and collapse that rocked the United States.

(3) One might argue that it's more efficient to have a single, all-powerful federal bank regulator than multiple state bureaucracies, an OCC, a central bank, and a deposit insurance agency all regulating at once.

However, as we've noted at length, it was precisely bad regulations that triggered the United States' seventeen banking panics from 1792 to 2008 (one possible exception: 1837-1839).

We've discussed several of America's old regulations already, but new bad regulations both forced and rewarded banks to lower lending standards on home mortgages during the 1990's and 2000's which led to massive real estate loan losses and ultimately the 2008 financial crisis. Canada avoided any crisis in 2008, all its banks remained profitable, and none of its banks took a penny in government bailout money.

In fairness to Canada, bad regulations *were* floated in the House of Commons in 1869: a bill to convert the Bank of Montreal into a central bank and condemn all remaining private banks to no branches (effectively recreating unit banking in Canada) but Parliament soundly rejected it.[158]

Which reveals the hazards of crediting Canada's stability to the "single regulator" concept. For the key is not the number of regulators but rather good versus bad regulations, and Canada has had mostly the former and very little of the latter.

In the Economics Correspondent's opinion Canada's success was rooted more in its decisions to avoid enacting bad bank regulations, not in adopting a centralized model with fewer agencies to administer bad regulations more efficiently.

(4) Even though the "Hamiltonian vision" crowd agrees with everyone else that the U.S. unit banking system was horrible all-around, unit banking laws were regulations too.

Once again the real issue is whether bad regulations were imposed on the banking sector or not, not whether a powerful central government or states/provinces enforced the rules. Canada's Parliament may have had fewer incentives to pass unit banking laws but it could just as easily have imposed a different set of bad bank regulations on the industry. Lawmakers had an opportunity to do just that in 1869 but voted not to.

Professor Joe Martin from the University of Toronto goes out of his way to reject the alternate "free banking" narrative of Canada's success —that Scottish immigrants emulated their native country's lightly regulated system when they arrived—and insists Canada followed the Hamiltonian model, not the Scottish one.[159]

The Economics Correspondent is impressed with Martin's breadth of knowledge and has enjoyed several of his articles and interviews, but based on the evidence and historical record maintains the Canadian banking system's first 118 years were molded more in the spirit of Adam Smith than Alexander Hamilton.

In summary the Economics Correspondent believes Canada's free banking era was so successful because it was, well… so free, not because the federal government borrowed Alexander Hamilton's vision. The one and only Hamiltonian feature of Canadian banking that can claim credit for stability is the national charter which prevented provincial-level unit banking from ever taking hold.

But that's all. Because there are many more traits of Hamiltonian banking that would have spawned crisis and panic as they did in the United States, but which Canada avoided precisely by not adopting them.

February 1, 2023

Bank of Canada head office, circa 1942

Chapter 34

Why Was the Bank of Canada Established?

Cautious Rockers who've even glanced at the Cautious Economics Correspondent for Economic Affairs' articles on Canadian free banking would be justified in asking a logical question:

"Given how well free banking worked for a century and even withstood the Great Depression without a single bank failure, why on earth did the Canadian government feel it necessary to open a central bank in 1935?"

Curious Rockers feel free to read on to learn more.

As we've covered in multiple past entries, Canada's banking system was the industrialized world's second least regulated from 1817 to 1844, and least regulated from 1845 to 1935. All throughout its entire 118-year free banking era the Canadian system was crisis-free in stark contrast to the heavily regulated United States which had already borne fifteen crises before 1935.

However the free banking era is universally viewed as abruptly ending in 1935 when Canada's first central bank, the Bank of Canada, opened for business by order of the 1934 Bank of Canada Act.

Why then, if Canada's free banking system was performing so well, did Canadian Parliament elect to establish a central bank?

As one might expect the decision was rooted in politics.

STEMMING RADICAL PARTIES

There were two primary political catalysts for Ottawa's embrace of a new central bank.

The greatest, by far, was domestic Great Depression politics.

In the depths of Canada's economic hardship an eccentric upstart party named the Social Credit Party (an interesting name given China's modern Social Credit System) won a large bloc of parliamentary seats, mostly in Alberta where it garnered 46% of the popular vote.[160]

The Social Credit Party's platform, based in the theory of social credit, was considered radical in its day.

Social Credit called for redistribution of wealth and mass printing of government "prosperity certificates" which would be doled out to the public and any business that sold below cost to consumers. Furthermore the party sold its platform in an agrarian Christian populist package, marketed with slogans hailing the national construction of "A Utopia of Our Own."

Compounding problems was the surging "Cooperative Commonwealth Federation" (CCF), a socialist party founded in 1932 on a platform that included nationalization of financial institutions.[161] Capitalizing on widespread public discontent with the depression, the CCF rose in just two years to official opposition status within the provincial governments of Ontario and Saskatchewan.

The rapid ascent of these fringe movements so alarmed the establishment Liberal and Conservative parties that they sought some form of political compromise to curb the most extreme elements of the Social Credit and CCF movements.

A linchpin of that compromise was the Bank of Canada.

Although the Canadian banking sector held up extremely well during the Great Depression and weathered the slump without a crisis, the public nevertheless largely blamed banks—a historically unpopular industry and easy political target—for the depression itself.

Hence the Liberal and Conservative parties believed the creation of a central bank to govern monetary policy would appease all disgruntled parties: not only the Social Credit Party and Cooperative Commonwealth Federation but restless Canadian voters as well.

GLOBAL PRESTIGE

A secondary impetus for the decision to establish a central bank was national prestige.

By the mid 1930's most developed countries were attending regular international monetary conferences. The post-1933 period saw a particularly rapid flurry of meetings where governments repeatedly worked to quell competitive "beggar thy neighbor" monetary policies—frequent cycles of national currency devaluations to boost exports and jumpstart economic growth at the expensive of other trading partners.

However only countries with central banks were invited.

Canadian officials felt they were being left off the world stage, so the two major political parties supported the Bank of Canada Act in order to secure conference invitations and bring Canada the worldly prestige they thought it was due.

According to Bordo and Redish (1986)...

> "The World Monetary and Economic Conference in 1933 had stated that all developed countries without a central bank should create them to facilitate monetary cooperation and recovery. In an article analyzing the need for a central bank, Queen's University economists had stressed the need for a central bank to send representatives to world monetary conferences; 'There are few countries... ...more vitally interested in international cooperation in the monetary and economic fields than Canada and yet we lack any institution which would permit effective participation in such cooperation.'" [162]

Shortly after a government commission headed by pro-central bank parliamentarian Hugh MacMillan handed down its central bank endorsement, Prime Minister R. B. Bennett...

> "...announced that he would introduce a Bill to establish a central bank, 'to regulate credit and currency in the best interests of the economic life of the nation, to control and protect the external value of the national monetary unit and to mitigate by its influence fluctuations in the general level of production, trade, prices and employment.'" [163]

Canada's banking sector had navigated the challenging depression economy successfully without a central bank, but Parliament created one anyway to satisfy politicians of all stripes: populist, socialist, international, and establishment.

RAPID GOVERNMENT SUPERVISION

Once opened the Bank of Canada rapidly took control of monetary functions previously performed by private competitive banks and the historic 118-year era of very light regulation abruptly ended.

(1) In 1935 the Bank of Canada became the official arbiter of banking system reserves and official lender of last resort.

(2) By 1936 the Bank of Canada was government-majority owned.

(3) In 1938 the Bank of Canada was completely nationalized by the federal government.

(4) By World War II private banknote issuance was effectively monopolized by the Bank of Canada, the last-ever private banknote issued in 1943 by the Royal Bank of Canada.

After World War II Canadian Parliament itself took a more active role in bank regulation.

Federal deposit insurance was introduced in 1967.

The Bank of Canada went completely off the last remaining vestiges of international gold after Richard Nixon effectively ended the Bretton-Woods international gold-exchange standard in 1971.

Today Canadian regulators dictate capital ratio and liquidity coverage requirements to banks, monitor their market shares for antitrust violations, and restrict Canadian banks from investing in what they view as risky assets.

And just like the Bank of England, Federal Reserve System and every other modern-day central bank, the Bank of Canada has embarked on a deliberate campaign of long-term price inflation to serve the central government's fiscal interests. Since 1935 prices in Canada have risen nearly 2,100% or an annualized inflation rate of 3.57%.

Stated another way, the Loonie has lost 95.4% of its value, much as the

U.S. dollar has lost 95.6% of its value during the same period.

However even with such a dramatic departure from free banking since the Great Depression, Canada's banking sector has still managed to avoid any systemic crises—unlike the United States which braved two more in 1990 and 2008.

What has Canada done differently even in the modern era to outperform the United States? We'll discuss that subject in our next two chapters.

February 7, 2023

Chapter 35

Canada's Post-1935 Success and the USA's Failures

The Cautious Optimism Correspondent for Economic Affairs and Other Egghead Stuff explains Canadian banking's modern-day success and stability with a brief summary of how subprime mortgages played out both in the USA and north of the border.

Before 1935 Canada possessed the industrialized world's least regulated banking system yet never experienced a financial crisis.

By then the United States, with the industrialized world's most regulated banking system, had already endured fifteen banking panics going back to 1792.

However since 1935 the Canadian government has caught up with the rest of the world and imposed a great deal more control over its banking industry. The Bank of Canada is now monopoly issuer of the currency, has unilateral control over the banking system's level of reserves and interbank lending rates, and provides a lender of last resort facility to member banks.

Federal deposit insurance was introduced in 1967 and today Canadian regulators impose legal capital ratio requirements on banks, inspect merger requests for antitrust violations, and dictate what types of bank investments are too risky. Yet even as the Canadian banking system increasingly resembles the USA's Canada has still managed to avoid a financial crisis—ever.

Meanwhile the United States, even with the imperfect but reasonably effective remedy of federal deposit insurance since 1934, has still managed to suffer through the S&L Crisis of the late 1980's and the Great Financial Crisis of 2008.

And while American banks received over $400 billion in bailout loans from the U.S. Treasury in 2008 and 2009, Canadian banks remained profitable during the global GFC and didn't take a penny from the Canadian government.

WHY STILL DIFFERENT OUTCOMES?

What's the difference between these two seemingly similar regulatory regimes? Why has Canadian banking continued to enjoy such stability and served as a model to the world while so many other countries, the USA included, have suffered 140 financial crises—defined as aggregate failed bank losses greater than 1% of GDP—since 1978?[164]

The answer again lies in good versus bad regulations.

First we'll concede that a monopoly central bank is generally an example of bad regulation, and Canada has one. The Bank of Canada has even recently done the country the disservice of inflating a huge housing bubble, the final disposition of which remains to be seen.

But even as central bank-induced asset bubbles are major contributing factors in creating financial crises they usually aren't enough to induce panic on their own. Most monetary economists know it takes more than just the central bank.

The other critical element, notably absent in Canada, is a lowering of lending standards. And historically the United States has had a lot of that, imposing lower lending standards on its banks via regulation.

For America's first 170 years state-level unit banking laws restricted bank branching making it difficult to impossible for banks to diversify their loan portfolios. Unlike the USA, Canada has never told its banks they can't branch.

Also unlike Gilded Age America, the Canadian government never restricted the national supply of currency based on the level of federal debt its banks held. And also unlike the United States, in recent decades the Canadian government hasn't imposed regulations to openly force banks to lower lending standards in the name of social justice.

MORE RECENTLY: CRA

During the years leading up to the 2008 financial crisis Congress was able to force American banks to either lend $1 trillion directly to uncreditworthy borrowers or to finance many subprime mortgages that were originated by mortgage lenders like Countrywide and GMAC.[165]

Much of this was mandated by 1995 revisions to the 1977 Community Reinvestment Act (CRA), a law that was originally passed during the Jimmy Carter administration in the name of anti-racial discrimination.

While commercial banks largely ignored the 1977 CRA legislation Congress' 1995 revisions imposed stiff penalties on banks that regulators deemed weren't lending generously enough to low-income borrowers. As policy analyst Edward Pinto pointed out in his 2009 Congressional testimony, from 1992 to 2008 U.S. banks acquiesed to:

> "...a total of $6 trillion in announced CRA commitments—680 times the cumulative volume of $9 billion during the entire first 15 years of CRA." [166]

Supporters of CRA argue Countrywide and other mortgage lenders were never CRA-regulated, only commercial banks. Therefore, they say, the public should blame the reckless greed of less-regulated mortgage lenders, and by extension the unregulated free market for making so many bad loans to uncreditworthy borrowers, not the government.

But it was the regulatory mandate that forced commercial banks to seek out poor-credit borrowers—who are not the banking industry's traditional clientele—from mortgage companies to begin with. Regulators imposed the mandates, mortgage lenders supplied the shaky borrowers, and CRA-regulated banks were obliged to provide the capital.

Hence pardoning CRA for bad loans originated by mortgage lenders is tantamount to exonerating the tax code for tens of millions of annual TurboTax and H&R Block tax returns. "Congress didn't force TurboTax and H&R Block to process all those returns" is the twisted logic, but of course it's the complex tax code that drives taxpayers into the arms of tax preparers every year just as CRA diverted commercial bank capital towards mortgage lenders.

The CRA-regulated bank/mortgage lender partnership has all but disappeared from marketing websites since the 2008 debacle, but the Correspondent saved one particularly large advertising campaign from the many he witnessed during the 2000's. From a major mortgage player offering to assist banks seeking to satisfy CRA mandates in 2004:

> "Countrywide's goal is to meet the Six Hundred Billion Dollar challenge, funding $600 billion in home loans to minorities and lower-income borrowers, and to borrowers in lower-income communities, between 2001 and 2010. As of July 31, 2004, the company had funded nearly $301 billion [!] toward this goal."

> "The result of these efforts is an enormous pipeline of mortgages to low-and moderate-income buyers. With this pipeline, Countrywide Securities Corporation (CSC) can potentially help you meet your Community Reinvestment Act (CRA) goals by offering both whole loan and mortgage-backed securities that are eligible for CRA credit."

-Countrywide marketing website (now defunct)

MORE RECENTLY: GSE'S

The Clinton and George W. Bush White Houses required Fannie Mae and Freddie Mac, via Department of Housing and Urban Development mandates, to purchase more and more low-quality mortgages from U.S. banks including CRA loans, bundle them into securities, and sell them off with implied taxpayer guarantees—all in the name of "affordable housing." From the October 30, 2000 American Bankers Association Conference:

> "We will take CRA loans off your hands–we will buy them from your portfolios, or package them into securities–so you have fresh cash to make more CRA loans. Some people have assumed we don't buy tough loans. Let me correct that misimpression right now. We want your CRA loans because they help us meet our housing goals." [167]

-Jamie Gorelick, Fannie Mae Vice Chairman

By the dawn of the financial crisis a minimum 56% of Fannie and Freddie's annual mortgage purchases were mandatory "below median income" and 24% were mandatory "special affordable," defined as very low income.

(See chart for visual and note mandate increases in 1996 and 2001)

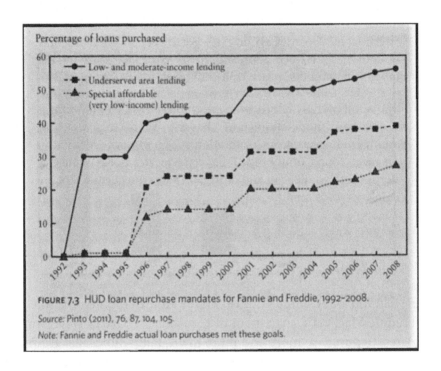

FIGURE 7.3 HUD loan repurchase mandates for Fannie and Freddie, 1992–2008.

Source: Pinto (2011), 76, 87, 104, 105.

Note: Fannie and Freddie actual loan purchases met these goals.

CANADIAN MORTGAGE LENDING

True to the historical pattern Canada avoided the 2008 crisis by never having any such laws let alone on such an immense scale.

There is a smaller version of Fannie Mae in Canada—the Canada Mortgage and Housing Corporation or CMHC—but it guarantees less than half the mortgages of Fannie Mae and Freddie Mac as a share of the market. To compare, by December 2007 Fannie and Freddie held or guaranteed $5.4 trillion in mortgage assets, about half the $11 trillion U.S. mortgage market at the time, including $3.5 trillion of mortgage-backed securities which they had packaged themselves from their low-to-moderate and very low-income mortgage purchases.[168]

(See regulator OFHEO's 2007 chart)

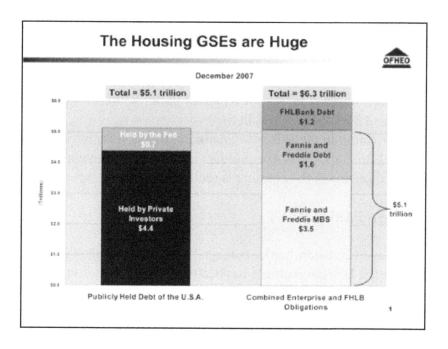

While CMHC is not in the business of holding lots of mortgages, in December of 2007 it did guarantee CA$165 billion or 20.8% of Canada's then CAD$792 billion of mortgage debt (source: CMHC and Statistics Canada).[169]

The United States GSE's and the Canadian CMHC: Half vs 20.8%. Big difference.

But the biggest difference of all is CMHC's mission. Unlike the Fannie and Freddie of the 2000's CMHC more resembles the pre-Clinton administration Fannie: guaranteeing quality mortgages instead of encouraging unsound lending by buying up huge quotas of junk mortgages to package and resell in a political social engineering scheme.

All throughout the housing bubble years and beyond, Canadian credit quality was and remains high. Just ask any Canadian homeowner about mortgage lending standards.

Canadian homeowners have to reapply and requalify for their mortgages every five years, effectively making all mortgages adjustable-rate.

There's no such thing as a 30-year fixed mortgage in Canada which is an almost uniquely American invention—introduced by FDR along with government mortgage guarantees during the Great Depression.

2% down, 1% down, and zero-down mortgages are unheard of in Canada, and the absolute minimum down payment in Canada has only recently been lowered to 5% for balances under $500,000 (10% above $500,000 and 20% above $1 million).

(Note to Cautious Optimism's Canadian readers: Never having bought a house in Canada, if the Correspondent has slipped up anywhere, please post your thoughts in the comments section.)

CANADIAN PARLIAMENT

How have Canadian banks managed to keep lending standards so high while the U.S. government has beaten American lending standards down?

Simple. Even though for decades there have been many populist bills floated in the Canadian House of Commons to force banks to lower lending standards they have been consistently blocked by the more level-headed Canadian Senate.[170]

Now before Canadian readers roll their eyes at the idea of their senators being "level-headed," I only ask them to compare their banking legislative edicts and the public demeanor of their senators to that of U.S. senators past and present like Bernie Sanders, Elizabeth Warren, Corey Booker, John Fetterman (may his health improve), Al Franken, or even Senator Barack Obama.

Over many decades the U.S. Senate has passed countless laws that forced or rewarded American banks for lowering lending standards including the creation of the GSE's, Federal Housing Administration, and the CRA.

But the Canadian Senate, which like the U.S. Senate prior to the U.S. Constitution's 17th Amendment (1913) is not directly elected by

Canadian voters, has been far less populist when it comes to tinkering with bank regulation.[171]

Which is why it was possible for American loan applicants with no job and no income to access vast pools of mortgage credit during the 2000's while Canadian banks were still allowed to tell such borrowers "no"—and did.

The Economics Correspondent doesn't know if Canada's winning streak will last forever. The Bank of Canada has inflated a housing bubble of its own, and should it deflate the banking industry will incur higher loan losses. But the size of such losses is less likely to be catastrophic when confining mortgage credit to more creditworthy borrowers— something Parliament has so far allowed the industry to keep doing.

In our next installment we'll discuss the question of Glass-Steagall restrictions and Canadian financial stability.

March 7, 2023

Senator Carter Glass and Representative Henry Steagall

Chapter 36

Did Canada's Glass-Steagall Safeguard Its Banks in 2008?

Spoiler: Canada didn't have a Glass-Steagall.

The Cautious Optimism Correspondent for Economic Affairs explores Glass-Steagall regulations as they relate to the Canadian banking industry and the 2008 financial crisis.

During the 2008 Global Financial Crisis it became stylish in some circles to blame the upheaval on the repeal of a single provision from the 1933 Glass-Steagall Act: the separation of commercial banking from investment banking. In the fifteen years since Senator Elizabeth Warren has been one of the loudest and most consistent voices blaming the 1999 partial repeal, known also as the Gramm-Leach-Bliley Act, for the crisis.

Aside from the fact Glass-Steagall never existed in most continental European countries including France, Germany, and the Netherlands, which avoided systemic financial crises for 75 years before 2008, there are also several problems with the "bring back Glass-Steagall" panacea.[172]

The six years between the enactment of Gramm-Leach-Bliley and the popping of the residential real estate bubble provided only a narrow window for mergers between large commercial and investment banks to introduce the risk that was allegedly responsible for the 2008 crisis. In those six years very little such banking integration took place, but critics blame the crisis on a massive union of business lines that didn't yet exist.

And an even bigger problem is that Canada has combined commercial and investment banking operations at its major banks for a much longer time than the USA. In stark contrast to the USA, by the 2000's decade all of Canada's "Big Five" commercial banks had already integrated investment banking into their operations.

According to the Glass-Steagall lobby Canadian banks should have suffered an even larger crisis than their U.S. counterparts in 2008, yet they experienced no crisis whatsoever.

GLASS-STEAGALL DURING THE GREAT DEPRESSION

First let's quickly review what Glass-Steagall was: a Great Depression-era series of banking reforms cosponsored by Senator Carter Glass (D-VA) and Representative Henry Steagall (D-AL) who chaired their respective Senate Appropriations and House Banking committees.

Also known as the Banking Act of 1933, Glass-Steagall contained four major provisions:

(1) The introduction of federal deposit insurance through the establishment of the FDIC.

(2) The creation of the central bank Federal Open Market Committee (FOMC) to conduct monetary policy.

(3) Regulation Q: Prohibiting banks from paying interest on demand deposits and strict limits on interest paid for other forms of deposits (repealed in 1980).

(4) The separation of commercial banking and investment banking activities within the same institution (repealed in 1999).

Ironically, only one of the four provisions did anything to help avert future banking panics (deposit insurance) and two of the provisions were actually anti-competitive measures designed to protect politically favored banks (deposit insurance and Regulation Q).

Both anti-competitive provisions were championed by Henry Steagall who represented an unstable unit banking state. Regulation Q was enacted to prevent monopoly unit banks from losing customers to other monopoly unit banks in neighboring localities, and deposit insurance was designed to protect unit banks from their own unstable structure: undiversified loan portfolios and undiversified depositors stemming from state laws limiting them to a single office in small rural towns.

As Steagall said himself during Congressional bill debate:

"This bill will preserve independent dual banking [i.e. unit banking] in the United States. That is what the bill is intended to do."

-"Deposit Insurance or Branching?" from "Compendium of Issues Relating to Branching by Financial Institutions," United States Senate Committee on Banking, Housing, and Urban Affairs (1976)

The creation of the FOMC can be argued to have actually made the banking system more unstable as monetary policy, the Fed's buying and selling of assets to manipulate both interest rates and the quantity of reserves in the banking system, has produced larger and more destructive credit boom-bust cycles.

And lastly the separation of commercial and investment banking activities was included at the insistence of one man: Carter Glass, who was steadfast in his strange belief that a crossover between lending deposits and underwriting securities had caused the great banking crises of the early 1930's.

However even mainstream economists have recognized for decades that the depression-era crises were due to unit banking laws and the multiple failures of the Federal Reserve. Of the over 9,000 banks that failed between 1929 and 1933 the vast majority were small unit banks in rural areas, hardly active in underwriting new Wall Street stock offerings or corporate bonds.

Nevertheless, Glass' powerful Appropriations Committee chair provided the clout to successfully push the investment banking provision though into law.

AMERICAN INVESTMENT BANKS IN THE 2000's

The legal barriers separating commercial and investment banking were repealed in November of 1999 meaning financial institutions only began working on large merger/acquisition prospects in 2000 and 2001.

Most did not.

And a key fact many proponents of Glass-Steagall fail to address is by early 2008 America's leading investment banks:

-Goldman Sachs
-Morgan Stanley
-Merrill Lynch
-Lehman Brothers
-Bear Stearns

…were still standalone entities with little to no crossover activity.

By early 2008 the top five U.S. commercial banks:

-Citigroup
-Bank of America
-JPMorgan Chase
-Wachovia
-Wells Fargo

...were a mixed bag, three with immature and still developing investment banking divisions.

Citigroup and JPMorgan Chase were exceptions. Citibank was granted a Glass-Steagall exemption by the Federal Reserve when it merged with Travelers Group in 1998. As a consequence of the deal the new Citigroup combined Citibank's commercial bank and Travelers' Salomon Smith Barney investment bank divisions. Chase Manhattan Bank also acquired investment bank J.P. Morgan in 2000 to create JPMorgan Chase.

Ironically, instead of being dragged down by its combined commercial and investment banking divisions, JPMorgan Chase fared better than any other major bank during the 2008 crisis with the possible exception of Wells Fargo. Citigroup, the only other fully integrated major bank, was a polar opposite, faring the worst and ultimately requiring $45 billion in Treasury TARP loans and massive Federal Reserve assistance.

But the great bulk of Citi's subprime losses didn't stem from investment banking activities. Rather its bad loans originated largely from within its own traditional mortgage arm (CitiMortgage) and the 2000 acquisition of Associates First Capital (aka. "The Associates"), a consumer finance company that had aggressively pursued subprime lending for years.

Citigroup also doubled down in 2007, buying $45 billion in distressed assets from what was the USA's largest subprime mortgage lender until 2005: Ameriquest.[173] Coincidentally $45 billion is the exact amount of TARP assistance Citigroup received from the U.S. Treasury a year later.

Pre-1999 Glass-Steagall restrictions didn't preclude any of these mortgage and lending acquisition activities.

Citigroup was also one of the first banks to agree to large Community Reinvestment Act commitments as a condition for regulatory approval of its merger with Travelers Group. In response to its announcement of $115 billion in loans to low-income communities politicians, activists, and academics criticized Citigroup's commitment for being too small. According to the New York Times:

> "The amount promised was less than what some community activists and others had expected... ...'They can do much better,' said Kenneth Thomas, a lecturer in finance at the Wharton School of the University of Pennsylvania. 'We expected to see $200 billion to $400 billion' in loan commitments, he said."
>
> -from "Communities to Receive $115 Billion, Citigroup Says"

And just two months after Citigroup's announcement some banks began to express concerns about increasing political pressure to lend more and more hundreds of billions of dollars to satisfy regulators.

> "'C.R.A. has become a volume-oriented game, with up being good and down being bad,' said Ms. Bessant of Nationsbank. 'I worry about crazy pricing and crazy credit as everybody tries to generate more loans in order to get a better [regulator] rating.'" [174]

In 2008 JPMorgan Chase's financial position was so strong that it rescued Bear Steans from collapse through an eleventh-hour government-brokered acquisition. Regulators hoped the buyout would avert a wider financial crisis (they were proven wrong a few months later).

Meanwhile the imminent failure of Merrill Lynch gave Bank of America an opportunity it had long coveted: to acquire a major investment bank and finally enter the securities underwriting, M&A, wealth and asset management, and sales and trading businesses writ large. In a hurried deal Bank of America rescued Merrill Lynch for $50 billion during the darkest hours of the 2008 crisis.

Incidentally the JPMorgan Chase/Bear Stearns and Bank of America/Merrill Lynch rescues would have been illegal under Glass-Steagall's original restrictions. Had the rules not been repealed in 1999 the number of major investment bank failures would have grown from one of the Big Five (Lehman Brothers) to three (Lehman, Bear Stearns, and Merrill Lynch), deepening the crisis and subsequent Great Recession.

Today only two of the original five investment banks remain independent entities: Goldman Sachs and Morgan Stanley.

RESILIENT CANADIAN INVESTMENT BANKS

Canada also once had its own version of Glass-Steagall: the so-called "Four Pillars" that separated commercial banking, investment banking, securities trading, and insurance.

In 1987 the conservative Mulroney government freed the first three pillars to be integrated (leaving insurance separated out). The so-called financial "Little Bang" allowed commercial and investment banks to merge a dozen years before President Bill Clinton signed the Gramm-Leach-Bliley Act into law.

Immediately Canada's "Big Five" commercial banks (plus number six National Bank of Canada) began acquiring securities trading and underwriting firms. Each of their first forays were:

-August 1987: Bank of Montreal acquires Nesbitt Thompson
-October 1987: Toronto-Dominion acquires Gardiner Group[175]
-December 1987: Scotiabank acquires McLeod Young Weir
-March 1988: Royal Bank of Canada acquires Dominion Securities
-June 1988: CIBC acquires Wood Gundy
-June 1988: National Bank of Canada acquires Levesque Beaubien

By the time the U.S. housing market collapsed four of Canada's Big Five banks had had two decades to fully integrate investment banking into their commercial banking businesses while all five had long since expanded into investment brokerage services, following the "financial supermarket" model that had already taken hold in Europe and Asia. U.S. banks only had six years which explains why only two bore any resemblance to universal banks by then. By 2008 two Canadian superbanks were also major players on the global investment banking stage: namely RBC Capital Markets and BMO Capital Markets.

Today each of the Big Five's integrated investment bank divisions are:

-RBC Capital Markets
-TD Securities
-Scotia Global Banking and Markets
-BMO Capital Markets
-CIBC World Markets

According to Glass-Steagall proponents Canada's megabanks should have gone down in flames in 2008, yet they all escaped the financial crisis unscathed, remaining profitable throughout with none taking even a penny of government money.

American Enterprise Institute scholar Alex Pollock summarizes this obvious dilemma for Glass-Steagall proponents when he writes...

> "Our neighbors to the north in Canada have a banking system that is generally viewed as one of the most stable, if not the most stable, in the world. The Canadian banking system certainly has a far better historical record than does that of the United States."

> "There is no Glass-Steagall in Canada: all the large Canadian banks combine commercial banking and investment banking, as well as other financial businesses, and the Canadian banking system has done very well. Canada thus represents a great counterexample for Glass-Steagall enthusiasts to ponder."

> -from "Glass-Steagall never saved our financial system, so why revive it?" (2017)

A FAMILIAR CULPRIT

So why, if Canada's combined commercial and investment banks didn't experience their own crisis in 2008, did so many of America's standalone commercial banks and investment banks fail or need government bailouts to survive?

The answer, once again, is bad regulations.

The American mortgage lenders, commercial banks, and investment banks that came under pressure in 2008 got that way not because of complex commercial and investment bank mergers but rather due to old-fashioned bad loans.

Federal government regulations forced U.S. lending standards down, particularly on residential mortgages, while GSE's Fannie Mae and Freddie Mac offered to buy up lousy loans, package them with better loans, and sell the bundled securities to investors to the tune of trillions of dollars. Bear Stearns, Merrill Lynch, and Lehman Brothers joined the securitization party and found themselves holding toxic mortgage paper when the music stopped.

Combined with a historic housing bubble inflated by Federal Reserve cheap money policies, U.S. lenders suffered huge losses when the bubble burst, housing prices plummeted, and uncreditworthy borrowers stopped paying their mortgages.

The culprits were simple and historically familiar: a central bank-induced bubble and bad loans on the traditional mortgage side.

And as we reviewed in a previous column the Canadian government, particularly the Canadian Senate, has been far less amenable to accommodating populist political movements seeking to transform banks into tools of social justice.

Hence when the financial crisis struck, Canadian banks held up—because they hadn't made nearly as many bad loans, or more precisely because they hadn't been compelled to make as many bad loans via regulation.

Far from the partial repeal of Glass-Steagall being the cause of the U.S. system's problems, the full integration of commercial and investment banking in Canada proves precisely the opposite: Canada's financial supermarket model held up in 2008 while in the United States, where few major commercial and investment banks had combined in the 2000's, the financial sector fell into disarray.

March 28, 2023

Did Canada's Glass-Steagall Safeguard Its Banks in 2008?

Silicon Valley Bank depositors queue up to withdraw cash

Chapter 37

What Does Silicon Valley Bank's Collapse Tell Us About Depositor Losses Under Canadian Free Banking?

The Cautious Optimism Correspondent for Economic Affairs has a few words to write about the warp speed collapse of Silicon Valley Bank (SVB), deposit insurance, and even a connection to his ongoing series on free banking in Canada.

The Economics Correspondent just read today that over 90% of failed Silicon Valley Bank's deposits are uninsured even though the bank is an FDIC member.

Over 90% of deposits are at risk because the FDIC only insures accounts up to $250,000 per depositor. And SVB, the 16th largest U.S. bank by assets, has many customers with higher than $250,000 balances including wealthy individuals and businesses who draw on deposit accounts to make payroll.

DEPOSIT INSURANCE

The Economics Correspondent had originally decided not to write in detail on the subject of deposit insurance and depositor losses during Canadian free banking, but SVB's sudden collapse has provided a timely segue to comment.

Canada had no deposit insurance until Parliament established the Canadian Deposit Insurance Corporation (CDIC) in 1967.

Although there was never a financial crisis during Canada's earlier free banking era (1817-1935), isolated bank failures did occur from time to time since banking is, after all, a profit/loss business just like any other.

Critics of free banking argue that absent deposit insurance customers can become unnerved during periods of stress, withdraw their funds en masse and set off a run which could spread to other banks and spawn systemic crisis (oddly, there has never been a financial crisis in Canada). Deposit insurance, they say, assuages such fears and makes the banking system more resilient to runs while protecting customers from losses.

Critics of deposit insurance argue it introduces moral hazard both to bankers and depositors since both sides, aware that government guarantees will cover their losses, become considerably less interested in managing risk.

The moral hazard story, they argue, was evident during the 1980's Savings and Loan Crisis. During the late 1980's thrifts that had gotten in trouble offered absurdly high deposit interest rates, attracting new funds to make extremely speculative all-or-nothing loans in a desperate attempt to avert otherwise certain failure.

Yet depositors happily handed their money to institutions they knew were failing, indifferent to anything but high yields since they knew the government would cover their losses if the thrift folded. Instead of prudence S&L depositors cared only if there was an FDIC or FSLIC sticker in the bank's front window.

Subsequently the final cost of the S&L depositor bailout swelled by tens of billions of dollars, a substantial sum back in the 1980's and a paradigmatic example of deposit insurance enlarging both a financial crisis and its bailout price tag.

But critics of uninsured deposits have one more, undeniable piece of evidence to support their case: the empirical history of Canada. During free banking some depositors did lose money in the isolated bank failures that occurred from time to time.

Using historical records economists have estimated that during the latter third of the 19th century total Canadian depositor losses totaled less than 1% of failed bank liabilities across the period.[176]

Canadian losses were so small precisely *because* there was no deposit insurance. Instead of an insurance fund it was the bank owners and directors who were liable for depositor losses; up to double their paid-in capital stake (i.e. double liability). Having their personal assets at stake proved very effective at focusing Canadian bank owners and directors like a laser on sound lending and credit quality.

(Note: During the same period the United States endured several banking panics where estimated depositor losses totaled 57% of failed bank liabilities.)[177]

A Federal Reserve report confirmed the Canadian trend all the way until 1931 using assets, which are a rough analog to liabilities, bringing the total sample to 64 years:

> "For the period 1901 to 1920 the assets of suspended banks in Canada amounted to about one-half of one percent of the average yearly banking assets of the country... ...For the eleven year period 1921-1931 the assets of suspended banks in Canada were again equal to about one-half of one per cent of the average yearly banking assets of the country while the corresponding figure in the United States was about twenty times as high, or 10.7 per cent." [178]

> -"Branch Banking in Canada," Federal Reserve Committee on Branch, Group, and Chain Banking (1932)

Nevertheless, proponents of deposit insurance maintain that even losses of less than 1% are unacceptable. Depositors, they say, should enjoy guarantees they will lose nothing in the event their bank fails. And the FDIC has made good on that promise, emphasizing no one has ever lost a penny in insured deposits since its inception in 1934.

INSURED VS UNINSURED

The key FDIC phrase the Correspondent would like to stress here is *insured* deposits. Because deposit balances over the FDIC limit ($250,000 per depositor since 2008) are uninsured and therefore ineligible for compensation.

The Economics Correspondent hasn't been able to find total U.S. *uninsured* depositor losses during the 90 years the FDIC has been in business, and the FDIC is understandably reluctant to announce such numbers loudly.

However the recent SVB story is quite informative.

SVB's most recent annual report reveals that in December of 2022 at least 90% of its deposits were above the FDIC limit and therefore uninsured.

Out of curiosity the Economics Correspondent checked JPMorgan Chase's most recent annual report and found over $1 trillion in uninsured deposits.

Given the sheer amount of money wealthy and business clients have in U.S. banks the Economics Correspondent would venture that uninsured depositor losses in America's two post-1933 crises—the S&L Crisis and the Great Financial Crisis—have exceeded 1% of liabilities.

In fact we already know something about S&L Crisis losses.

Depositor losses were so great in the late 1980's that the Federal Savings and Loan Insurance Corporation (FSLIC) itself went bankrupt and had to be absorbed into the FDIC. The failure of the government's insurance agency left S&L depositors holding the bag and the U.S. taxpayer was forced to make up the difference.

The S&L bailout ultimately cost taxpayers $132 billion or roughly 15% *of the entire industry's liabilities*[179] (not just failed institutions, which would have raised the percentage even higher).

Cautious Rockers may also remember the taxpayer was on the hook for over $400 billion in capital injections during the 2008 financial crisis to prevent bank failures that would easily have bankrupted the FDIC.

Ultimately the $400+ billion was repaid with interest, so unlike 1990 taxpayers weren't forced to permanently subsidize depositors, but the point is without putting a huge amount of taxpayer money at risk the FDIC itself would have become insolvent and uninsured depositor losses would have exploded.

And these estimates don't include losses associated with the smaller waves of bank failures that occurred in the mid/late 1930's plus the decades worth of intermittent bank failures that have occurred since then such as Franklin National in 1974 and Continental Illinois in 1984.

Hence, even though the Economics Correspondent is having trouble finding all uninsured depositor losses for the 1934-2023 period, he'll still wager a steak dinner with anyone that depositors fared better under Canadian free banking with no deposit insurance (< 1% losses) than they have in the United States even with the FDIC and FSLIC.

SILICON VALLEY BANK

As for Silicon Valley Bank itself, the Economics Correspondent is confident that not all of its 90% in (uninsured) deposits will go unpaid. But there is a reasonable chance that there will be *some* losses.

It all depends on the final disposition of the bank.

If the FDIC can find a buyer for SVB, a large firm that's willing to take over its assets and liabilities and enter into a loss-sharing agreement with the agency, all in exchange for SVB's branch network footprint and customer base, then even uninsured deposits might be made whole.

But if the bank has to be wound down—its assets sold and its liabilities paid off—uninsured depositor losses become much more likely.

SVB's balance sheet claims assets in excess of liabilities, but in the rapidly rising interest rate environment of late 2022/early 2023—which is rumored to have triggered the bank's difficulties to begin with—the mark-to-market value of those assets comes into question.

SVB is a bit different from your average bank in that over half of its assets are securities, not loans, such as Treasuries and mortgage-backed securities.

As the Federal Reserve has rapidly hiked interest rates the value of those securities has fallen, and if SVB were to wind down and sell all its securities at depressed rates there might not be enough cash to pay off all depositors.

Of course the FDIC will make up the difference for every depositor up to $250,000 apiece, but anyone with more at stake will be out of luck.

And the FDIC won't mention those losses… at least not very loudly. And neither will critics of free banking.

Postscript: For anyone wondering if the Economics Correspondent is advocating the abolishment of deposit insurance in the United States, the answer is a qualified no.

The pros and cons of deposit insurance can be complicated, but in a single phrase the Correspondent's opinion is this: So long as a monopoly central bank, politicians, and all their destabilizing regulations exist, then deposit insurance serves as an imperfect, liability-laden, but nevertheless effective remedy for quelling the panics created by Washington, D.C.

However history clearly demonstrates that when politicians haven't interfered with banking systems the industry has functioned far better on its own. Deposit insurance has therefore not only been unnecessary, it has actually introduced moral hazard and greater risk to the system.

In fact the moral hazard problem is precisely why U.S. Congress rejected 150 separate bills attempting to establish federal deposit insurance legislation between 1880 and 1933. It's also why most developed countries didn't introduce deposit insurance until the late 20th century—the U.S. being one of the first in 1934 only after Czechoslovakia. Canada was next more than three decades later, and Australia and New Zealand last in 2008.

March 11, 2023

What Does SVB Tell Us About Free Banking Depositor Losses?

POSTSCRIPT:
THE GREAT DEPRESSION

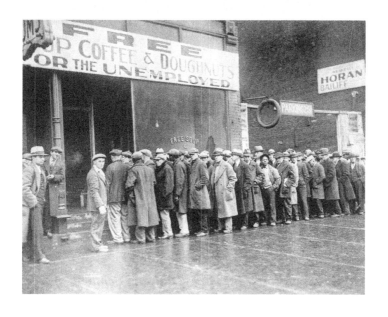

New York City meeting of four top central bankers:
(left to right) H. Schacht, B. Strong, M. Norman, C. Rist

Original photo caption: "On July 1, 1927, Montagu Norman of Britain was accompanied by Hjalmar Schacht, head of the German Reichsbank. They were joined by Charles Rist, [deputy] governor of the Banque de France. All three went into conference with Benjamin Strong to discuss the weak reserve position of the Bank of England and capital flight from Europe to America. It was hoped that lowering interest rates would deflect the capital inflows from Europe."

Chapter 38

What Really Started the Great Depression? Part 1

No, it wasn't income inequality which was just a symptom of the real cause: expansionary monetary policy and transatlantic Anglo-American central bank cooperation.

The Cautious Optimism Correspondent for Economic Affairs continues his series on the Great Depression addressing the pesky and poorly understood question of what started the whole sorry affair.

NEW YORK CITY: JULY 1, 1927

Meeting in the New York Federal Reserve Building the heads of the world's four largest central banks convened to discuss a major policy change in the new era of international monetary cooperation. Attending were:

Benjamin Strong: Governor of the New York Federal Reserve
Montagu Norman: Governor of the Bank of England
Hjalmar Schacht: Governor of the German Reichsbank
Charles Rist: Deputy Governor of the Bank of France

Fed governor Strong and his British counterpart surprised their French and German opposites with a startling announcement: the Federal Reserve would launch an aggressive asset purchase and monetary easing campaign, effectively bolstering U.S. inflation in an effort to curtail Great Britain's chronic trade deficits with the United States.

The meeting itself was a fait accompli, a mere formality as the new policy had already been privately consummated between Strong and Norman who were close working associates and personal friends.

Germany's Schacht and France's Rist, hard-money advocates who preferred adherence to the traditional workings of the pre-WWI classical gold standard and minimal state interference, were shaken by the development which they viewed as potentially destabilizing to the international monetary system. But powerless to do anything about it they reluctantly agreed—at which point Strong turned to Rist and excitedly announced:

"I'm going to give a little coup de whiskey to the stock market!" [180]

Strong kept his word. In the eighteen months that ensued the Federal Reserve expanded its holdings of securities from $1.175 billion to $1.824 billion—an increase of 55%—and the U.S. money supply ballooned at its fastest rate of the entire 1920's decade.[181]

Newly created money and bank credit quickly spilled over into asset markets fueling speculation as the Dow Jones Industrial Average advanced from an all time high of 175.35 in July 1927 to 386.10 by September 1929, a stunning advance of over 120% in just 26 months. Real estate speculation pushed commercial and particularly residential property prices into record territory. Cheap credit spawned irrational business investment projects such as factory overexpansion and competitive groundbreakings for "world's tallest building" in New York City.

And the rich—who by definition own assets—got a lot richer while the poor—who by definition don't own assets—saw only meager gains. Thus wealth inequality, which today's progressives obsess over and claim in and of itself causes recessions, widened due to the central bank induced inflow of money.

The climax of the Roaring Twenties was underway.

Oddly enough, since most of the new money flooded into asset speculation the wholesale and consumer price indexes signaled only subdued inflation. Fooled by ostensibly moderate price pressures,

America's greatest contemporary economist Irving Fisher concluded the U.S. economy had entered a new era of prosperity, famously declaring in the New York Times that "Stock prices have reached what looks like a permanently high plateau" on October 21, 1929—six days before the Black Tuesday crash.

Misled by holes in his own Quantity Theory of Money, it was a mistake that Fisher's Monetarist successors would go on to make decades later, including the great Milton Friedman himself who saw little inflation in 2005 and declared "The stability of our economy is greater than it has ever been in our history. We really are in remarkable shape." [182]

But back to the 1920's. Benjamin Strong, who had always suffered from poor health, died from tuberculosis in October of 1928 leaving it to his successor George L. Harrison to wind down the Fed's easing campaign at the end of the year, tightening credit and raising interest rates in 1929. Starved of plentiful new money to fuel the credit boom the economy began to sink into recession by the summer of 1929, and dangerously overvalued asset market bubbles began to burst, culminating with the famous stock market crash in October.

The 1927 secret meeting is only known to us because Charles Rist recorded it in his personal diaries. And the Fed as policy culprit rings with depressing familiarity from other such episodes in economic history. But the story behind the 1927 Fed's easy money policy is truly unique among history's credit-induced tragedies. Its origins ultimately laid the groundwork that dragged two continents into a cataclysmic monetary collapse that transformed what should have been just another credit-fueled recession (in the tradition of 1719, 1797, 1819, 1825, 1837, 1873, 1893, and 1921) into the Great Depression.

And the ill-fated joint decision by the Federal Reserve and Bank of England would prove so fatal that it would force the world off the centuries-long venerable gold standard only a few short years later—ironically because Strong and Norman attempted to "cheat" with policies that the traditional gold standard would never have allowed.

This column tells that story, because it's impossible to truly understand what started the Great Depression and particularly why its severity and duration were so unprecedented without grasping first its unique monetary policy origins.

BEFORE THE ROARING TWENTIES: THE INTERNATIONAL CLASSICAL GOLD STANDARD

To understand why Great Britain asked the Federal Reserve for inflationary assistance it's essential to revisit the global economy before 1914 when the industrialized world operated under the 19th century classical gold standard, defined roughly as 1870-1914 with Britain first to adopt it de jure in 1816 and the United States last in 1879.

Under the classical gold standard every country's currency was defined as a unit weight of gold. For example, the U.S. dollar was not a piece of paper but rather the dollar was literally about 1/20th an ounce of gold—or 23.22 grains to be exact. The British pound sterling was defined as approximately 1/4th an ounce of gold or 113.00 grains. Francs, marks, lira, etc… were also literally unit weights of gold.

Paper banknotes and demand deposit balances were simply claims on dollars, pounds, francs, etc… hence the reason old banknotes of the 19th century bore the promise "Will pay the bearer on demand five dollars."

Because both the dollar and the pound were defined as unit weights of gold, the exchange rate between the two was fixed. And since one pound sterling contained 4.86 times more gold than a dollar, the pound sterling equaled $4.86, an exchange rate that had been unchanged since the U.S. Coinage Act of 1834.

Another important attribute of the classical gold standard was that any institution that issued paper banknotes or demand deposit balances (usually created when that institution loaned money) was obligated to convert those notes or deposits on demand into gold coin. In the U.S. that commonly meant gold eagle coins equal to $20 in gold, or in Britain the gold sovereign containing one pound sterling equivalent in gold. Other countries' currencies followed the same rules.

The constant threat of on-demand redemption by holders of paper liabilities was critical as it kept issuing institutions "honest." That is, whether they were commercial banks—as was the case in the USA and Canada—or central banks such as the Bank of England, the threat of redemption served as a natural check against overissuance, inflation, or overexpansion of credit.

The handful of pre-WWI examples of irresponsible overexpansion were virtually always the consequence of government intervention overturning private redemption contracts such as legally suspending gold convertibility (Great Britain during the French Revolutionary and Napoleonic Wars 1797-1821 or the USA during the War of 1812) or attempts to substitute government paper for gold (USA: "Greenback" paper money during the Civil War). But in the relatively free and undisturbed periods of money and banking, institutions were kept in check by market forces that prevented inflationary overexpansion.

The same rules applied to entire nations. If one country's commercial banks or central bank printed too many banknotes or created too much demand deposit checkbook money (i.e. inflation), prices would rise in that country and, given fixed exchange rates, competing imported products became cheaper.

For example, if Britain inflated paper credit then her consumers shifted to less expensive imports, sending their British pounds across the English Channel. French exporters would receive pounds and, through the French banking system, redeem them at the Bank of England. The result: gold would flow across the Channel from Britain to France.

With its gold reserves declining, the British banking system would be forced to end its overexpansion or even contract and prices would fall back into line. Conversely, with French gold reserves now growing the resulting increase in the money supply would make French products more expensive leading to higher British imports and an equilibrium would ensue.

Scottish philosopher David Hume observed this phenomenon, recording his thoughts in the 1750's. The tendency for freely moving international commerce to put a check on overexpansion of money and credit vis-à-vis a country's gold reserves has been known since as the Hume price-specie-flow mechanism.

And under this self-regulating international monetary system—even with occasional destabilizing interventions by governments—the world witnessed an explosion in wealth creation and international trade. For example, from 1870 to 1914 worldwide foreign investment rose from 7% of GDP to 18%.[183] That's a near tripling not of foreign investment, but of its share of world GDP.

Since world GDP increased by approximately 147% during the same period (A. Maddison-2001), actual foreign investment rose by 530% in just 44 years.

The same is true of total world trade. From 1870 to 1914 global trade rose from 10% of GDP to 21%, or in absolute terms an expansion of 419%.[184] And these gains were accompanied by a dramatic decline in major European wars during the latter half of the 19th and early 20th centuries.

So understanding what made the classical gold standard work so well in the late 19th century is also essential for identifying what went wrong in the 1920's, a tragic story that we will visit in Part 2 of this series.

_____

November 1, 2018

Chapter 39

What Really Started the Great Depression? Part 2

The Cautious Optimism Correspondent for Economic Affairs continues with his analysis of what really started the Great Depression. Or what he modestly refers to as "the most important chapter in the world history of money."

In Part 1 we outlined the rules governing the international classical gold standard up to 1914 and foreshadowed the means by which bad monetary policy led to its demise while setting the stage for the beginning of the Great Depression. We continue now with the end of the classical gold standard and the paperized "gold-exchange" standard that replaced it in the 1920's.

WORLD WAR I: THE WORLD GOES OFF GOLD

The outbreak of World War I ended the idyllic global classical gold standard arrangement. As with all large-scale wars the belligerent governments went off the gold standard and freed their central banks to inflate aggressively as a means to finance war expenditures without the level of taxation that would otherwise be required. The only participant country that remained on gold was the United States, in part because it entered the war later. But even the U.S. government imposed a ban on international gold exports so for all practical purposes the U.S. was on an exclusively domestic gold standard.

As the war dragged on European governments inflated profusely and the value of their currencies plummeted. By the time of the Treaty of Versailles so much unbacked paper money had been created that the British pound had lost 35% of its prewar value. But the pound's loss was insignificant compared to the French franc (-64%), Belgian franc (-62%), Italian lira (-71%), and German mark which had depreciated by 96% even before the Weimar hyperinflation of 1921-23.[185]

Given the enormous increase in European paper money and demand deposit balances, it was practically impossible for most nations to return to the gold standard at their prewar pars for that would require a sharp deflationary contraction of prices. Also many had gone heavily into debt to the United States (Great Britain being a major debtor) or Great Britain (most European allies) meaning rising gold stocks were unlikely to come to their aid for some time. Present and prospective gold reserves could simply not support inflated money supplies if each unit of money was to serve as a claim on the prewar gold weight.

So European countries took the only option available to them: they returned their currencies to gold but at a sharply lower unit weight definition (i.e. devaluation). Permanent devaluation was the formal nail in the coffin that consummated the inflationary tax imposed on European citizens to pay for the Great War, but there was really no other option other than going off gold completely.

The two exceptions were Great Britain and of course the United States (we'll exclude Canada from the discussion as it was a unique case). The United States, despite inflating heavily itself to finance wartime expenditures, still had sufficient gold reserves to redeem at 1/20th of an ounce to the dollar throughout. Great Britain was a more complex problem and chose an ill-advised workaround solution that would sow the seeds for what would become the Great Depression.

BRITAIN RETURNS TO GOLD SANS RULES

Great Britain was determined to return the pound sterling to gold at the prewar par in an attempt to recapture London's status as the world's financial center from New York. But given such an inflated money supply she faced a difficult choice.

Her two options were:

(1) Maintain the current money supply by returning to gold at a devalued par, but blemish the pound's international reputation.

(2) Return to gold at the more prestigious prewar par but accept a painful deflation returning to some semblance of the prewar money supply.

Devaluation would certainly compromise Britain's attempts to leapfrog New York as the world's financial capital and was quickly ruled out. But could she return to gold at the prewar par and endure the accompanying deflation and likely recession?

She had before. After the Napoleonic Wars Great Britain returned to gold at the 1797 par and the result was a contraction of the money supply as commercial banks and the Bank of England were forced to reduce credit to realign their paper claims with actual gold reserves. The contraction produced a painful recession followed by a long period of stable expansion. The United States had taken the same medicine after the War of 1812, the Civil War, and even World War I with the deflationary Depression of 1920-21.

But the British political landscape was notably changed by the 1920's. Trade unions, emboldened by Labour policies, resisted falling wages even if the overall price level fell accordingly and resulted in no real change to wages. National unemployment insurance now empowered workers to ride out prolonged joblessness and thus refuse to accept jobs with lower nominal wages, even those unchanged in real terms.

And a new generation of economists berated the evils of deflation and espoused the virtues of inflation—among them Ralph Hawtrey and John Maynard Keynes—both products of Cambridge (interestingly neither Hawtrey nor Keynes ever earned an economics degree). In the eyes of British policymakers a solution had to be found that allowed Britain to return to gold at the old $4.86 par, but without accepting the politically problematic deflation.

It was Hawtrey and Keynes who would devise, foster, and successfully effectuate the solution.

First, Britain would return not to the traditional gold-coin standard whereby holders of banknotes and demand deposits redeemed their pounds in small denomination coins. Rather, the British government would mandate that all gold be centralized at the Bank of England, melted down into large gold bars of at least 400 ounces weight, and requests for redemption accommodated at minimum into one bar of gold bullion.

Hence the gold-coin standard, the product of the previously more laissez-faire system, was replaced with the gold-bullion standard.

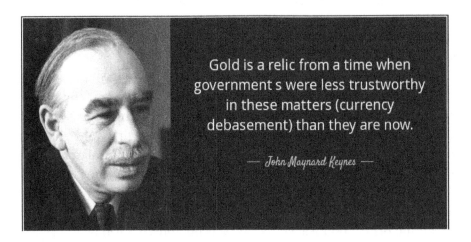

Gold is a relic from a time when government s were less trustworthy in these matters (currency debasement) than they are now.

— *John Maynard Keynes* —

The strategy behind the gold-bullion standard was clear: The overwhelming share of British citizens were simply not wealthy enough to afford gold redemptions of that size. 400 ounces was the equivalent of £1,701 in the 1920's, an astronomical sum at the time.

To put it into present-day perspective, a 400-ounce bar of gold bullion is worth approximately $500,000 today. Thus the number of American citizens who have the spare cash lying around to convert a minimum of $500,000 to gold is completely negligible from a policy standpoint—which was the whole objective of adopting bullion over coin: to disqualify most of the British public from even the possibility of redeeming their Bank of England liabilities.

Therefore under gold bullion, the Bank of England would not have to devalue and in fact could continue with a policy of inflating even more pound banknotes and credit atop the same insufficient gold reserves.

For, as the thinking went, gold reserves would no longer be insufficient given that nearly all British citizens would be unable to exercise their legal rights and the central bank's gold would go mostly unclaimed.

As contemporary Princeton economist and interwar gold-bullion observer Edwin Walter Kemmerer wrote:

> "It is obviously easier... ...for a government to debase its monetary unit under a gold-bullion or gold-exchange standard than under a gold-coin standard... ...[the masses] have not in their power, through the privilege of ready redemption, the ability continually to bring pressure against inflationary trends." [186]

-from *Gold and the Gold Standard* (1944)

By 1925 the façade was ended completely and British citizens were legally prohibited from redeeming their money into gold at all, freeing the Bank of England completely from a huge disciplinary obstacle that had kept it in check during the classical gold standard era.

Now Britain's only remaining concern was overseas holders of pound sterling liabilities, the largest of whom were central banks.

For that problem Hawtrey and Keynes recommended another rule-skirting solution: Britain would replace the old classical gold standard—where overseas holders of paper pound sterling notes or demand deposit balances could convert those liabilities into gold—with the new "gold-exchange" standard.

The gold-exchange standard was a cunning ruse designed to circumvent the discipline of the classical gold standard by replacing gold reserves with paper pound sterling reserves. Under this new system the Bank of England would inflate pound banknote and deposit balances atop its centralized gold reserves.

Unsurprisingly the resulting price inflation would continue to induce more imports than exports and British pounds would still flow overseas. But instead of its trading partners submitting their accumulated sterling balances to the Bank of England for gold, the countries of continental Europe would be pressured to accept pounds sterling as "equal to gold" and use the paper liabilities as a pseudo-gold base to inflate their own own paper currencies.

Although European central banks could technically redeem their sterling balances for gold, the gold-exchange standard allowed their governments to augment their own depleted gold reserves with a paper substitute and pursue their own inflation.

This way Britain could have its inflationary cake and eat it too, printing more paper liabilities without losing gold overseas—effectively "exporting" its inflation and short-circuiting the Hume price-specie-flow market mechanism (see Chapter 38 to review David Hume's price-specie-flow system).

Hard money opponents of the scheme quipped that a gold-bullion-exchange system that substituted paper reserves for gold ones was really no gold standard at all, devoid of the traditional gold standard's anti-inflationary checks and balances. But they were swiftly brushed aside by the plan's architects including Keynes himself who had long argued that...

> "A preference for a tangible gold currency is... ...a relic of a time when governments were less trustworthy in these matters than they are now." [187]

-from *Indian Currency and Finance* (1913)

In the third and final chapter we will review the consequences of the British international pound-sterling gold-bullion-exchange standard when European central banks all ran for the exits in 1931.

November 9, 2018

1931: Great Britain is forced off its novel gold-exchange standard

Chapter 40

What Really Started the Great Depression? Part 3

The Cautious Optimism Correspondent for Economic Affairs concludes his series on what really started the Great Depression. Monetary policy wonks, goldbugs and economic history buffs will be gripped by the collapse of the 1925-31 European gold-exchange standard and the subsequent deflation's role in enabling the rise of fascism.

In Part 2 we described the novel gold-exchange standard that Britain invented to displace the traditional classical gold standard which had governed global trade for nearly half a century. We conclude with Britain's monetary subjugation of Europe, the collapse of the new gold-exchange standard after only six years, and the subsequent lessons that were willfully unlearned by the postwar economics profession.

FORCING GOLD-EXCHANGE UPON EUROPE

As Britain engineered its novel gold-exchange standard to foist paper pounds sterling on Europe as a substitute for traditional gold reserves, the plan's architects brushed aside economists who appropriately called the plan a paper-hybrid standard.

But while dismissing academics and dissenting policy critics was one thing, convincing European governments to go along with the gold-exchange standard was another matter entirely.

Much of Europe would demand a return to the more honest classical gold standard and prefer to redeem in tangible reserves instead of hoarding paper obligations that Britain could produce without limit.

(See Chapter 39 for more on the gold-exchange standard)

The British Treasury's Ralph Hawtrey and Bank of England Governor Montagu Norman were called upon to overcome the international political obstacles.

Due to its status as a wartime creditor to many near-bankrupt European nations and its influential position heading the League of Nations Financial Committee, Great Britain relentlessly strongarmed over thirty countries into accepting gold-exchange including Germany, Austria, Hungary, Belgium, France, the Netherlands, Greece, Italy, Norway, Poland, Portugal and more.

Hawtrey worked out the technical details during the 1922 Genoa financial conference while Norman pressured finance ministers and his counterparts at other central banks. Paris reluctantly went along with Bank of France Governor Emile Moreau complaining in his diary that:

> "England having been the first European country to reestablish a stable and secure money has used that advantage to establish a basis for putting Europe under a veritable financial domination. The Financial Committee at Geneva has been that policy. The method consists of forcing every country in monetary difficulty to subject itself to the Committee at Geneva, which the British control. The remedies prescribed always involve the installation in the central bank of a foreign supervisor who is British or designated by the Bank of England, which serves both to support the pound and to fortify British influence... ... The currencies [of Europe] will be divided into two classes. Those of the first class, the dollar and pound sterling, based on gold, and those of the second class, based on the pound or the dollar." [188]

The final formality was to gain approval from Parliament and His Majesty's Government.

In one of his famous policy dinners Chancellor of the Exchequer Winston Churchill was persuaded by Hawtrey, Keynes, and banking and commercial interests of the benefits of the new gold-bullion-exchange standard. Churchill, never sophisticated in technical financial matters, deferred to the experts; pleased to hear only that the British pound would soon be returned to international pre-eminence.

The pound officially went back on gold at the old prewar par of $4.86 under the 1925 Gold Standard Act—although the new gold-bullion-exchange standard was a gold standard in name only, bearing almost no resemblance to the classical gold coin standard that had preceded it and devoid of the traditional rules that had previously imposed anti-inflationary checks on governments and central banks for centuries. As Austrian economist Murray Rothbard eloquently summarized Britain's new policy:

> "They were attempting to clothe themselves in the prestige of gold while trying to avoid its anti-inflationary discipline. They went back, not to the classical gold standard, but to a bowdlerized and essentially sham version of that venerable standard." [189]

Thus British policymakers believed they had shirked all the deflationary consequences of returning to gold at the old par of $4.86 while successfully pursuing a contradictory policy of persistent inflation. European trading partners were effectively bullied into accumulating pound sterling liabilities and treating them as equal to gold.

Over the next several years the Bank of England would pursue a consistently inflationary monetary policy, its paper liabilities piling up ever higher in the central banks of Europe—liabilities that it was hopelessly ill-equipped to redeem should financial difficulty strike one day.

And those liabilities, serving as a reserve "equal to gold" on the continent, induced another layer of inflation in Europe itself. Other governments found themselves flush with new paper reserves to pyramid their own domestic banknotes and demand deposits upon.

Little did Britain know how soon the day of reckoning—when she would be asked to make good on her unworkable promises—would come and which her own inflationary policies would help to bring about. But unconcerned about the prospect of future consequences, Threadneedle

Street contentedly kept the printing press rolling.

However there remained one major trading partner that refused to treat sterling as a reserve and stubbornly insisted on gold redemption. As Britain continued to inflate and her exports became more expensive on the world market, sterling liabilities promptly returned from that country's uncooperative central bank demanding prompt conversion and sustaining Britain's chronic gold drains.

That troublesome country was the United States, and in British eyes something had to be done to solve the so-called American problem. Thus Montagu Norman would appeal to his old friend New York Federal Reserve Governor Benjamin Strong for a favor: to engineer a major Fed intervention to assist Great Britain.

EUROPEAN RECESSION AND THE COLLAPSE OF THE GOLD-EXCHANGE STANDARD

Montagu Norman traveled to New York in 1927 and convinced his friend and colleague Benjamin Strong to launch an aggressive asset purchase campaign to raise American prices alongside Britain's in an attempt to curb its trade deficits (see Chapter 38 for more on the New York Fed's inflation).

The ruse worked. It balanced trade flows between the two nations, but as Alan Greenspan wrote in 1966:

> "It [the Fed's inflation] stopped the gold loss, but it nearly destroyed the economies of the world in the process. The excess credit which the Fed pumped into the economy spilled over into the stock market, triggering a fantastic speculative boom."

-from "Gold and Economic Freedom"

We all know the boom led to the famous crash in October of 1929 which coincided with America entering recession that same summer.

Europe, also dealing with the consequences of gold-exchange inflation, fell into recession shortly thereafter and central banks which had accumulated enormous sterling liabilities began to approach the Bank of England to cash in some of their credits.

But London had inflated far beyond any credible capacity to redeem its liabilities (that was the whole point of the gold-exchange standard it had forced upon Europe), and even modest claims on gold were quickly draining its woefully inadequate reserves.

In August of 1931 Bank of France Governor Emile Moreau sought to redeem some of his country's vast sterling balances which by then constituted one-fifth of France's monetary reserves and a full two-thirds of Britain's entire gold holdings.

Montagu Norman, knowing full well that his central bank would be bankrupted if only two or three major central banks converted their sterling balances, resisted Moreau and threatened to devalue the pound if France went through with its demands. Norman even lectured Moreau that more sterling paper was actually good (!) for France.

Moreau backed down and trimmed his remittance calls.

On September 18, 1931 Bank of Netherlands Governor Gerard Vissering also expressed concerns about rising sterling balances. Montagu Norman cajoled his old friend into abstaining and assured him the Bank of England would remain on the gold standard "at all costs."

But even the slowed pace of redemption was enough to alarm the Bank's directors and British policymakers. The quantity of liabilities they had printed simply overwhelmed their tangible gold reserves which were quickly evaporating. Britain was reaping the consequences of the European inflation that she herself had promoted.

On September 20th, two days after Norman assured the Netherlands that he would uphold the gold standard forever, the Bank of England suspended convertibility and promptly devalued. For the first time in its 237-year history, Great Britain failed to make good on a peacetime pledge to fully redeem its notes and deposits in gold to resolve balance of payments (its own citizens lost that right for good in 1925).

Britain could have avoided all the tragedy if, at the end of the Great War, she had simply accepted the traditional policy options of devaluation or deflation instead of adopting the gold-exchange standard to pursue two contradictory policy goals of prewar gold convertibility and perpetual inflation.

And even as late as 1931 as its gold reserves were falling, the Bank of England could still have salvaged the gold standard by raising interest rates to stop the inflation and attract gold inflows from overseas.

But proto-Keynesian cheap money theories had by then conquered domestic politics and Britain was wedded to an inflation-at-all-costs policy. Hence she took the easy-out of virtual bankruptcy and Europe was plunged into monetary chaos.

GLOBAL CONSEQUENCES AND CONTEMPORARY MISINTERPRETATIONS

As the economy slowed on the continent and bank failures multiplied—including the spectacular and far-reaching collapse of Austria's Kreditanstalt—citizens began to redeem their national currencies for gold at European central banks. Given the scale of the preceding inflation, and the short supply of gold due in part to Britain's refusal to meet its redemption commitments, a continuous drain of reserves from the financial system precipitated painful deflations across the continent.

In one of the more consequential cases the German Brüning deflation of the early 1930's produced high unemployment and fertile economic ground for the rise of Nazism. While historians famously blame the Versailles Treaty for Hitler's ascendancy, the truth is Britain's own interwar monetary policy was equally or even more culpable.

Facing harsh deflations which, given Britain's gold default, governments were unable to stem or reverse, European central banks went off gold one by one and launched a series of competitive devaluations, the last being France in 1936.

The United States, which held the world's largest gold reserves and had not participated in the ruinous gold-exchange scheme, could have remained on gold and avoided Great Depression with proficient monetary policy from its entrusted Federal Reserve Board. However, well-documented and nearly criminally negligent incompetence at the Fed led to a series of spectacular banking panics in 1930, 1931, and 1933 (nearly 10,000 American banks failed in total) and the U.S. went off gold in April of 1933. That is another story for a future column on American monetary policy during the 1930's.

So the gold standard as the world had known it died in the early years of the Great Depression.

Sadly, even the lessons of the sorry affair were soon to be lost or deliberately covered up. In the 1947 edition of his book *The Gold Standard in Theory and Practice* Ralph Hawtrey, co-architect of gold-exchange himself, explained that…

> "The cause of the failure of the gold standard was simple. It was the appreciation of the value of gold in terms of wealth [i.e. deflation]. Gold had not supplied a stable unit for the measurement of values." [190]

…without making any reference to the fatal flaw within the gold-exchange ploy itself: that it spurred British inflation that necessarily would reverse itself into painful deflation the moment a few central banks lost confidence in Britain's ability to make good on its impossible pledges.

Contemporary mainstream economists, mostly apologists for fiat money and staunch gold opponents, bemoan that the gold standard "failed" in the 1930's or that "the gold standard caused the Great Depression." Former Federal Reserve Chairman Ben Bernanke writes on his Brookings Institute blog that:

> "The gold standard of the 1920's was brought down by the failure of surplus countries to participate equally in the adjustment process." [i.e. inadequate central bank cooperation]

> -from "Germany's Trade Surplus is a Problem" (2015)

Aside from the fact that central bank cooperation was not required under the traditional classical gold standard, anyone familiar with the pre-1931 European gold-exchange standard and the 1927 New York conference can see the core problem was not failure by European central banks to abstain from cashing in their legal claims on gold. Rather the 1920's gold standard was brought down by its own perverse design: a "managed" sham of a gold-exchange standard that replaced gold with unlimited quantities of paper and freed Britain to issue far more banknote and deposit liabilities than she could ever possibly repay.

Thus to blame "the gold standard" is to embrace a fallacious misnomer, just as it would be a grave error to argue "commercial aviation failed" after central banks removed engines, wings, and landing gear from jetliners while they were in midair flight.

George Mason University's pro-gold economist Lawrence H. White has more astutely noted that...

> "The interwar period shows us a case where central banks—not the gold standard—ran the show." [191]

...and...

> "Several authors identify genuine historical problems that they blame on the gold standard, when they should instead blame central banks for having contravened the gold standard." [192]

And more forthright is prominent Austrian economist Ludwig von Mises who wrote in 1965:

> "The gold standard did not fail. Governments deliberately sabotaged it, and still go on sabotaging it." [193]

Note: The Cautious Optimism Economics Correspondent credits the late Professor Murray Rothbard for much of the content in this article. Rothbard's 1963 book, *A History of Money and Banking in the United States,* and in particular Chapter 4: "The Gold-Exchange Standard in the Interwar Years," remains the best text the Correspondent has read on this important episode in monetary and Great Depression history.

Rothbard's text also draws from the work of Dr. Melchior Palyi who served as chief economist at Deutsche Bank and advisor to the German Reichsbank during the gold-exchange standard's collapse.

November 18, 2018

NOTES

1. Calomiris-2010, p. 5.
2. Ibid.
3. Bowman-1937, p. 41.
4. Bowman-1937, p. 54.
5. Bowman-1937, p. 61.
6. Bowman-1937, p. 71.
7. Calomiris and Haber-2014, p. 95.
8. Bowman-1937, p. 141.
9. Bowman-1937, p. 142.
10. Andreadas-1909, p. 253.
11. Ibid.
12. Bowman-1937, p. 229.
13. Calomiris and Haber-2014, p. 118.
14. White-1984, p. 35.
15. Bowman-1937, p. 238.
16. White-1984, p. 86.
17. Bowman-1937, p. 242.
18. Turner-2014, p. 45.
19. Bernanke. *The Courage to Act*-2015, p. 469.
20. Bernanke. *The Courage to Act*-2015, p. 45.
21. Bagehot-1873, p. 97.
22. *Bloomberg*-2010.
23. Kovacevich-2012.
24. Grant-2019.
25. Ibid.
26. White-1984, p. 23.
27. White-1984, p. 24.
28. Calomiris and Haber-2014, p. 102.
29. White-1984, p. 24.
30. White-1984, p. 26.
31. White-1984, p. 31.
32. Smith-1776, p. 329. "The late multiplication of banking companies... instead of diminishing, increases the security of the public. It obliges all of them to be more circumspect in their conduct, and, by not extending their currency beyond its due proportion to their cash, to guard themselves against the malicious runs which the rivalship of so many competitors is always ready to bring upon them."

33. Smith-1776, p. 297. "That the trade and industry of Scotland, however, have increased very considerably during this period, and that the banks have contributed a great deal to this increase, cannot be douted."
34. White-1984, p. 43.
35. White-1984, p. 44.
36. Ibid.
37. McCulloch-1826, p. 19.
38. White-1984, p. 44.
39. Graham-1911, p. 242.
40. Shah-1997, p. 2.
41. Smith-1776, p. 315. "They seem to have intended... ...to supplant all the Scottish banks, particularly those established in Edinburgh."
42. Clapham-1944, p. 243.
43. Goodspeed-2015.
44. Fraser-2014, p. 456.
45. Selgin. "Scottish Banks and the Bank Restriction"-2018.
46. Thornton-1803, p. 112.
47. Selgin. "Scottish Banks and the Bank Restriction"-2018.
48. Calomiris-2010, p. 5.
49. Sylla, Legler and Wallis-1987, p. 401.
50. Calomiris and Haber-2014, p. 166.
51. Nadler and Bogen-1933, p. 29.
52. Ibid.
53. Calomiris and Haber-2014, p. 181.
54. Patterson-1917, p. 68.
55. Calomiris and Haber-2014, p. 164.
56. Calomiris and Haber-2014, p. 308.
57. Selgin. "Rare Beasts" from "The Fable of the Cats"-2021.
58. Carlson and Michener-2007, p. 44.
59. Selgin. "Abolish Banking Insurance?"-2017.
60. Mengle-1990, p. 6.
61. Calomiris and Haber-2014, p. 191.
62. Friedman and Schwartz-1963, p. 436.
63. *Wikipedia*. "The Glass Bill" from "The Banking Act of 1933."
64. Hayashi, Li, and Wang-2017, p. 6.
65. Chernow-2004, p. 393.
66. Ibid.
67. Taylor, Brian-2016.
68. Curott and Watts-2016, p. 24.

69. Hamilton-1781.

70. Bowers-1925, p. 47.

71. Ibid.

72. DiLorenzo-2008, p. 42.

73. Taylor, Brian-2016.

74. Hamilton-1781.

75. Taylor, Brian-2016.

76. Ibid.

77. Ibid.

78. *Wikipedia.* "Later Life" from "William Duer."

79. Curott and Watts-2016, p. 25.

80. Curott and Watts-2016, p. 11.

81. Curott and Watts-2016, p. 29.

82. *MeasuringWorth.*

83. Ibid.

84. Officer-2010.

85. Curott and Watts-2016, p. 22.

86. Sumner. *Robert Morris*-1892, pp. 161-162.

87. Chernow-2004, p. 480.

88. Rothbard. A *History of Money and Banking in the U.S.*-1963, p. 84.

89. Sumner. *A History of Banking in All Leading Nations*-1896, p. 98.

90. Rothbard. A *History of Money and Banking in the U.S.*-1963, pp. 86, 88.

91. Rothbard. A *History of Money and Banking in the U.S.*-1963, p. 87.

92. Rothbard. A *History of Money and Banking in the U.S.*-1963, p. 88.

93. Rothbard. *The Panic of 1819: Reactions and Policies*-1962, p. 10.

94. Rothbard. A *History of Money and Banking in the U.S.*-1963, p. 87.

95. Rothbard. A *History of Money and Banking in the U.S.*-1963, p. 89.

96. Ibid.

97. Rothbard. A *History of Money and Banking in the U.S.*-1963, p. 90.

98. Rothbard. *The Panic of 1819: Reactions and Policies*-1962, p. 16.

99. Ibid.

100. Davies-2008.

101. Campbell-2021.

102. Ibid.

103. Ibid.

104. Remini-1965, p. 126.

105. Taylor, George Rogers-1949, pp. 5-6.

106. Taylor, George Rogers-1949, p. 19.

107. *MeasuringWorth.*

108. Temin-1969, p. 71.
109. Ibid.
110. Rockoff-1971.
111. Bowman-1937, p. 238.
112. Ibid.
113. Temin-1969, p. 129.
114. Calomiris and Haber-2014, p. 170.
115. Selgin. "U.S. and Canada Free Banking Episodes"-2021.
116. Surro-2015, p. 1.
117. Rockoff-1975, p. 3.
118. Ibid.
119. Selgin. "New York's Bank"-2016, p. 4.
120. Calomiris and Haber-2014, p. 179.
121. Hoyt-1965, p. 281.
122. *MeasuringWorth.*
123. Selgin. "Price Stability and Financial Stability Without Central Banks," IEA Hayek Lecture-2016.
124. Selgin. "New York's Bank"-2016. Core sources: C.A. Curtis "Statistical Contributions to Canadian Economic History, Volume 1"-1931, and St. Louis Federal Reserve "Annual Report of the Comptroller of the Currency 1863-1930."
125. Rothbard. A *History of Money and Banking in the U.S.*-1963, pp.136-138.
126. Calomiris and Gorton-1991, p. 130
127. Lowenstein-2015, pp. 84-86.
128. Hoyt-1965, p. 227.
129. Powell-2005, p. 2.
130. Powell-2005, p. 5.
131. Powell-2005, p. 7.
132. Powell-2005, p. 9.
133. Schull and Gibson-1982, p. 5.
134. Denison-1966, pp. 94-97.
135. Denison-1966, p. 73.
136. Schull and Gibson-1982, pp. 6-16.
137. Calomiris and Haber-2014, p. 181.
138. Patterson-1917, p. 68.
139. Federal Reserve. "Branch Banking in Canada"-1932, p. 11.
140. Federal Reserve. "Branch Banking in the United States"-1932, p. 25.
141. Curtis-1948.
142. Breckenridge-1895, pp. 32-33.

143. Shearer-1994. "There followed a period of severe credit and monetary contraction... ...this would have created difficult times for a small bank. However, all other Canadian banks survived; the Agricultural Bank did not."

144. Breckenridge-1895, p. 40.

145. Fung, Hendry, and Weber-2017, p. 9.

146. Fung, Hendry, and Weber-2017, p. 6.

147. Fung, Hendry, and Weber-2017, p. 7.

148. Selgin. "Entry into Canadian Banking 1870-1935"-2018.

149. Ibid.

150. Calomiris and Haber-2014, p. 307.

151. Fung, Hendry, and Weber-2017, p. 8.

152. Lavoie-2020.

153. Canadian Bankers Association website. "CBA History."

154. Carr, Mathewson, and Quigley-1995, p. 1143.

155. Calomiris and Haber-2014, p. 310.

156. Carr, Mathewson, and Quigley-1995, p. 1153.

157. Calomiris-2010, p. 5.

158. Martin-2014.

159. Martin, Darroch, and Ecker-2021.

160. Bordo and Redish-1986, p. 14.

161. Ibid.

162. Ibid.

163. Bordo and Redish-1986, p. 16.

164. Calomiris-2010, p. 5.

165. Taylor, John-2010.

166. Pinto-2009.

167. *Yale University EliScholar*-2000.

168. Katopis-2011, p. 3.

169. Canada Mortgage and Housing Association-2007, p. 44.

170. Calomiris and Haber-2014, pp. 308, 310.

171. Calomiris and Haber-2014, p. 296.

172. BBC-2010. "'There is no groundswell of opinion in Europe to break up the banks-there just isn't the same political pressure [as in the UK and the US]. Banks in Europe are national institutions there to support industry.' He [MF Global's Simon Maughan] points out there was no Glass-Steagall Act in Europe, a piece of legislation introduced in the US in the aftermath of the Great Depression to separate retail and investment banking, which was abolished by Bill Clinton in 1999. European banks have always integrated commercial and investment operations."

173. *Reuters.* "Ameriquest closes, Citigroup buys mortgage assets"-2007.
174. *New York Times.* "For banks, a big nudge to do more"-1998.
175. Martin-2012, p. 12. It's worth noting that Toronto-Dominion was a sole outlier. While the then fifth largest Canadian bank entered discount brokerage in the 1980's and full service brokerage in 2000, it only expanded into investment banking with its 2000 with the acquisition of Newcrest Capital.
176. Selgin. "An Unnecessary Evil: How Canada Ended up Insuring Bank Deposits"-2021.
177. Ibid.
178. Federal Reserve. "Branch Banking in Canada"-1932, p. 26.
179. *Washington Post*-1996.
180. Rothbard. *America's Great Depression*-1963, p. 155.
181. Grant-2015, p. 210.
182. Friedman. Charlie Rose interview-2005.
183. Lewis-2007.
184. Estevadeoral, Frantz, and Taylor-2002, p. 36.
185. Palyi-1972, pp. 28-39.
186. Kemmerer-1944, p. 144.
187. Keynes-1913, p. 73. "A preference for a tangible gold currency is no longer more than a relic of a time when Governments were less trustworthy in these matters than they are now."
188. Rothbard. *America's Great Depression*-1963, p. 152.
189. Rothbard. A *History of Money and Banking in the U.S.*-1963, p. 381.
190. Hawtrey-1947, p. 137.
191. White-2012, p. 16.
192. White-2012, p. 1.
193. Von Mises-1965.

SOURCES: BOOKS

Andreadas, Andreas Michael. *History of the Bank of England,* 1909.

Bagehot, Walter. *Lombard Street, A Description of the Money Market,* 1873.

Bernanke, Benjamin S. *The Courage to Act: A Memoir of a Crisis and its Aftermath,* 2015.

Bowers, Claude G. *Jefferson and Hamilton: The Struggle for Democracy in America,* 1925.

Bowman, William Dodgson. *The Story of the Bank of England,* 1937.

Breckenridge, R.M. *The History of Banking in Canada,* 1895.

Calomiris, Charles, Steven Haber. *Fragile by Design: The Political Origins of Banking Crises and Scarce Credit,* 2014.

Chernow, Ron. *Alexander Hamilton,* 2004.

Clapham, John. *The Bank of England: A History, Volume 1 1694-1797,* 1944.

Denison, Merrill. *Canada's First Bank: A History of the Bank of Montreal,* 1966.

DiLorenzo, Thomas J. *Hamilton's Curse: How Jefferson's Arch Enemy Betrayed the American Revolution--and What It Means for Americans Today,* 2008.

Fenstermaker, Joseph Van. *The Development of American Commercial Banking, 1782-1837,* 1963.

Fraser, Ian. *Shredded: Inside RBS, the Bank That Broke Britain,* 2014.

Friedman, Milton, Anna Schwartz. *A Monetary History of the United States, 1867-1960,* 1963

Graham, William. *The One Pound Note in the History of Banking in Great Britain,* 1911.

Grant, James. *Bagehot, The Life and Times of the Greatest Victorian,* 2019.

Grant, James. *The Forgotten Depression. 1921 the Crash That Cured Itself,* 2015.

Hawtrey, R. G. *The Gold Standard in Theory and Practice,* 1947.

Hoyt, Edwin P. *The House of Morgan,* 1966.

Kemmerer, Edwin Walter. *Gold and the Gold Standard: The Story of Gold Money, Past, Present, and Future,* 1944.

Keynes, John Maynard. *Indian Currency and Finance,* 1913.

Lowenstein, Roger. *America's Bank: The Epic Struggle to Create the Federal Reserve,* 2015.

Maddison, Angus. *The World Economy: A Millennial Perspective,* 2001.

McCulloch, John Ramsay. *Fluctuations in the Supply and Value of Money,* 1826.

Nadler, Marcus, Julius I. Bogen. *The Banking Crisis: The End of an Epoch,* 1933.

Palyi, Melchior. *The Twilight of Gold, 1914-1936: Myths and Realities,* 1972.

Patterson, Edward Lloyd Stewart. *Banking Principles and Practice,* 1917.

Remini, Robert. *Andrew Jackson and the Bank War,* 1965.

Rockoff, Hugh. *The Free Banking Era: A Re-examination*, 1975.

Rothbard, Murray N. *A History of Money and Banking in the United States*, 1963.

Rothbard, Murray N. *America's Great Depression*, 1963.

Rothbard, Murray N. *The Panic of 1819: Reactions and Policies*, 1962.

Schull, Joseph, J. Douglas Gibson. *The Scotiabank Story: A History of the Bank of Nova Scotia 1832-1982*, 1982.

Smith, Adam. *An Inquiry into the Nature and Causes of the Wealth of Nations*, Glasgow Edition, 1776.

Sumner, William Graham. *A History of Banking in all the Leading Nations, Volume 1*, 1896.

Sumner, William Graham. *Robert Morris*, 1892.

Taylor, George Rogers. *Jackson Versus Biddle*, 1949.

Temin, Peter. *The Jacksonian Economy*, 1969.

Thornton, Henry. *An Enquiry into the Nature and Effects of the Paper Credit of Great Britain*, 1803.

Turner, John D. *Banking in Crisis: The Rise and Fall of British Banking Stability, 1800 to the Present*, 2014.

White, Lawrence H. *Free Banking in Britain: Theory, Experience and Debate*, 1984.

SOURCES: PAPERS, ESSAYS, ARTICLES, INTERVIEWS

BBC. "Obama's banking proposals: The impact on Europe," 2010.

Bennett, Robert. "A Banking Puzzle: Mixing Freedom and Protection," *New York Times*, 1984.

Bernanke, Benjamin S. "Say it Ain't So Jack," 2015.

Bloomberg. "GE Borrowed $16 Billion in Commercial Paper Plan, Fed Data Show," 2010.

Boettke, Peter J, Steven Horwitz. "The House That Uncle Sam Built," 2010.

Bordo, Michael D, Angela Redish. "Why Did the Bank of Canada Emerge in 1935?" 1986.

Brown, Abram. "The High Crimes and Misdemeanors of William Duer, The Founding Father Who Swindled America," 2019.

Calomiris, Charles. "Banking Crises Yesterday and Today," 2010.

Calomiris, Charles, Gary Gorton. "The Origins of Banking Panics: Models, Facts, and Bank Regulation," National Bureau of Economic Research, 1991.

Campbell, Stephen. "Nicholas Biddle," 2021.

Canada Mortgage and Housing Association. "2007 Annual Report."

Canadian Bankers Association. "CBA History" from cba.ca website.

Carlson, Mark, Kris James Mitchener. "Branch Banking as a Device for Discipline: Competition and Bank Survivorship During the Great Depression," 2007.

Carr, Jack, Frank Mathewson, Neil Quigley. "Stability in the Absence of Deposit Insurance: The Canadian Banking System, 1890-1966," 1995.

Curott, Nicholas, Tyler A. Watts. "What Caused the Recession of 1797?" 2016.

Curtiss, C.A. "History of the Banking System of Canada," 1948.

Davenant, Charles. "An Essay Upon Ways and Means for Supplying the War," 1695.

Davies, Phil. "The Rise and Fall of Nicholas Biddle," Federal Reserve Bank of Minneapolis, 2008.

Estevadeordal, Antoni, Brian Frantz, Alan M, Taylor. "The Rise and Fall of World Trade, 1870-1939." NBER working paper, 2002.

Fisher, Gerald C, Carter H. Golembe. "Deposit Insurance or Branching?" from "Compendium of Issues Relating to Branching by Financial Institutions," U.S. Senate Committee on Banking, Housing, and Urban Affairs, 1976.

Federal Reserve Committee on Branch, Group, and Chain Banking. "Branch Banking in Canada," 1932.

Federal Reserve Committee on Branch, Group, and Chain Banking. "Branch Banking in the United States," 1932.

Friedman, Milton. Charlie Rose interview, 2005

Fung, Brian, Scott Hendry, Warren E. Weber. "Canadian Bank Notes and Dominion Notes: Lessons for Digital Currencies," Bank of Canada, 2017.

Goodspeed, Tyler. "Lessons from the Ayr Bank Failure," 2015.

Greenspan, Alan. "Gold and Economic Freedom," 1966.

Gross, Daniel. "The Horsetrading that gave birth to the Federal Reserve," *Washington Post*, 2015.

Hamilton, Alexander. Letter to Robert Morris, April 30, 1781.

Hayashi, Fumiko, Bin Grace Li, Zhu Wang. "Innovation, Deregulation, and the Life Cycle of a Financial Service Industry," Federal Reserve Bank of Richmond, 2017.

Jefferson, Thomas. "Explanations of the Three Volumes Bound in Marbled Paper," 1818.

Katopis, Chris. Executive Director Association of Mortgage Investors, testimony at U.S. House Financial Services Committee, 2011.

Kovacevich, Richard. "The Financial Crisis," *Frontline* interview, 2012.

Krugman, Paul. "Why We Regulate," *New York Times*, 2012.

Lavoie, Marc. "Canadian Central Bank Policy, Real-time Payments, and the Post-Keynesian Tradition" (Mercatus Center interview), 2020.

Lewis, Nathan. "The 1870-1914 Gold Standard; The Most Perfect One Ever Created," 2007.

Martin, Joseph E, James Darroch, Janet Ecker. "150 Years of Canadian Banking and a Look Into the Future," 2021.

Martin, Joseph E. "The Toronto-Dominion Bank and Canada's 'Little Bang' of 1987," 2012.

Martin, Joseph E. "Who's the father of Canada's banks?" 2014.

MeasuringWorth. Pre-1929 U.S. real GDP and real per-capita GDP estimates.

Mengle, David L. "The Case for Interstate Branch Banking," Federal Reserve Bank of Richmond, 1990.

Mises, Ludwig von. "The Gold Problem," 1965.

New York Times. "Communities To Receive $115 Billion, Citigroup Says," 1998.

New York Times. "For Banks, A Big Nudge To Do More," 1998.

Officer, Lawrence H. "The Annual Consumer Price Index for the United States, 1774-2009," 2010.

Pinto, Edward J. "Proposals to Enhance the Community Reinvestment Act," testimony at U.S. House of Representatives hearings, 2009.

Pollock, Alex J. "Glass-Steagall Never Saved Our Financial System, So Why Revive It?" 2017.

Powell, James. "A History of the Canadian Dollar," Bank of Canada, 2005.

Reuters. "Ameriquest closes, Citigroup buys mortgage assets," 2007.

Rockoff, Hugh. "Money, Prices, and Banks in the Jacksonian Era," 1971.

Selgin, George. "Abolish Banking Insurance?" Soho Forum Debate, 2017.

Selgin, George. "Entry Into Canadian Banking: 1870-1935," 2018.

Selgin, George. "New York's Bank," 2016.

Selgin, George. "Price Stability and Financial Stability Without Central Banks," IEA Hayek Lecture, 2016.

Selgin, George. "Scottish Banks and the Bank Restriction," 2018.

Selgin, George. "The Fable of the Cats," 2021.

Selgin, George. "An Unnecessary Evil: How Canada Ended Up Insuring Bank Deposits," 2021.

Selgin, George. "U.S. and Canada Free Banking Episodes," Juan de Mariana Institute Lecture, 2021.

Settle, Russell F. "The Impact of Banking and Fiscal Policies on State-level Economic Growth," 1999.

Shah, Parth J. "The option clause in free-banking theory and history: A reappraisal," 1997.

Shearer, Ronald A. "Notes on Free Banking in Canada in the 1830's," 1994.

Social Democracy for the 21st Century: A Realist Alternative to the Modern

Left. "Canada's Banking Stability in the Early 20th Century and the 1930s," 2011.

Surro, Chris. "Free Banking in America: Disaster or Success?" 2015.

Sylla, Richard, John Legler, and John Wallis. "Banks and State Public Finance in the New Republic: The United States, 1790-1860," 1987.

Talton, Jon. "Trump's reshaped Fed won't reveal itself until the next crisis," *Seattle Times,* 2017.

Taylor, Brian. "The Panic of 1792," 2016.

Taylor, John, President and CEO National Community Reinvestment Coalition, testimony at FDIC Community Reinvestment Act Hearings, 2010.

Washington Post. "An S&L Crisis Congress Can Avert," 1996.

White, Lawrence H. "Recent Arguments Against the Gold Standard," 2012.

Wikipedia. "The 1933 Banking Act."

Wikipedia. "William Duer."

Yale University EliScholar. "James S. Gorelick Remarks at the National Community and Economic Development Conference," 2000.

IMAGE CREDITS

1. Bank of England façade (cover), *The New Statesman* via Getty Images

2. Bank run (p. 10), National Archives "Unwritten record" blog.

3. Parliamentary debates (p. 22), National Portrait Gallery, London

4. Walter Bagehot (p. 28), *Financial Times*

5. Ben Bernanke (p. 34), American Institute for Economic Research

6. Bank of Scotland office (p. 44), *BBC* via Getty Images

7. 1825 Crisis (p.50), *Blue Anchor Corner*

8. RBS protest (p. 56), N/A

9. William Pitt the Younger (p. 62), Bank of England Museum

10. Canada vs USA crises (p. 70), *Wall Street Journal* via Calomiris & Haber

11. Branch vs Unit Banking (p. 74), *Diffen.com*

12. 1931 bank branching laws by state (p. 82), Federal Reserve Committee on Branch, Group, and Chain Banking

13. Branching laws by state (p. 89), Federal Reserve Bank of Richmond

14. Henry Steagall (p. 90), U.S. House of Representatives

15. Hamilton and Jefferson (p. 96), Rutgers University Alumni Association

16. Massachusetts war bond (p. 102), *Bidsquare* auction

17. William Duer (p. 108), *Forbes* via Jeffrey Smith

18. First BUS and industrial production (p. 116), Joseph H Davis and *USHistory.org*

19. Second BUS (p. 124), *Wikipedia* via S.G. Goodrich
20. Second BUS banknote (p. 130), Allen's Inc
21. Jackson and Biddle (p. 136), Museum of American Finance and *Brittanica.com*
22. Depression of 1837 (p. 144), Public domain via Edward Williams Clay
23. Panic of 1857 (p. 152), Public domain via Library of Congress
24. U.S. vs Canadian banknotes (p. 165), CATO via George Selgin
25. New York Times currency headline (p. 166) CATO via George Selgin
26. War of Wealth (p. 172), Library of Congress via Charles Turner Dazey
27. Benjamin Harrison (p. 180), Public domain via Library of Congress
28. 1890 Treasury note (p. 183), National Numismatic Collection at the Smithsonian Institution.
29. Bank of Montreal (p. 186), *le Devoir* via Olivier Zuida
30. Parliament & U.S. Capitol (p. 194), NA
31. John Richardson (p. 202), Public domain via McCord Stewart Museum
32. Bank of Montreal banknote (p. 208), BMO website
33. Marc Lavoie (p. 214), Institute for New Economic Thinking
34. Lord Keynes (p. 223), *Social Democracy for the 21st Century: A Realist Alternative to the Modern Left*
35. Macdonald & Hamilton (p. 230), *TheTyee.ca*
36. Bank of Canada (p. 238), The Canadian Encyclopedia via Bank of Canada Archives
37. HUD/GSE directives (p. 248), Edward Pinto and Charles Calomiris
38. GSE liabilities (p. 249), *Drhousingbubble.com* via OFHEO
39. Carter Glass & Henry Steagall (p. 252), *DW.com*
40. SVB queue (p. 262), Business Insider via Justin Sullivan/Getty Images
41. Great Depression food line (p. 271), Brittanica via Everett Historical
42. Central banker meeting (p. 272), Researchgate via Priscilla Roberts
43. Keynes on gold (p. 282), *AZquotes.com*
44. Britain off gold newspaper (p. 286), *Financial Post*

INDEX

Adams, John–46, 98-99, 106, 112, 117, 121-122 ,134
Adams, John Quincy–106, 138
Aldrich, Nelson W.–169-170
American Bankers Association–247
American International Group (AIG)–38, 61
Ameriquest–256
Andreadas, Andreas–19
Apple Inc.–224
Arthur, Chester–182
Asian Financial Crisis (1997)–176
Associates First Capital–256
Astor, John Jacob–128
Ayr Bank (Douglas Heron & Company)-59
Bagehot, Walter–28-30, 32, 35-37, 39-41, 113
Bagehot's Dictum–30,32, 36-39, 41, 60
Bank Act of 1927 (Canada)–225
Bank Holding Act of 1956 (U.S.)–94
Bank of America–77, 86, 192, 195, 256-257
Bank of Canada (central bank)–189, 200, 210, 225, 244-245, 251
    Founding–238-242
Bank of Canada (commercial bank)–189
Bank of England–20, 22-23, 41, 45-46, 48, 52-53, 62, 72, 110, 125, 170, 200, 222, 242, 276-277
    Alexander Hamilton's model–98-100, 232
    Bagehot's Dictum–29-31, 35, 40
    Dominates Scotland–60
    Federal Reserve assists in 1927-272-273, 275
    Founding–15-17
    Gold bullion and gold-exchange–281-283, 288-291
    Panic of 1837 role–145-146, 148-151
    Parliamentary criticism–24
    Peel's Act monopoly–25-27, 228
    Six Partner Rule monopoly–18-19
    Suspension of 1797–64-65, 121

Bank of France–125, 149, 170, 273, 288, 291
Bank of Halifax–85
Bank of Ireland–64
Bank of Maryland–113
Bank of Montreal (BMO)–72, 86, 188-192, 195, 197, 202, 204, 218, 221, 236, 258
Bank of Netherland (aka. Netherlands Bank)–291
Bank of New Brunswick–189
Bank of New York–77, 111, 113
Bank of Norfolk–85
Bank of North America–97, 119
Bank of Nova Scotia (Scotiabank)–190-192, 195, 197, 218, 258
Bank of Quebec–189
Bank of St. Louis–85
Bank of Scotland (aka. "Old Bank")–24, 45-49, 59-61
Bank of the West–192
Bank of Toronto–85-86, 191, 197
Bank of Upper Canada–189
Bank Restriction Act of 1797 (Great Britain)–64, 66
Banking Act of 1871 (Canada)–209-210, 217, 223, 232
Barclay, James–25
Barclays Plc–25, 30
Bear Stearns–38, 255, 257, 259
Beckworth, David–217
Bell, Robert–54, 150
Bennett, Richard Bedford–241
Bernanke, Benjamin–34, 36-38, 41, 113-114, 216, 293
Bethlehem Steel–84
Biddle, Nicholas–136, 138-141, 149
Biden, Joe–57, 86
Booker, Corey–250
BMO Capital Markets–258
BMO Harris Bank–191
BNP Paribas (Banque National de Paris)–191
Bordo, Michael–215-216, 231, 241

Bowers, Claude–105
Bowman, William Dodgson–19
Brainard, Lael–86
Bretton-Woods Agreement–73, 242
British Linen Company–48-49
Brookings Institute-293
Bryan, William Jennings–175
Buchanan, James–132
Buchanan, James A.–132
Buren, Martin Van–138
Burr, Aaron–122
Bush, George W.–247
California Gold Rush–148, 174
Calomiris, Charles–8, 13, 92, 95, 170, 232
Campbell, Stephen–139
Canada Mortgage and Housing
Corporation (CMHC)–248-249
Canada Rebellions-150, 206
Canadian Bank of Commerce–83, 191, 197
Canadian Bankers Association (CBA)–224
Canadian Deposit Insurance Corporation
(CDIC)–263
Canadian Imperial Bank of Commerce
(CIBC)–191-192, 195, 218, 258
Carter, Jimmy–246
Chase Bank/Chase Manhattan Bank–49, 64,
256
Cheves, Langdon–137
Churchill, Winston–288-289
CIBC World Markets–258
Citigroup/Citibank–38, 64-65, 86, 195, 256-
257
CitiMortgage–256
City Bank of Glasgow–60
Civil War, U.S.–39, 45, 76, 92, 153, 158, 167,
173, 182, 198, 233, 277
National Banking Acts–160-161
Classical gold standard–13, 32, 73, 274
Operation–276, 278-279
Replaced with gold-exchange–283, 287-
289, 293
Clay, Henry–138-140
Clearinghouses–26, 47-48, 52, 59, 80, 177,
200, 206

Cleveland, Grover–177-178
Clinton, Bill–94, 247, 258
Clinton, George–106, 122
Clydesdale Bank–48-49, 60
Coinage Act of 1792 (U.S.)–174
Coinage Act of 1834 (U.S.)–276
Community Reinvestment Act (CRA)–95,
246-247, 250, 256
Confederacy, American–160-161
Confederation, Canadian–191, 196, 206-
207, 209, 233
Constitutional Convention of 1787–98
Coolidge, Calvin–182
Cooperative Commonwealth Federation
(CCF)–240
Corrupt Bargain of 1824–138
Countrywide Financial–246-247
Dallas, Alexander J.–127-128
Darroch, James–231
Davenant, Charles–16
Democratic-Republican Party–122
Deposit Insurance–32, 51-52, 60, 63-64, 71,
198, 235, 242, 244-245
Implied in Canada–224-225
Introduction in U.S.–92-93, 171, 254
Losses under–263-268
Depository Institutions Deregulation and
Monetary Control Act of 1980–94
Depression of 1920-21 (U.S.)–281
Dominion Bank–191, 197
Dominion notes (Canada)–210, 226-228
Dominion Securities–258
Duer, William–108, 111, 114
Dundee Bank–49
Eisenhower, Dwight D.–182
Fannie Mae–247-249, 259
Federal Bankruptcy Act of 1800–122
Federal Deposit Insurance Corporation
(FDIC)–11, 49, 93, 198, 233-234, 254, 263-
267
Federal Open Market Committee (FOMC)–
254-255
Federal Reserve Bank of Minneapolis–138
Federal Reserve Bank of New York–273, 290

Federal Reserve System–11 26, 31, 36, 38-39, 41, 80, 92, 113-114, 118, 121, 138, 140, 175, 182, 197-221-222, 233-234, 242, 256, 260, 265, 292-293
    1927 inflation–200, 272-276, 290
    Great Depression bank failures under-73, 88, 232, 255
    Reasons for adoption–160, 165, 167, 171, 212
Federal Savings and Loan Insurance Corporation (FSLIC)–93, 264, 266
Fetterman, John–250
Finance Act of 1914 (Canada)–227
First Bank of the United States (BUS)–95, 97, 107, 122, 127, 161, 190, 199, 233, 235
    Founding and structure–100-101
    Jefferson's opposition to–99-100, 113-114
    Panic of 1792–109-113, 117, 125, 158, 169, 234
    Panic of 1797–116-117, 119-120, 125, 158, 169, 234
    Powers–117-118
    Share subscription–103-105
    Stephen Girard's ownership–128
Fisher, Irving–275
Four Pillars (Canadian finance)–258
Fowler, Charles–166
Franklin, Al–250
Franklin, Benjamin–46
Freddie Mac–247-249, 259
French-Indian War–188
Friedman, Milton–36, 92, 101, 215, 275
Gardiner Group-258
General Electric–38, 224
General Motors Acceptance Corporation (GMAC)–246
Genoa Economic and Financial Conference of 1922–288
Genworth–38
Girard, Stephen–128
Glasgow Bank–49
Glass, Carter–93, 252, 254-255
Glass-Steagall Act (aka. U.S. Banking Act of 1933)–90-93, 251, 253-260
Gold-bullion standard–282
Gold-coin standard–281-282, 289
Gold-exchange standard–32, 242, 279, 283, 286-288, 290-294
Gold Standard Act of 1900 (U.S.)–177
Gold Standard Act of 1925 (Great Britain)–289
Goldman Sachs–61, 255, 257
Gore, Christopher–106
Gore Bank of Canada–206
Gorelick, Jamie–247
Gouge, William–131, 135
Graham, William–54, 150
Global Financial Crisis (2008)–11, 31-32, 36, 53, 60, 64, 72, 75, 95, 113, 140, 235, 243, 245-248, 253, 256-257, 266
Gramm-Leach-Bliley Act of 1999–253, 258
Graybacks (currency)–161
Great Depression–10, 30, 45, 134, 171, 173, 181, 200, 204, 232, 234, 250, 254, 273, 275
    Bank of Canada–239-240, 243
    Canadian banks–197-198, 217, 219, 222-223, 225-226
    Glass-Steagall–254
    Gold standard–279-280, 287, 292-294
    Introduction of deposit insurance–91-92
    U.S. bank failures–12, 73, 87-88, 197
Greenbacks (currency)–39, 160, 168, 182, 277
Greenspan, Alan–290
Gresham's Law–148, 174, 176
H&R Block–246
Haber, Stephen–13
Halifax Banking Company-190
Hamilton, Alexander–30, 96, 116
    Buying state government debt–102, 104-107
    Canadian banking model–231-236
    First Bank of the United States–98-101, 103
    Panic of 1792–109-114, 117, 125
    Panic of 1797–118-120, 122, 125

Index

Harrison, Benjamin–174-175, 180-182
Harrison, George L.–275
Hartford, The–38
Hawtrey, Ralph–281, 283, 288, 293
Hayes, Rutherford B.–182
Hitler, Adolf–292
Home Bank of Canada–225-226
Hoover, Herbert–182
Hoyt, Edwin–163
Hume, David–49, 277
Imperial Bank of Canada–191
Independent Bankers Association–94
Industrial revolution–53
Internal Revenue Service (IRS)–246
Jackson, Andrew–114, 136-142, 145-146, 150-151, 159
James II, King–15
Jay, John–112
Jefferson, Thomas–46, 96, 109, 112, 117, 121-122, 131, 133, 134, 138
    Opposition to central banking–96, 98-101, 103, 105, 109, 113-114, 122, 232
Jones, William–127, 137
JPMorgan Chase & Co.–192, 195, 256-257, 266
Kemmerer, Edwin Water–283
Kennedy, John F.–182
Keynes, John Maynard–216, 281-284, 288
Kreditanstalt bank (Austria)–292
Krugman, Paul–11-13, 73, 86, 159, 216
Lancaster Turnpike Company–120
Lavoie, Marc–214, 216-218
Law, John–39
Lehman Brothers–61, 255, 257, 259
Levesque Beaubien–258
Liability, double–206, 264
Liability, full–51-52, 58
Liability, limited–52, 58
Lincoln, Abraham–182
Lincoln Financial–38
Little Bang (Canadian finance)–258
Liverpool, Earl of–23, 54
Lloyds Bank–25, 30, 61
Louis XIV, King–15

Louisiana Purchase–133
Macdonald, John–204
Mackenzie, Alexander–204
Mackenzie King, William Lyon–204
Macleod, Henry Dunning–25, 148
MacMillan, Hugh–241
Macomb, Alexander–111, 114
Madison, James–46, 114, 127
Marine Midland Bank–94
Martin, Joe–231, 236
Mary, Queen–16
McCulloch, John Ramsay—54
McCulloch, William–132
McFadden Act of 1927 (U.S.)–82, 87
McGill, James–204
McKinley, William–175, 182
McLachlan, Sarah–204
McLeod Young Weir–258
Merrill Lynch–38, 255, 257, 259
Midland Bank–30
Mises, Ludwig von–294
Mississippi Company (or Bubble)–39, 99, 133
Modern Monetary Theory (MMT)–216, 220
Montagu, Charles–16
Montesquieu–99
Moreau, Emile–288, 291
Morgan, John Pierpont–80, 84, 163, 177-178
Morgan Stanley–255, 257
Morris, Robert–97, 104-106, 111, 119-121
Mosler, Warren–73, 217
Nadler, Marcus & Jules Bogen–79
Napoleon Bonaparte–23, 66, 125-126
Napoleonic Wars–20, 64, 121, 277, 281
National Bank of Canada–197, 258
National Bank of Scotland–49
National Banking System (U.S.)–95, 158, 160, 165, 167, 169-171, 173-174, 176, 182, 199, 232
    Bondholding mandate–161-164, 167, 198
    Tiered system–168, 170

National City Bank–38
National Monetary Commission–169-170
National Provincial Bank–30
NatWest–61
Neal, James, Fordyce and Down Bank–59
Nesbitt Thompson–258
New York Stock Exchange–133
New York Times–13, 73, 75, 147, 166, 257, 275
Nicholson, John–121
Nixon, Richard–242
Norman, Mike–73
Norman, Montagu–272-275, 288, 290-291
Northern Inland Navigation Company–120
Obama, Barack–250
Office of Federal Housing Enterprise Oversight (OFHEO)–249
Office of the Comptroller of the Currency (OCC)–11, 232-235
Office of the Superintendent of Financial Institutions (OSFI)–233
Option clause (banknote)–47-48, 58
Quantity theory of money–275
Palyi, Melchior–294
Panic of 1792–107, 109, 112, 114, 169, 235
Panic of 1797–72, 114, 116-117, 120-122, 125, 169, 200, 234
Panic of 1819–125, 128, 134-135, 137, 158, 169, 200, 234
Panic of 1837–54, 145-146, 149-150, 153, 158, 206
Panic of 1839–145-146, 149
Panic of 1857–152, 158
Panic of 1893–80, 167, 172-173, 176-177, 181-182, 199
Panic of 1907–80, 163, 169, 212
Paterson, William–16
Patriots War (Canada)–150, 206
Patterson, Edward Lloyd Stewart–83, 197
Peel, Sir Robert–24-26, 54
Peel's Acts (British Bank Charter Acts of 1844 and 1845)–25-27, 29, 60, 228
Pinto, Edward–246
Pitt the Younger, William–62

Pollock, Alex–259
Post-Keynesian economics–216, 220
Powell, Jerome–100
Randolph, Edmund–112
RBC Capital Markets–258
Redish, Angela–215, 231, 241
Regulation Q–91, 93-94, 254
Reichsbank (German central bank)–170, 272-273, 294
Remini, Robert–138, 141
Revolutionary War (U.S.)–101-103
Ricardo, David–54
Richardson, John–189, 202, 204
Riegle-Neal Interstate Banking and Branching Efficiency Act of 1994–94
Rist, Charles–272-275
Rockefeller, John D.–46
Rockoff, Hugh–157, 215-216, 231
Rothbard, Murray–128, 132-135, 289, 294
Roosevelt, Franklin D.–182-183, 250
Roosevelt, Theodore–182
Royal Bank of Canada (RBC)–191, 195, 197, 218, 242, 258
Royal Bank of Scotland (aka. "Royal Bank") –46-49, 56, 59-61
Salomon Smith Barney–256
Sanders, Bernie–250
Santa Anna, Antonio Lopez–148
Savings and Loan (S&L) Crisis–72, 93-94, 235, 245, 264, 266
Schacht, Hjalmar–272-274
Schuler, Kurt–231
Schuyler, Philip–120
Schwartz Anna–92, 101
Scotia Global Banking and Markets–258
Scottish Enlightenment–46, 48, 99, 203
Schuylkill & Susquehanna Company–120
Second Bank of the United States (SBUS)– 95, 98, 122, 124, 125, 153, 161, 190, 199, 233
    Bank War with Andrew Jackson–137-138, 140-141, 159
    Founding and structure–127-128, 130-134, 137
    Panic of 1819–158, 169, 234

Panic of 1837–145-147, 149
Second Bank of Upper Canada–189
Selgin, George–8, 88, 157, 164, 221-222, 231
Settle, Russell–76
Sherman Silver Purchase Act–175, 177, 182
Silicon Valley Bank (SVB)–262-263, 265-267
Silver certificates (currency)–182
Six Partner Rule (Bank of England Act of 1708)–18-20, 24-27, 31, 49, 53
Six Percent Club–111, 114
Smith, Adam–52-53, 99, 236
Social Credit Party–240
South Sea Bubble–99, 133
Specie Circular of 1836–145-146, 150-151
Standard Oil–18, 46
Steagall, Henry–90, 93, 252, 254
Stephen, George–204
Strong, Benjamin–272-275, 290
Stuart, James Edward Francis–17
Suffolk Bank–85-86
Summers, Larry–216
Surro, Chris–157
TD Securities–258
Temin, Peter–147, 150
Thornton, Henry–30, 65
Toronto-Dominion Bank (TD)–191, 195, 218, 258
Travelers Group–256
Treasury General Account (TGA)–140
Treasury notes (Canadian currency)–188
Treasury notes (U.S. currency)–175-177 180, 182-183
Treasury Tax and Loan (TT&L) accounts–140
Treaty of Ghent–126
Treaty of Versailles–280
Trump, Donald–140, 146
Trump Derangement Syndrome–146
TurboTax–246
Turgot, Anne Jacques Robert–99
Union Bank of Scotland–49
Unit banking–87, 95, 97, 118, 146, 150, 167-168, 170-171, 173-174, 176, 196-197, 199,

211, 218, 233-234, 236-237, 245
  Demise–93-94
  Glass-Steagall protections–90-93, 254
  Great Depression–87-88, 90-93, 255
  None in Canada–170, 196-197, 236-237
  Origins–76-78
  Problems with–79-80, 83-86
  With "free banking"–154-155, 158
United States Bank of Pennsylvania (USBP)–145, 149
U.S. Bancorp–192
Victoria, Queen–29, 49
Vissering, Gerard–290
Volcker, Paul–121
Wachovia–38, 256
War of 1812–125, 126, 128, 160, 277, 281
Warren, Elizabeth–250, 253
Washington, George–98, 101-101, 103-106, 109
Washington Mutual–38
Washington Post–147
Weimar hyperinflation–280
Wells Fargo–39, 192, 195, 256
Western Bank of Scotland–60
Western Inland Navigation Company–120
Westminster Bank–30
Whiskey Rebellion–105
White, Eugene–215
White, Lawrence H.–8, 26, 55, 58, 231, 294
Wildcat banking–86-87
William III, King–15-17, 46
William and Mary–15
Wilson, James–121
Wilson, Woodrow–171
Wood Gundy–258
World Monetary and Economic Conference of 1933–241
World War I–27, 30, 121, 227, 279, 281
World War II–204, 242
Yancey, Charles–131, 133
Yellen, Janet–100, 216

Made in the USA
Las Vegas, NV
26 March 2024

87782371R00174